Beyond Disfluency

Advances in Interaction Studies (AIS)
ISSN 1879-873X

Advances in Interaction Studies (AIS) provides a forum for researchers to present excellent scholarly work in a variety of disciplines relevant to the advancement of knowledge in the field of interaction studies. The book series accompanies the journal *Interaction Studies: Social Behaviour and Communication in Biological and Artificial Systems*.

The book series allows the presentation of research in the forms of monographs or edited collections of peer-reviewed material in English.

For an overview of all books published in this series, please see
benjamins.com/catalog/ais

Editors

Kerstin Dautenhahn
University of Waterloo

Angelo Cangelosi
The University of Manchester

Editorial Board

Henrik Christensen
University of California, San Diego

Harold Gouzoules
Emory University

Takayuki Kanda
Kyoto University

Tetsuro Matsuzawa
California Institute of Technology

Giorgio Metta
IIT, Genoa

Adam Miklosi
Eötvös Loránd University

Robert W. Mitchell
Eastern Kentucky University

Chrystopher L. Nehaniv
University of Waterloo

Stefano Nolfi
CNR, Rome

Pierre-Yves Oudeyer
INRIA, Bordeaux

Irene M. Pepperberg
Harvard University & Brandeis University

Kerstin Severinson Eklundh
KTH, Stockholm

Stefan Wermter
University of Hamburg

Volume 11

Beyond Disfluency. The interplay of speech, gesture, and interaction
by Loulou Kosmala

Beyond Disfluency

The interplay of speech, gesture, and interaction

Loulou Kosmala
Université Paris Nanterre

John Benjamins Publishing Company
Amsterdam / Philadelphia

The paper used in this publication meets the minimum requirements of the American National Standard for Information Sciences – Permanence of Paper for Printed Library Materials, ANSI z39.48-1984.

DOI 10.1075/ais.11

Cataloging-in-Publication Data available from Library of Congress:
LCCN 2023053070 (PRINT) / 2023053071 (E-BOOK)

ISBN 978 90 272 1450 8 (HB)
ISBN 978 90 272 4726 1 (E-BOOK)

© 2024 – John Benjamins B.V.
No part of this book may be reproduced in any form, by print, photoprint, microfilm, or any other means, without written permission from the publisher.

John Benjamins Publishing Company · https://benjamins.com

Table of contents

List of abbreviated terms — IX

Acknowledgments — XI

Introduction — 1
I. Introducing inter-(dis)fluency: Beyond cognitive oriented models of speech production — 1
II. Data under study — 7
III. Preview of the book — 8

CHAPTER 1. Theoretical background — 10
I. What is disfluency? A psycholinguistic production model — 11
    1.1 Disfluency as a deviation in speech from the ideal delivery — 11
    1.2 The role of disfluencies in speech production — 12
    1.3 Major disfluency types and classifications — 12
II. Fluency, disfluency, and hesitation: A terminological debate beyond terminological issues — 14
    2.1 Definitions of L1 and L2 fluency — 14
    2.2 Approaches to L1 disfluency — 16
    2.3 Summary of the overlapping terms and my choice of terminology — 23
III. Beyond the psycholinguistic model: An interdisciplinary approach to inter-(dis)fluency — 25
    3.1 Cognitive grammar and usage-based linguistics — 25
    3.2 Interactional linguistics and conversation analysis — 32
    3.3 Gesture studies and multimodal interaction — 38
IV. Summary of the approaches adopted in this book — 51
V. Towards an integrated framework of inter-(dis)fluency — 53
    5.1 Definition of inter-(dis)fluency — 54
    5.2 Main theoretical assumptions — 55

CHAPTER 2. Inter-(dis)fluency across languages and settings: A literature review — 57
  Introduction to the chapter — 57
I. Research on L2 fluency and gesture — 57
    1.1 L2 fluency, accuracy, and proficiency — 57
    1.2 L2 fluency, interactional competence, and "CA-for-SLA" — 60
    1.3 Gesture production in Second Language Acquisition — 63

II. Effects of task type, discourse domain, and style   66
    2.1 Type of delivery and speech mode   66
    2.2 Evidence from experimental and corpus-based studies   67
    2.3 Effect of style and setting on gestures: A gap in the literature   70

CHAPTER 3. Corpus and method   73
  Introduction to the chapter   73
I. Data   73
    1.1 The SITAF corpus   74
    1.2 The DisReg corpus   79
    1.3 Motivations for working on a "small" corpus   82
II. Annotation protocol for the quantitative analyses   86
    2.1 (Dis)fluency annotation   86
    2.2 Tools   98
III. Methods for qualitative analyses   100
    3.1 Conversation-analytic methods   100
    3.2 Multimodal analysis: Use of PRAAT for the vocal dimension   101
  Conclusion to the chapter   101

CHAPTER 4. Inter-(dis)fluency in native and non-native discourse   103
  Introduction to the chapter   103
I. Research questions and hypotheses   103
II. Quantitative findings   105
    2.1 Marker level: Rate, form, and duration of individual fluencemes   105
    2.2 Sequence level: Type, length, position, and patterns
        of co-occurrence   113
    2.3 Visuo-gestural level: Gesture production and gaze behavior   116
III. Qualitative analyses   124
    3.1 Communication management: Overview of the data   124
    3.2 Non-native speakers' multimodal communication strategies   125
IV. Discussion   137
    4.1 Specificities of L1 and L2 fluency   137
    4.2 How L2 learners deal with language difficulties: Beyond lexical
        retrieval   142
  Conclusion to the chapter   143

CHAPTER 5. Inter-(dis)fluency across communication settings   146
  Introduction to the chapter   146
I. Research questions and hypotheses   146

II. Quantitative findings   148
    2.1 Marker level: Rate, form, and duration of individual fluencemes   149
    2.2 Sequence level: Type, length, position, and patterns of co-occurrence   155
    2.3 Visuo-gestural level: Gesture production and gaze behavior   158
III. Qualitative analyses   166
    3.1 Overview of Communication Management in the two situations   166
    3.2 The case of tongue clicks: Blending vocal and kinetic behaviors   167
    3.3 Embodied displays of intersubjectivity in storytelling: The interactive dimension of fluencemes   170
    3.4 The interplay of vocal and material resources in the course of class presentations   176
IV. Discussion   180
    4.1 Effect of style and setting on fluency and gesture   181
    4.2 The importance of audience design   185
Conclusion to the chapter   189

CHAPTER 6. On the relationship between Inter-(Dis)fluency and gesture **191**

Introduction to the chapter   191
I. Synchronization of speech and gesture   191
    1.1 Hold and retraction: Suspension and interruption in the two modalities   192
    1.2 Preparation: Preparing speech and gesture in tandem   196
II. On the visual-gestural practices embodying inter-(dis)fluency   198
    2.1 Doing thinking as an interactional practice   198
    2.2 Embodied displays of stance and intersubjectivity   211
Conclusion to the chapter   214

General conclusion   **216**
I. Beyond disfluency: Towards a multidimensional framework   216
II. Summary of the main findings   217
    2.1 Study on the SITAF corpus: Native versus non-native productions   218
    2.2 Study on the DisReg corpus: Individual class presentations versus dyadic conversations   219
    2.3 Synthesis   221
III. Perspectives for future work   222

References   **225**

Appendices 245
  Appendix 1   246
  Appendix 2   247
  Appendix 3   257

Index 263

List of abbreviated terms

AM	American
CA	Conversation Analysis
CL	Cognitive Linguistics
EDT	Explicit Editing Phrase
EFL	English as a Foreign Language
FIG	Figure
FP	Filled Pause
FR	French
ICM	Interactive Communication Management
IL	Interactional Linguistics
IR	Identical Repetition
L	Line
L1	First Language
L2	Second Language
LH	Left Hand
LRH	Lexical Retrieval Hypothesis
MLU	Mean Length Of Utterance
MS	Morpho-syntactic Marker
NL	Non-Lexical Sound
NNS	Non-Native Speaker
NS	Native Speaker
OCM	Own Communication Management
EN	English
POH	Palm Open Hand
PUOH	Palm-Up Open Hand
PHW	Per Hundred Words
RH	Right Hand
PR	Prolongation
SLA	Second Language Acquisition
SI	Self-Interruption
SR	Self-repair
SRB	Scope of Relevant Behavior
TCU	Turn-Constructional Unit
TR	Truncated Word
UP	Unfilled Pause
VOC	Vocal Marker

Acknowledgments

This book is a revised version of my Ph.D thesis, completed at the Université Sorbonne Nouvelle (France) in December 2021. This work could not have seen the light of day without the tremendous support of my two advisors Aliyah Morgenstern and Maria Candea. Their continuous guidance, enthusiasm, insight, and sympathy, whether it was online or in person, has truly helped me complete this journey. This work would also not have been possible without the financial support of my university and my Doctoral School *MAGIIE*, as well as the research grant provided by the LABEX EFL.

Warm thanks to colleagues from *SeSyLiA*, especially Céline Horgues and Sylwia Scheuer for giving me access to the SITAF corpus and for their valuable insight on tandem interactions. I would also like to express my gratitude towards Pauline Beaupoil Hourdel who has been my mentor since my research internship.

I am also deeply grateful to members of the (dis)fluency community who have all helped me complete my study in their own way: special thanks to my other mentor, Ludivine Crible, for her insightful comments, suggestions, and assistance at different stages of my research project; big thanks to friends and colleagues from Bielefeld (Simon Betz, Loredana Schettino); I am also deeply thankful to Christelle Dodane, Ivana Didirková and Fabrice Hirsch from the *BENEPHIDIRE* project. My thanks also go to people from the *Gesture and Multimodality Group* at UC Berkeley, and more specifically Eve Sweetser who supervised me during my research stay.

Big thanks to my London friends who were the very first participants who accepted to take part in my experiment as part of my Master's project in 2015. Big thanks to my Parisian friends from *La Maison de La Recherche* who have made this adventure truly memorable. Much love to friends and family who have been following me in the past ten years, even before I started my Ph.D. Special thanks to Guillaume, my role model, who taught me so much. And of course, I wish to thank *my* Hugo, who despite his constant teasing, has always genuinely shown his support.

Lastly, I would like to thank you all, speakers of this world, for speaking, gesturing, laughing, saying *uhm*, and interacting in your first, and second, or third – who knows how many- language; without you I could have never found such a fascinating topic of research.

Singing for me is -s -s sweet relief (…) it is the only -s -s time when I (…) fff feel -f -f fluent. (Megan Washington, *Ted Talk Radio Hour with NPR*, 2014)[1]

The laughter died out, and only gestures of arms, movements of bodies, could be seen shaping something in the room. Was it an argument? A bet on the boat races? Was it nothing of the sort? What was shaped by the arms and bodies moving in the twilight room? (Virginia Woolf, *Jacob's Room*, 2008 Penguins edition, p. 56.)

---

[1]. Retrieved from https://www.npr.org/2014/11/21/364151177/how-does-singing-help-achieve-stillness (August 16th 2021)

Introduction

I. Introducing inter-(dis)fluency: Beyond cognitive oriented models of speech production

What happens when we speak? To put it simply, according to previous models of word production (e.g. Levelt, 1983, 1989, 1999), our brains go through a series of mental operations, as we first select and activate a lexical item stored in our minds, assess its morphological and phonological code, then formulate and articulate the intended expression in the speech channel. While spoken languages typically follow a linear order, as speakers utter one word after the other in the acoustic channel, they are in fact governed by a number of nonlinear processes, since speakers constantly work on their production to re-shape the course of their delivery. They may pause to think about what to say next, re-start a previously uttered constituent, add a new item, or abandon a current utterance. Spoken languages are thus typically governed by cycles of what have commonly been labeled "fluent" (grammatically correct syntactic structures with lexical content) versus "disfluent" speech (non-lexical items which add no propositional content and disturb the fluidity of the surface structures). However, spoken speech production covers a multiplicity of genres, from theatrical performance, talk show, prayer, to spontaneous face-to-face encounter, film interview, political speech, etc., which inevitably affects how we speak. In early psycholinguistic work on disfluency phenomena, a common distinction was often drawn between "spontaneous" and "prepared" speech, with a clear focus on the recognition of disfluency phenomena in spontaneous productions, i.e., productions elicited spontaneously with no preparation beforehand, as opposed to read or laboratory speech. As many researchers (e.g. Bailey & Feirrera; Shriberg, 1994, among others) have claimed, unprepared spontaneous speech necessarily gives rise to many disfluencies, such as "uh" and "um", self-repairs, repetitions, truncations, and the like. Indeed, disfluencies are a very common part of human speech, and are said to occur at the rate of six to ten per hundred words (Bortfeld et al., 2001; Dollaghan & Campbell, 1992; Fox Tree, 1995; Shriberg, 1994). Disfluencies are virtually everywhere, not only in our spontaneous exchanges, but in TV shows, video games, or animated films. These markers of spontaneity, which help distinguish between careful read speech and spontaneous speech events, are also what makes us human. In fact, a number of new technologies have emerged recently and aimed to model disfluencies for speech synthesis, such as the *Google Duplex*, an Artificial Intelligence system using conversational data and its many disfluencies to model natural sounding speech, to carry out "real world" tasks over the phone.[2] Speech disfluency has also been a popular topic of research in speech modelling and human-machine dialogue since the late 1990s, with the rise of computer technology (to name but a few, Betz et al., 2018; Eklund, 2004; Eklund & Shriberg, 1998). In sum, the study of disfluency is gaining more and more attention in various fields, such as psycholinguistics, cognitive science, or computational linguistics, and is now recognized as a legitimate topic of research, with the recurrent *DiSS* workshop (Disfluency in Spontaneous Speech)[3] first held in 1999, which brings together researchers from various academic disciplines interested in topics and issues surrounding disfluency. This common interest is mainly due to the large role disfluencies are said to play in speech production and comprehension, as Shriberg (2001, p. 53) reported: "disfluencies provide a window onto underlying processes affecting human speech and language production". But what exactly is disfluency? Where does the term come from? What are its implications for current linguistic research?

The term "disfluency" initially stems from a departure of the notion of *ideal delivery*, an expression used to describe the seemingly continuous *fluent* flow of speech, marked by an absence of "noise" in the signal or the presence of ungrammatical structures (Clark, 1996). Similarly, in Second Language Acquisition, the notion of "fluency" refers to ideally effortless native-like speech, which contains very few errors, as opposed to non-native speech, which is not yet "fluent" in the acquisition process (Lennon, 1990). In addition, "fluency" can also refer to the ability to produce wellformed expressions in a persuasive and stylistic manner, using rich vocabulary and eloquent utterances (Fillmore, 1976). As this book will show, the constructs of "fluency" versus "disfluency" have different definitions, and they have constantly been subject to a binary opposition in the literature across several theoretical fields, based on the monolithic and mythical assumption that a speaker is either fluent or disfluent, that a structure either reflects fluency or disfluency, or that certain phenomena are either deemed lexical (e.g. verbs, nouns, adjectives etc.) or non-lexical (e.g., breathing, laughter, clicking sounds and the like). The main goal of this book is to go beyond this common opposition, and further explore the complexity of these phenomena by offering an integrated and multi-level approach, combining different frameworks and methodologies. The main issue with previous studies, as will be high-

---

2. Information retrieved from https://ai.googleblog.com/2018/05/duplex-ai-system-for-natural-conversation.html (August 16th, 2021)

3. Information concerning the workshop series can be found in Ralph Rose's website https://filledpause.org/diss/ (last retrieved on August 16th, 2021)

lighted throughout this book, is that so-called disfluency markers (e.g., "uh", "um", pauses, repairs, repetitions, truncations, and the like) have too often been exclusively restricted to the level of *speech* analysis. But language is so much more than a series of spoken words in decontextualized utterances. Language is an embodied experience, grounded in our overall environment comprised of our own bodies, our movement in space, the people and objects around us, and our social background. Following the frameworks of interactional linguistics, linguistic anthropology, cognitive linguistics, and gesture studies, it will be maintained throughout this book that the complexity of human communication can only be fully understood in richly contextualized situations, where all semiotic features (voice, gaze, face, gesture, icons) are deployed together at a specific moment in time to build meaning that is relevant to the task at hand. The present work is thus deeply influenced by the work of researchers who do not only consider language as a verbal or vocal phenomenon, but a multimodal one, deeply embedded within social structures (Candea, 2000; Cienki, 2015a, Goodwin, 1981, Morgenstern, 2014; Morgenstern et al., 2021, Streeck, 2009b, Sweetser, 1998, among others).

These assumptions have a number of consequences for the study of so-called disfluency phenomena. The issue with the term "disfluency" is that it presupposes a problem to be fixed, or a disruption, which is too restrictive, and does not truly capture the complexity of these phenomena. A novel term will thus be introduced in this book to describe these processes, following previous authors' initiatives (Candea, 2000; Crible et al., 2019; Allwood, 2017; McCarthy, 2009) labeled *inter-(dis)fluency*. Following Crible et al.'s (2019) functionally ambivalent approach to (dis)fluency, the "dis" in brackets captures the ambivalence of fluency and disfluency phenomena, without systematically opposing them, hence regarding them as dynamic systems, with the potential for the same a priori "disfluent" forms to serve both "fluent" and/or "disfluent" functions. The prefix "inter", as will be further explained in the first Chapter, captures the interactive process of *doing fluency*, or *confluence* (McCarthy, 2009) where several levels of analysis (speech, gesture, and interaction) are combined to build the overall flow of communication. The core term "fluency" is to be understood here not as second language proficiency, but as a metaphor embodying the notions of continuity, flow, progressivity, and fluidity. This metaphor will be found throughout the analyses. Let us illustrate this idea with a short example, which can be analyzed in many different ways, depending on the approach taken:

```
*SPK1: &uh (..) well you'd have [//] you wouldn't &hav [/] you wouldn't [//] you'd
       have to ask &uh other people on that.
*SPK1: &uh I always seem you know growing up in &b +//.
*SPK1: I think [/] I think in fact [/] I think that's my house over there.
```

These three utterances are taken from an interview recorded in 1992 with American film director Tim Burton, transcribed with CHAT transcription conventions (cf Appendix 1). An expert in disfluency research would commonly make the following observations regarding: the number of occurrences found in this passage (10 in total in bold, one pause, three filled pauses, two truncations, one repair, one self-interruption, two repetitions), where they are located in the utterance (utterance-initial, medial, and final), and whether they co-occur with one another or appear isolated, forming more complex sequences (e.g. a truncation clustered with a repair). Drawing from this type of analysis, we can make the preliminary observation that this particular speaker is highly *disfluent*, given the number of disfluencies found in his speech. We may thus wonder, how come this American native speaker, who was already quite famous at that time, and who was used to doing interviews on TV, produces so many "unwanted" "non-lexical" items in his speech? Does it reflect a lack of confidence? Stress and anxiety? Difficulties in grammatical encoding? While there is no straightforward answer to this question, we soon realize that this type of analysis is too restrictive, as it completely disregards other fundamental aspects of face-to-face communication, mainly visible bodily behavior and interactional dynamics. Let us now reconsider this example by taking into account these two additional layers of analysis, using a multimodal transcription system:

Tim Burton – 1992 interview[4]

```
1 *INT: How strange were you as a child?
            ((gazes at TIM))
2 *TIM: uh (…) well you'd have you wouldn't h(ave) you wouldn't
                        ((aborted gesture))
hhh. you'd have to ask uh other people on that
((brings down his right palm facing sideways in a rapid motion))
```

---

4. Tim Burton on Bob Costas, 1992 late night interview. The full video can be found at https://www.youtube.com/watch?v=krc8NVKtAoE&t=71s (last retrieved on August 16th, 2021)

```
3 *TIM: uh I always seem you know growing up in B(urbank)
((bent fingers brought forward in his central gesture space with a series of
repetitive beat motions))
```

```
4 *TIM: I think I think in fact I think that's my house over there.
((points to the transistor next to him with his index finger))
```

```
5 *INT: ((laughs))
```

Tim Burton was first asked a rather blunt question by the interviewer about his childhood (l.1), projecting a question-answer sequence. Tim Burton's utterance in line 2 is first delayed with a turn-initial filled pause clustered with an unfilled pause, indexing an initiation to take the turn and provide an answer to the interviewer's prior question. What is relevant to note here is that the director is not asked a question about his films or his career as a filmmaker, but a personal one regarding his private life, accounting for a change of participant's status or discourse identity (from "film director" to perhaps "intimate friend"). All these features (turn-taking, participation framework, sequence formation, etc.,) which are highly common characteristics of talk-in-interaction in *Conversation Analysis* (Sacks et al., 1974), are altogether essential to further our understanding of this excerpt. In this view, Tim Burton is thus not solely a highly "disfluent" speaker, but the co-participant of a conversation, more specifically a film interview, who is recorded live on television, and who is expected to provide answers to a number of questions asked by the interviewer in a timely manner. He may decide, however, to display dispreferred actions by rejecting the current topic of conversation, which is what he does here, as he refrains from providing a straightforward answer to the interviewer's question. In this view, the notion of *fluency* may thus also be applied to the *flow* or *progressivity* of the interaction, going beyond the level of speech analysis.

We can further note that the speaker displayed different forms of participation towards the task at hand, reshaping the course of his emerging talk and redirecting his attention to external objects. These manifestations are conveyed in his visual-gestural behavior, as depicted in the illustrations within the transcript. We can see him moving his hands in space in an orchestrated manner with his speech: in line 2, Tim dismissed the previously asked question with a negative statement ("I wouldn't") then shifted the topic ("you'd have to ask other people on that") while producing a sort of "brushing away" gesture (Bressem & Müller, 2014), synchronized with an audible inbreath ("hhh.") moving his hand away from his body in a rapid motion, as to negatively assess the current topic of conversation. He further makes use of his surrounding space to build meaning with his hands: he places his right hand with bent fingers opposite him in the gesture space to refer to a specific location (probably his hometown Burbank, in line 3, but the word was truncated), and then points towards an external object (the transistor in the studio) to direct the interviewer's attention towards an imaginary location (his house). In sum, the speaker does so much more than producing a series of "disfluent" utterances in this excerpt, he in fact *languages* his experience (Morgenstern, 2020) with his hands, making use of his body and his surrounding material environment to build meaning. As Jürgen Streeck beautifully said, "the world of artifacts was not built by brains, but hands" (Streeck, 2020, p. 2). Hands, and arms, among other parts of the body (e.g. trunk and shoulders) thus play a fundamental role in the interactive process of building language. In this sense, spoken words are not only generated by a series of mental processes working in the brain, they are captured in situated discourse, experienced by living embodied human beings in the world. While the study of embodiment and gesture is now being more and more recognized as a legitimate and full-fledged topic of research, with for instance the *International Society for Gesture Studies*,[5] the journal *Gesture*[6] and the book series *Gesture Studies*,[7] co-edited by Sotaro Kita and Adam

---

5. https://www.gesturestudies.com (las consulted on August 17th 2021)
6. https://benjamins.com/catalog/gest (last consulted on August 17th 2021)
7. https://benjamins.com/catalog/gs (last consulted on August 17th 2021)

Kendon, their relationship to (dis)fluency remains still quite underexplored in the literature.

To address this gap, it will be argued in this book that the constructs of fluency and disfluency should *not* be restricted to the level of speech production, reflecting a mental cognitive process associated with difficulty or uncertainty, but should include other fundamental features as well, illustrated in this short example. The speaker may have sounded "disfluent" from a verbal or vocal perspective, but he also performed a series of *fluid* actions embodied in his *gestural flow*. So where exactly do we draw the line between "fluency" and "disfluency"? Is it in fact even relevant to oppose these notions? The present work calls for further investigation and stresses the need to consider all aspects of multimodal communication to explore the complexity of inter-(dis)fluency phenomena.

II. Data under study

The aim of this book is to explore the ways in which the different dimensions outlined above (speech, gesture, interaction) may interact with one another to build the fluency, fluidity, or flow, of multimodal discourse, by targeting different languages and types of situations in a dataset of videorecorded productions. Starting with the assumption that inter-(dis)fluency is a multimodal, dynamic and ambivalent system, I expect a high degree of variability and dispersion in the distribution of (dis)fluency markers (which will be labelled *fluencemes*, further explained in Chapters 2 and 3), as well as gestures, according to task type, or language. To that aim, this study will focus on a specialized video dataset of university students engaged in different activities in their first and second language.

The first dataset under study is a selected sample of the SITAF corpus (Horgues & Scheuer, 2015) which includes video recordings of 21 French and American students from Sorbonne Nouvelle University engaged in an argumentative task. The students interacted in pairs in L1-L2 settings, alternating between their first and second language in French and English. The students were asked to debate on a given topic and decide on their level of agreement. The pair knew each other fairly well, since they met once a month as part of a tandem exchange program to practice their second language. During the exchanges, they were thus invited to share and co-construct ideas on a given topic (i.e. do prisoners have the right to vote, are teenage years the best years of your life, etc.) leading to joint multimodal productions.

The second dataset under study is a selected sample of the *DisReg corpus*, collected by myself for this study (Kosmala, 2020a), which comprises video recordings of 12 French students from Sorbonne Nouvelle University engaged in two different tasks in different settings. The students were first recorded during their presentation of a graded oral assignment in class, performed in front of the teacher and the whole classroom. They were then recorded face-to-face in pairs, and asked to discuss everyday topics (last film seen on TV, funny anecdote at university, etc.). Just like the participants from the SITAF corpus, the pairs knew each other from university, and could hence discuss their common experience and display several tokens of understanding, leading to the *co-fluency* of discourse.

This dataset was compiled for its multimodal quality, as well as for the number of similarities found between the two data samples (similar speaker profiles, discourse identities, university setting, etc., see Chapter 3) which enables to triangulate evidence from language proficiency, setting, task type, genre, and setting, as to capture the multifunctionality and multimodality of inter-(dis)fluency across different contexts of use.

III. Preview of the book

This book comprises six different chapters, which all target both theoretical and methodological issues regarding the multimodal and multidimensional status of fluency, as well as its place in linguistic research.

The first two chapters are mainly theoretical, reviewing a number of interdisciplinary research fields relevant to the study of (dis)fluency, mainly psycholinguistics, usage-based linguistics, second language acquisition, gesture studies and interactional linguistics. In particular, the first chapter contributes to the current terminological debate regarding the use of the term "disfluency" in the literature, further justifying my choice of terminology, leading to the construction of my integrated framework. The second chapter reviews a number of studies conducted in L1 and L2 fluency as well as gesture research in order to acquire a holistic understanding of these phenomena within diverse linguistic frameworks and contextual environments.

The third chapter is methodological, and presents the mixed-methods methodology used in the study which relies on quantitative treatments performed with several tools and softwares (ELAN, CLAN, Excel, and statistical tests) as well as micro analyses of the data, using conversation-analytic tools borrowed from Conversational Analysis (Mondada, 2007; Sacks et al., 1974).

The last three chapters are empirical, and present the results of the two corpus-based studies conducted on the *SITAF* and *DisReg corpus*. Chapter 4 focuses on the *SITAF corpus*, targeting aspects of native versus non-native language use. Chapter 5, which focuses on the DisReg corpus, follows the same structure as Chapter 4. The aim of this chapter is to draw potential differences in fluency and visual-gestural behavior across two distinct styles and settings (individual graded class presentations versus face-to-face casual conversations). Lastly, Chapter 6 presents a number of analyses from the two data samples, focusing this time exclusively on micro qualitative analyses of the data in order to shed light on the multiple features affecting the use of fluencemes in multimodal discourse.

All the findings are then discussed in the *General Conclusion*, where the main results obtained in Chapters 4 and 5 are summarized, and the two datasets are compared. A number of recurrent characteristics differentiating fluency and gesture behavior across languages and settings is further presented, based on the different variables used in the annotation model. Specific attention is also paid to individual differences, which play a fundamental role in corpus-based research. Lastly, the *General Conclusion* presents a multidimensional approach to inter-(dis)fluency, evaluating different degrees of fluency and disfluency in a tridimensional continuum based on the different dimensions explored throughout the chapters (speech, gesture, interaction).

CHAPTER 1

Theoretical background

The aim of this chapter is to discuss the different theoretical and methodological frameworks grounding the concepts of fluency and disfluency in the study of spoken language. It will review very different theoretical backgrounds such as psycholinguistics, cognitive usage-based linguistics, and second language acquisition, but other academic fields will also be reviewed, some of which have not as often been in the scope of "traditional" disfluency research, mainly interactional linguistics and gesture studies. The overview of these various theoretical approaches will highlight the need to view inter-(dis)fluency phenomena as complex, dynamic, multi-level, and multi-modal processes.

This chapter thus also aims to contribute to the terminological debate regarding the use of the term "disfluency". We may ask ourselves whether it is really accurate to use such a "negative" (but common) term, which originally referred to stuttering and verbal blundering, when dealing with spontaneous face-to-face spoken interaction. Isn't it time, as Allwood (2017) or Tottie (2014) suggested, to make a change in the terminology? While there is no straightforward answer to this question, this chapter will still attempt to paint a consistent picture of the diverse and complex phenomena related to the construct of fluency and disfluency. This multi-approach construct will not be restricted to the verbal and vocal dimensions of speech, but will incorporate other relevant visible features of face-to-face communication as well.

This chapter is structured as follows: first, I begin with the traditional production-based approach to disfluency phenomena, related to speech planning and cognitive processes; secondly, I sketch out the different terms associated with these phenomena and their different approaches, and I discuss my choice of terminology; thirdly, I review three other theoretical frameworks (Cognitive Grammar, Interactional Linguistics, and Gesture Studies) relevant to the present study of inter-(dis)fluency. Finally, I conclude this chapter with an introduction to my integrated framework, and address my main theoretical assumptions.

I. What is disfluency?: A psycholinguistic production model

The study of disfluency has been analyzed thoroughly over the past sixty years by a number of researchers in different academic fields, such as speech pathologists, speech scientists, phoneticians, and psycholinguists (Goldman-Eisler, 1958; Johnson, 1961; Lickley, 2015; Maclay & Osgood, 1959; Shriberg, 1994; to name but a few). The present section will focus on the theoretical framework mainly adopted by (but not restricted to)[8] psycholinguists, and will present a brief review of their theoretical and methodological approaches to disfluency.[9]

1.1 Disfluency as a deviation in speech from the ideal delivery

In the field of pycholinguistics, the study of disfluency, or *speech errors* (see Levelt, 1983, 1989; Menn & Dronkers, 2016) has been of particular interest with regard to how speakers' brains create and understand meaningful language, based on different speech production models (Menn & Dronkers, 2016). Psycholinguist Levelt (1983, 1989, 1999) discussed, for instance, the *speakers' linearization problem*, mainly that the channel of speech prohibits the simultaneous expression of multiple propositions; consequently, a linear order has to be determined, which compels speakers to constantly work on their production. In order to do so, speakers can monitor their own speech (Levelt, 1983) by following several steps (*message construction, formulating, articulating, parsing*, and *monitoring*). Thus arises the notion of "ideal delivery": every use of a word, phrase or sentence has an ideal delivery, defined as "a single action with no suspensions – no silent pauses, no fillers, no repeats, no self-corrections, no delays except for those required by the syntax of the sentence" (Clark, 1996, p. 253). When conversing, the primary goal of speakers is to produce maximally acceptable speech in both content and form (Hieke, 1981, p. 150). However, despite speakers' efforts to be in control of the communication channel and remain intelligible, they are often obliged to stop, backtrack, or interrupt their current planning, which often leads to utterances which turn out to be very different from their initial ideal delivery (Hieke, 1980). Given the fluctuating nature of speech production (moving backwards and forwards from *conceptualization* to *articulation*) it first appears that the construct of disfluency is originally based on a reflection of the non-linearity of speech, but also on a departure from the representation of this

---

[8]. This section will also mention the work of computational linguists (e.g. Shriberg, 1994).
[9]. The field of pathological "dysfluency" (typically concerned with pathological speech such as stuttering or aphasia) goes beyond the scope of this book so it will not be reviewed in this chapter.

ideal delivery. In fact, Ferreira & Bailey (2004, p. 234) defined disfluency as "any deviation in speech from the ideal delivery". They also claimed that some disfluencies (such as repeats, abandonments and repairs) create *ungrammatical utterances*, which further implies that disfluency constitutes a deviation from an ideal, grammatical, and well-formed utterance.

1.2 The role of disfluencies in speech production

Disfluency, "when speech breaks down" (Lickley, 2015, p. 12), thus very often describes an interruption in the speech flow (Fox Tree, 1995; Merlo & Mansur, 2004). "Disfluent" utterances tend to follow the same surface structure (Shriberg, 1994) which can be divided into different parts, or regions: (1) the original delivery, (2) the reparandum, (3) the edit term, (4) repair, and (5) resumption. The *reparandum* region shows the item that needs to be repaired. This region ends at the *interruption point* (or *suspension point*), the point in which the speech flow breaks down. It is then followed by the *editing phase* (also called *interregnum*, or *hiatus*) which can be empty, or contain a silent or filled pause. When the interregnum is filled, the utterance does not necessarily have to be followed by a disruption, but can be resumed with no repair (*suspensive interruption*). However, in some cases, a repair (or *reparans*) does occur (*disfluent interruption*), which will then lead to the *resumption* of fluency (i.e. the fluent delivery).

1.3 Major disfluency types and classifications

One of the first major studies conducted on disfluency phenomena dates back to the 1950s with Maclay & Osgood's (1959) seminal paper entitled *Hesitation Phenomena in Spontaneous Speech*. In this paper, the authors provided a formal categorization of disfluency (or "hesitation") phenomena, based on Mahl's (1956) categorization of "disturbances",[10] mainly: (1) filled pause, (2) unfilled pause, (4) false starts and (4) repeats.

A few decades later, with the rise of speech technology and computerized applications, disfluencies were annotated at a much larger scale and more systematically by a number of speech technologists who were interested in the annotation of natural speech data (e.g., Meteer et al., 1995). One of the first major and highly influential annotation schemes in this area was introduced by Shriberg (1994), who worked on a large dataset comprising different types of corpora (human-human and human-computer dialogues. Her annotation model, which initially targeted

---

10. These terminological differences (*hesitation* and *disturbances*) will be discussed in Section II.2.1.

"disruptive" features of spoken speech (i.e. repetitions, substitutions, insertions, misarticulations, word fragments etc.), relied on a complex and efficient classification system, which paved the way for later annotation models of disfluency (e.g., Christodoulides et al., 2018; Eklund, 2004; Moniz, 2013; Pallaud et al., 2013). More recently, the DUEL (*Disfluency, Exclamation, and Laughter in Dialogue*) project (Hough et al., 2016) introduced a crosslinguistic annotation model of disfluency and laughter for practical and computational dialogue modelling, which included the annotation of several disfluencies (e.g. filled pauses, repairs, and restarts, among others).[11] The main commonality between the different disfluency annotation models is the systematic reference to Levelt (1983)'s Repair Model which introduced the different Disfluency regions in their surface structure (i.e. *reparandum, interruption point, interregnum, repair*; cf Section I.1.2).

As Pallaud et al., (2019) noted, disfluencies are concerned with phonetic, acoustic, and prosodic levels, as well as morpho-syntactic ones. For instance, Guaïtella (1993) emphasized the acoustic and perceptible features of vocal "hesitations" (e.g. filled pauses, prolongations etc.) which have specific acoustic features (Guaïtella, 1993, p. 131), such as decreasing of pitch or diminution of subglottal pressure. Conversely, Pallaud et al., (2019, p. 1) rather focused on *morpho-syntactic disruptions*, which have specific morpho-syntactic and syntagmatic effects (with regard to their position within the different disfluency regions).

Disfluencies, which are very frequent in natural language production, include several markers (e.g. filled and unfilled pauses, substitutions, deletions, interruptions), and they can be seen as the hallmarks of speech production processes (i.e. planning, processing, articulating, monitoring etc.). They are inherent to spontaneous spoken speech, and consequently, as many psycholinguists have argued (e.g. Clark, 2002; Pallaud et al., 2013), there is nothing dysfunctional about them, despite what the prefix "dis" suggests. There are, however, several issues regarding the term disfluency, and there are a number of overlapping terms used in the literature to describe the same phenomena.

---

11. This is a reference to the 3-year collaborative project between Université Paris Diderot and Bielefeld University (information found on this website https://www.dsg-bielefeld.de/DUEL/, last retrieved on August 26th 2021). Its aim was to model disfluencies in different spoken languages (German, French, and Chinese) and create formal models and computational systems on speech processing.

II. Fluency, disfluency, and hesitation: A terminological debate beyond terminological issues

The confusion and lack of consensus over the terminology have been pointed out by several researchers (to name but a few, Allwood, 2017; De Jong, 2018; Eklund, 2004; Kormos & Dénes, 2004; Lickley, 2015). The choice of terminology (e.g. *fluency, disfluency, hesitation, communication management* etc.), as we shall see, will reflect the different theoretical views of these phenomena.

2.1 Definitions of L1 and L2 fluency

2.1.1 *Smoothness of speech versus language competence*

As pointed out earlier, the notion of disfluency has often been associated with a deviation in speech from the "ideal delivery", in other words, a *fluent* delivery. But what does the term *fluency* suggest precisely? If we look at a dictionary entry, "fluency" is defined as "a smooth and easy flow; readiness, smoothness of speech" (Oxford English Dictionary). This concept of "smoothness" was also taken up by Lickley (2015, p. 2) who regarded speech fluency as multidimensional. He listed three different dimensions of fluency, where the notion of smoothness is recurrent:

1. Planning fluency: smoothness of the speech flow.
2. Surface fluency: a smooth flow from one sound to the next.
3. Perceived fluency: the listener's impression that the speech they are listening to has been produced smoothly.

As Lickley observed, an "intuitive" definition of fluency is based on the listener's perception of the speech flow. From the listener's perspective, fluency can be viewed as "an impression on the listener's part that the psycholinguistic processes of speech planning and speech production are functioning easily and efficiently" (Lennon, 1990, p. 291). Once again, the idea of speech being produced "easily" and "efficiently" seems to some degree related to the notion of "smoothness", and perhaps again the construct of an ideal and uninterrupted delivery of speech. Additionally, Fillmore (1976, p. 93) gave four different definitions of fluency:

1. The ability to talk at length with few pauses and fill time with talk.
2. The ability to express a message in a coherent manner with "semantically dense" sentences.
3. The ability to talk in a wide range of contexts.
4. The ability to be creative and imaginative in language use.

These four aspects of fluency seem to strongly rely on the speakers' "abilities" to perform a series of actions in different contexts of language use, but not as much of on the flow of speech (except, perhaps, in 1). As Kormos & Denès (2004) pointed out, there are two main approaches to fluency, one which regards it as a *temporal phenomenon*, and another one as a *spoken language competence*. The latter suggests a speaker's level of proficiency (e.g. "I speak English fluently"), which is in sharp contrast with the first definitions given by Lickley (2015).

2.1.2 Fluency in Second Language Acquisition

Within an EFL (*English as a Foreign Language*) environment, Lennon (1990, p. 389) explained that the term "fluency" has a narrow and a broad sense. The broad sense is a general cover term for oral proficiency, and is usually used for academic reference with entries such as "fair", "good", "fluent". The narrow sense, on the other hand, is one component of oral proficiency, which can be found in procedures for grading oral examinations used by teachers.

In SLA, many studies on fluency aim to find objective measures of a speaker's speech fluency in order to evaluate their speaking proficiency (De Jong, 2018). These measures include speech rate (the number of syllables articulated per minute), mean length of utterance (average number of syllables produced in utterances), and number of filled pauses, silent pauses, repetitions, and repairs per minute, (for an extensive review see De Jong, 2018, p. 4). The rate of disfluency markers is thus a key component of speech fluency, and is often used as a measure to subjective ratings of perceived fluency (see Riggenbach, 1991; Watanabe & Rose, 2012). To that end, the goal for L2 learners would be to "produce speech at the tempo of native speakers, unimpeded by silent pauses and hesitations, filled pauses ("ers" and "erms"), self-corrections, repetitions, false starts, and the like" (Lennon, 1990, p. 390). However, Lennon also pointed out the mystical monolithic view of fluency as a target to "native-like levels". He argued: (p. 292)

> It is often assumed that the fluency target of the language learner is "native-like levels". However, a moment's reflection shows that the idea of monolithic and unitary fluency for native speakers is mythical. Native speakers clearly differ among themselves in fluency, and, more particularly, any individual native speaker may be more or less fluent according to the topic, interlocutor, situation, "noise", stress, and other factors.

Consequently, the concept of fluency is difficult to grasp because it is originally based on the realization of an ideal and "native-like" fixed language. But how can we measure the proficiency of a non-native speaker based on measures that are also inherent to native speech? As Lickley (2015, p. 2) observed, there can be a "mismatch" between "the flow of the processes underlying speech production" and "the listener's perception of fluency". He added:

> An utterance that is perceived as fluent may still have contained hitches during the production processes. Minor disturbances in the flow of overt speech are easily missed by the listener, and may be detectable only on close inspection of the acoustic signal.

This further justifies Lickley's argument in favor of a multidimensional view of fluency, which includes the planning level, the surface level, and the perception level. As we shall see throughout this book, the notions of fluency and disfluency should not only be restricted to levels of production or perception but should include other dimensions as well, such as interaction. For instance, McCarthy (2009), in his paper entitled *Rethinking Spoken Fluency*, re-examined the notion of fluency by putting forward its interactive dimension. While fluency has typically been conceived as a monologic achievement, essentially judged with temporal measures (e.g. speed of delivery, number of pauses etc.), McCarthy focused on the *co-creation* of fluency in a conversation, rather than the fluency of an individual speaker. Therefore, he offered the metaphor of "confluence" to replace the term "fluency".

2.2 Approaches to L1 disfluency

If fluency embodies the ideal, efficient, and smooth delivery of speech, then disfluency presents a "failure" to maintain the smoothness of speech. We are now faced with a challenging question, raised by Lickley (2015, p. 13):

> Is fluent speech the norm? If a speaker can produce a stream of spontaneous speech without having second thoughts about whether they are conveying the correct message at the right time, without spotting and reacting to an inaccuracy in the message or an error in its production, without struggling to find the right words and getting the sounds right, and without being interrupted by another speaker or some other distraction, then that stream of speech is likely to be completed smoothly, without interruption or revision: Fluently, in other words. However, both casual observation and corpus studies of unrehearsed speech suggest that such fluency is the exception, rather than the rule.

The issue with the term disfluency[12] is that it entails a pathological problem, or something dysfunctional (which was originally the case with the term "dysflu-

---

12. We also find the term "non-fluency" in the literature, which is explained in more detail in Eklund's dissertation (Eklund, 2004, p. 158).

ency" used to refer to speech pathologies and stuttering). But disfluencies are also inherent to spontaneous speech and play a large role in speech production. In fact, disfluencies can be used to restore *continuity* in speech (e.g. Clark & Wasow, 1998). This view is in sharp contrast with the view of disfluency as a negative *disruption* or *interruption*. Consequently, two different views on disfluency phenomena have emerged in the literature, resulting in radically different theoretical implications, and thus further questioning the use of the term *disfluency*. These views are presented below.

2.2.1 *The two main views of disfluency*

In her doctoral dissertation, Nicholson (2007, p. 94) pointed out two main views of disfluency: the first one, called the *Strategic Modelling* view, suggests that disfluencies are used for strategic and communicative purposes in order to signal their commitment to the listener. The second view, called the *Cognitive Burden view*, considers the speech production process as a highly complex one which can be cognitively overburdened, thus leading to the production of disfluencies. Disfluencies are thus viewed as a manifestation of cognitive load. Similarly, Clark & Fox Tree (2002) shed light on the different conceptions of one specific class of disfluency markers, mainly filled pauses. They presented three views, labeled (1)" filler-as-symptom", (2) "filler-as-signal", and (3) "filler-as-word". In the first view, "fillers"[13] are seen as symptoms of problems in speaking. In the second view, they are regarded as nonlinguistic signals which initiate a delay in speech. The third view, which has led to numerous debates (see Corley & Stewart, 2008; Kowal et al., 1983; Tottie, 2016) states that "uh" and "um" should be seen as word interjections commenting on a speaker's performance. While the third view could only be applied to filled pauses (and hardly to other disfluency markers such as repetitions, self-repairs or silences), I will examine the two views proposed by Nicholson (2007), which are similar to (1) and (2).

The *Cognitive Burden* (or *disfluency-as-symptom*) view is essentially reflected in the work of psycholinguists who explored and investigated the contextual, lexical, and cognitive determinants of disfluencies. Beattie (1979), who worked on *hesitation phenomena* (I will discuss the choice of the term "hesitation" in the following subsection), has shown that long clauses (containing 6–10 words) were more likely to contain more pauses than short ones (2–5 words). This is supported by the hypothesis that hesitation pauses occur at high points of uncertainty: unpredictable or infrequent lexical items are more likely to be preceded by pauses than frequent ones (Beattie & Butterworth, 1979). Consequently, hesitation disfluencies are said to reflect "an act of choice" (Beattie & Butterworth, 1979, p. 202)

---

13. Note that the authors used the term "fillers" in their paper to refer to filled pauses.

between different lexical items. More evidence suggests that lexical access problems and planning difficulties often lead to disfluencies (Brennan & Schober, 2001; Hartsuiker & Notebaert, 2009; Schnadt & Corley, 2006). For instance, Hartsuiker & Notebaert (2009) conducted an experimental study in which participants were asked to describe networks of lines, drawings, and paths connecting these drawings. Results indicated that pictures which had a low name agreement led to more disfluencies than those with high name agreement. They concluded that difficulties at certain stages of language production (i.e., lexical access) resulted in distinct patterns of disfluencies (i.e. self-corrections and repetitions).

In sum, a number of studies have insisted on the fact that disfluencies reflect signs of "trouble", "problems", and "difficulties" in speech. They occur when speakers detect *trouble* in processing: as Levelt (1983) suggests, "uh" is a symptom of recency of *trouble* indicating that the trouble is still present at the moment of interruption. Similarly, filled pauses are said to provide a consistent picture of *difficulties* encountered in sentence planning (Holmes, 1988), as they are consistently affected by message-levels *difficulties* (Fraundorf & Watson, 2014). Furthermore, disfluencies indicate the depth of speakers' retrieval *problems* (Smith & Clark, 1993), reflect cognitive *difficulty* (Finlayson & Corley, 2012) and production *difficulty* (Fraundorf & Watson, 2011). Merlo & Mansur (2010, p. 491) define them as *"verbalized difficulties* in which the speaker notices a problem after or during the speech".

However, advocates of the *Strategic Modelling* view (or disfluency-as-signal) suggest that disfluencies have little to do with trouble. Disfluencies can serve a wide array of pragmatic functions, such as initiating a turn (Schegloff, 2010), keeping the floor (Kjellmer, 2003; Maclay & Osgood, 1959; Tottie, 2014), or managing interpersonal relations (Fischer, 2000). Tottie (2011, 2014, 2015, 2016, 2019) conducted several studies dedicated to the *pragmatic* uses of filled pauses in British and American English. In her work, which focuses primarily on the distribution of filled pauses in naturally occurring conversation, she put forward the idea that "uh" and "um" should be considered as a class of pragmatic markers, which are strongly determined by setting and register.[14] Indeed, her corpus-based studies revealed effects in age, gender, socio-economic class, context, and register (Tottie, 2011, 2014). In line with Clark & Fox Tree's (2002) hypothesis that "uh" and "um" signal a delay in speech in order to keep or cede the floor, or to attract attention (Kjellmer 2003), Tottie (2011) stressed the fact that "uh" and "um" functioned as a *planning* device, and thus suggested the term *planner*. She argued that filled pauses could serve several overlapping functions: they can help structure upcoming discourse (following Swerts, 1998), but they can also be used intentionally with a stylistic purpose. She further stated (Tottie, 2014, p. 21):

---

14. The effect of setting and register on disfluency will be examined in Chapter 5.

> Uhm can be much more than a filler of pauses, a sign of hesitation or disfluency: as a stance marker, it can be used to initiate discourse paragraphs, to clarify meanings, to correct an utterance, to achieve precision, and to mark stance, among other functions.

This view of filled pauses, which is not restrictive to situations of cognitive load or production difficulties (put forward by the *Cognitive-Burden* view), takes into account the pragmatic dimension of speech, and thus defends a more positive approach to these phenomena.

In light of this approach, the terms *disfluency* or *hesitation* are often found to be inadequate. In fact, Tottie (2014, p. 26) suggested that "uhms" should deserve to be called markers of *fluency* rather than *disfluency*. While her suggestion only concerns filled pauses and does not cover the rest of the disfluency markers (e.g. prolongations, silent pauses, repairs, repetitions etc.) Moniz et al., (2009) classified all disfluency phenomena as *fluent* communicative devices. Similarly, Hieke (1981) argued that disfluencies formed an integral part of speech production in a *positive* sense, and should thus be viewed as "a normal component of fluency" and "wellformedness phenomena rather than disfluencies, at least as far as they serve as devices by the speaker to produce more error-free, high-quality speech." (Hieke, 1981, p. 150).

Further in line with the view of disfluency as a signal, Clark (1996, 2002) put forward the idea that disfluencies should be considered as *collateral signals*. Clark distinguished between primary signals (i.e. the linguistic devices by which speakers accomplish discourse) and collateral signals, which are lexical, syntactic, prosodic, and gestural devices which help coordinate speakers' primary signals. They are used by speakers to manage their on-going performance, and fall into four main categories, inserts, juxtapositions, modifications, and concomitants (read Clark & Fox Tree, 2002, p. 78). This approach to disfluencies as collateral signals offers a much broader perspective as it incorporates the visual-gestural modality of speech.

Similarly, Allwood et al., (2005) pointed out the pragmatic and multimodal dimensions of disfluency in their study of *communication management*. Communication management, or *speech management* (Allwood et al., 1990) are defined as a "linguistic and other behavior which gives evidence of an individual managing his own communication while taking his/her interlocutor into account". Allwood et al., (1990) argued that speakers can manage their own communication with the use of gaze aversion, pausing, repetitions, and the like. They further distinguished between own *communication management* (OCM) and *interactive communication management* (ICM) (Allwood et al., 2005). OCM is concerned with how speakers continuously manage the planning and production of their own communication, while ICM pertains to the management of the interaction through turn-taking, feedback, and sequencing. Once again, we can note the use of the term *fluent*, which suggests a more positive viewpoint: "OCM, contrary to what this term [disfluency] suggests, often contributes to the fluency and flexibility of speech" (Allwood et al., 2005).

To conclude, the study of disfluency, which was originally investigated in the field of psycholinguistics, is not only restricted to cognitive and internal speech processes, (in line with the Cognitive Burden view) but can include other dimensions of communication as well, such as pragmatics and gesture, which accounts for a more positive approach.

2.2.2 *Disfluency or hesitation?*

Another traditional term found in the literature to describe spontaneous speech phenomena is *hesitation*. Lickley (2015, p. 21) defined it as the following:

> Hesitation usually involves the temporary suspension of flowing speech. It may be achieved by stopping altogether and remaining silent for a moment, by prolonging a syllable, by producing a filled pause or a lexical filler or by repeating the onset of the current phrase.

This definition seems to relate to previous definitions of disfluency with the notion of speech suspension, and it also includes the major disfluency types (mainly filled and unfilled pauses, prolongations, and repetitions). However, there are many inconsistencies regarding what types of markers should be included in the "disfluency" or "hesitation" category. For example, some authors have included filled and unfilled pauses in their taxonomy of hesitation/disfluency phenomena (e.g., Beattie, 1979; Ginzburg et al., 2014; Riggenbach, 1991; Vasilescu & Adda-Decker, 2007, among others) while others have studied "uh" and "um" specifically without labeling them as hesitation or disfluency markers, but "fillers" (e.g. Clark & Fox Tree, 2002; Merlo & Mansur, 2004) or "uhm" (e.g. Schegloff, 2010; Tottie, 2014). Conversely, other researchers have chosen not to include silent pauses in their taxonomy of disfluencies (e.g., Bortfeld et al., 2001; Boulis et al., 2005; Nicholson, 2007), while others distinguished between different types of pauses (e.g. silences, gaps, and lapses; cf Edlund et al., 2009 or lexicalized versus non-lexicalized pauses, cf Schettino et al., 2020). Similarly, repetitions are sometimes included or excluded from hesitation phenomena (e.g. Lickley, 2015; Ginzburg et al., 2014). Another striking observation is the fact that in some cases the term "hesitation" is not only used to cover a (temporal) feature of disfluency, but also a function. Lickley (2001, p. 93) claimed that the two major functions of disfluency were "hesitation" and "self-repair", although he also gave a formal description of hesitation (characterized by filled and unfilled pauses, word prolongations, or a combination of all). Therefore, the function of "hesitation" is not very clear.

Shriberg (2001, p. 155) made a striking distinction between disfluency and hesitation on the basis of time and duration. When speakers detect a problem in speech, they can either repair or repeat the previous constituent, or they can insert a filled or unfilled pause. The latter is more likely to be interpreted as a hesitation. Similarly, Betz (2020, p. 11) defined hesitation as "anything that temporally extends the delivery of the intended message". In this sense, hesitations are viewed as a *temporal extension* of the message, which may help speakers to buy time in order to solve problems when speaking. Therefore, the notion of hesitation is closely related to the concept of *buying time* (Brennan & Schober, 2001; Fehringer & Fry, 2007).

Candea (2000) investigated so-called hesitation phenomena in French spontaneous speech and emphasized the differences found in the terminology. She argued that the term "hesitation" was more adequate than "disfluency" because it did not entail a problem or a speech pathology. However, Candea (2000, p. 18) further pointed out that the term "hesitation" was still too broad, and had two underlying problems (ambiguity and restriction). The term presupposes that a specific class of markers, which are very common in spoken spontaneous speech (such as "uh" and "um"), are systematically associated with the cognitive notion of "hesitation" which is, according to Candea, too simplistic and not often the case. In other words, saying "uhm" does not necessarily imply that speakers are currently "hesitating" in the strict sense (i.e. making a difficult choice). As we have seen earlier with the work of Tottie (2014, 2016, 2019) or Clark & Fox Tree (2002), "uh" and "um" can serve many pragmatic functions other than "hesitation".

For these reasons, Candea (2000) refrained from using the term "hesitation" or "disfluency" in her work, as the latter failed to truly embody these different dimensions of language. Therefore, she opted for the term "travail de marque de formulation" (*formulation marker*) instead, following Morel & Danon-Boileau (1998). This novel term further integrates the different cognitive, enunciative and interactional mechanisms associated with the production of so called "hesitation" phenomena, without being contingent upon error or indecision.

2.2.3 *Beyond terminological issues: A functionally ambivalent approach to (dis)fluency*

Given the complexity and multiplicity of processes underlying the concept of the phenomena under study, as well as the range of perspectives and angles adopted by different researchers, the overlapping terms "fluency", "disfluency" or "hesitation" may be too restrictive, and at times even confusing. For this reason, a new body of research emerged (in line with the *Strategic Modelling View*) and offered new terms to define these phenomena. I have briefly sketched out some of these novel terms introduced in the literature more or less recently, such as "planner" (exclusively for filled pauses; Tottie, 2016; Jucker, 2015), "collateral signals" (Clark, 2013) "travail de formulation" (Candea, 2000; Morel & Danon-Boileau, 1998), "wellformedness phenomena" (Hieke, 1981) "own communication management" (Allwood et al., 1990, 2005), or "confluence" (McCarthy, 2009). All of these terms are a blatant departure from the initial term "disfluency" or "hesitation", as they account for a more positive approach to these phenomena.[15]

More recently, another body of research, partly based on the work of Götz (2013) on fluency enhancing strategies in SLA, put forward the term *(dis)fluency*, with the prefix "dis" in brackets (Crible, 2018; Crible et al., 2019; Dumont, 2018; Grosman, 2018; Notarrigo, 2017). This term captures both the notion of fluency *and* disfluency, and goes beyond the binary divide between the two concepts. Instead of opposing fluency with disfluency, or arguing in favor of a positive versus a negative view of disfluency (cf Section 2.2.1), Crible et al. (2019) argued that this duality should be considered on a scale or a continuum of (dis)fluency. This implies that the same forms, called "fluencemes" (suggested by Götz, 2013), vary systematically according to language, context, and genre. Fluencemes are defined as "an abstract and idealized feature of speech that contributes to the production or perception of fluency, whatever its concrete realization may be" (Götz, 2013, p. 8). The choice of the term *fluenceme* is central because, unlike *disfluency marker* or *hesitation marker*, it avoids the underlying notion of dysfunction, problem, or uncertainty.

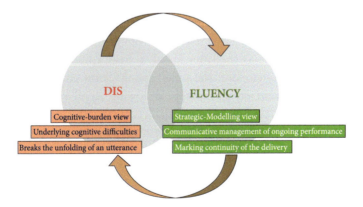

Figure 1. An ambivalent approach to (dis)fluency: Two sides of the same coin (following Crible et al., 2019)

---

15. I will also mention the term "repair" used by conversation analysts in Section III.3.2.2.

Additionally, the term *(dis)fluency* implies that disfluency and fluency reflect *two sides of the same coin* (Crible et al. 2017, p. 71); in other words, it does not disregard the Cognitive-burden view nor the Strategic-Modelling view altogether, but considers them both: the same forms have the potential to perform both fluent and/or disfluent functions (cf Figure 1).

Even though Allwood (2017) fervently argued in favor of a positive view of disfluency embodying efficient mechanisms to interactive communication, he raised a more nuanced point when discussing the fact that speakers were not necessarily fluent or disfluent in all types of communicative activities; he noted (p. 3):

> It seems fairly clear that most of them would be "disfluent" in written language, if we are not trying to capture authentic speech in writing. It also seems clear that many of them might be disfluent in many types of public speaking. But this does not mean that they are disfluent in interactive (small) talk, where it is important that you are able to hesitate, change your mind, repeat for clarity, be flexible, and non-categorical and give continuous unobstrusive feedback.

Once more, the idea that speakers are deemed "fluent" or "disfluent" does not only rely on temporal measures of fluency (e.g. length and frequency of pauses), but on contextual features as well, such as the type of communicative activity or register. Additionally, it also relies on the social expectations and conversational constraints in a given situation. Fluencemes thus emerge from speakers' intentions and expectations in a specific context, which can potentially lead to (un)successful communication.

2.3 Summary of the overlapping terms and my choice of terminology

While some authors have chosen the term *hesitation* to refer to an act of choice (e.g. Beattie, 1979; Goldman-Eisler, 1968) or the acoustic and phonetic features of pauses (e.g. Duez, 2001a, 2001b), others focus on the surface structure of *disfluency* which embodies an interruption point (e.g. Pallaud et al., 2019; Shriberg, 1994). Conversely, several authors refused to use the term *disfluency* or *hesitation*, and coined novel terms, such as *communication management, confluence,* or *collateral signals*. Allwood (2017) even suggested to change the terminology and abandon the term *disfluency* altogether for a more positive and neutral one (*communication management*). However, the latter may be too large, and does truly not capture the notion of *flow* which will be put forward in this book. A list of the main existing terms is summarized in Table 1, including a "tentative" definition of the terms, and a (non-exhaustive) list of the authors who have used them.

The reason for the term *disfluency* to be an overarching term in the literature is certainly related to the fact that it has been the most widely used since the

Table 1. Summary of the overlapping terms used in the literature

Term	Tentative definition	Authors
Disfluency	A deviation in speech from the ideal delivery. A temporary suspension or interruption of the speech flow.	Shriberg (1994) Eklund (2004) Lickley (2015) Feirrera & Bailey (2004)
Fluency	Ideal delivery of speech, global impression of smooth speech. One component of oral proficiency.	De Jong (2018) Lennon (1990) Fillmore (1976)
Hesitation	Temporal extension of the message (through pausing and delaying), often associated with uncertainty and an act of choice.	Gilquin (2008); Maclay & Osgood, (1959) Duez (1991) Betz (2020)
Confluence	Co-creation of fluency in a conversation.	McCarthy (2009)
(Dis)fluency	Functionally ambivalent phenomena made of fluencemes which can potentially serve fluent and/or disfluent functions.	Götz (2013) Crible et al., (2019)
Communication Management	Linguistic and other behavior which gives evidence of a speaker managing his communication while taking his interlocutor into account.	Allwood et al. (1990, 2005) Ginzburg & Poesio (2016)
Wellformedness	Devices used by the speaker to produce more error-free and high quality speech.	Hieke (1981)
Travail de Formulation	Markers used for planning and formulation.	Candea (2000) Morel & Danon-Boileau (1998)
Collateral signals	Communicative signals which comment and manage speakers' ongoing performance.	Clark (1996, 2003)

late 1950s. As we have seen, despite what the negative prefix "dis" suggests, most researchers interested in disfluency phenomena do not view them as negative processes, but on the contrary, they consider them as an integral part of speech planning and processing. Moreover, from a strictly *formal* perspective, disfluencies do mark a disruption in the speech flow or in the acoustic signal, but that does not mean that they are necessarily *disruptive* per se, as they can serve communicative and interpersonal functions. Therefore, the real issue is not only terminological, but theoretical as well. The "dis" in disfluency, from a psycholinguistic point of view, refers to a breakdown in the speech flow, thus focusing primarily on the linear verbal and vocal channel of communication. Moreover, this breakdown is often understood at the surface level of the verbal *utterance*, thus disregarding all other aspects of communication at the level of the interaction. The integration of interactional dynamics was put forward in the work of Clark (1996);

McCarthy (2009); Candea (2000), or Allwood (2017), among others. This contribution is highly relevant to the present work, as it is believed that disfluency should be investigated at several levels of analysis, integrating the verbal, vocal, and visual-gestural communication channel, as well as the speech, visuogestural, and interactional level of fluency.

This leads us to my choice of terminology: because disfluency is such a complex and multi-faceted phenomenon, resulting from several cognitive, interactional, and speech processes, it cannot easily be categorized under one label. While the terms *confluence, communication management* and *collateral signals* are truly innovative, they do not quite grasp the functional ambivalence of these phenomena, put forward in the work of Götz (2013) and Crible et al. (2019). By keeping the core notion of *fluency*, understood here in broad terms (i.e. speech, discursive, interactional, and gestural fluency, or flow) and adding the "dis" (i.e. disruption, discontinuity) in brackets, I focus on the potential for the same fluencemes to serve fluent and/or disfluent functions, depending on contextual and situational features, in line with the tenants of Cognitive Grammar (described in Section III.3.1.3).

To conclude, the present study of inter-(dis)fluency phenomena, grounded in an integrated theoretical framework (further described in Section III and IV) aims to go beyond the traditional and "pathologized" view of disfluency as a speech disruption, and offer a fresh interactional and multimodal perspective.

III. Beyond the psycholinguistic model: An interdisciplinary approach to inter-(dis)fluency

The present section will focus on different theoretical approaches relevant to the present study, which I briefly touched upon in the previous subsection, mainly Cognitive Grammar and usage-based linguistics, Conversation Analysis and Interactional Linguistics, and Multimodality and gesture studies.

3.1 Cognitive grammar and usage-based linguistics

3.1.1 *Key principles of Cognitive Grammar and usage-based linguistics*

Cognitive Grammar, initially introduced by Langacker, (1987, 1995, 1999), provides a framework to language which considers grammar as not built up out of syntax and semantics respectively, but consisting of symbolic units, made of form-meaning pairings. The main linguistic components of a language, such as grammar, lexicon, and phonology, are not independent, but inter-related. The understanding of these linguistic components relies essentially on speakers' general cognitive abilities, such as perception, attention, and categorization. The semantics of a language, for instance, can be related to some of these cognitive abilities, such as perception; i.e. the way speakers draw on their perceptual experience to conceive and construe a situation. In this view, meaning is primarily based on usage and deeply rooted in experience. Speakers' experience of a language is thus based on its actual use in real life conversations, not on word entries in a vocabulary, or syntactic structures in a grammar book. In light of this approach emerges the framework *of usage-based linguistics* (e.g. Barlow, 2013; Bybee, 2008; Croft, 2000) which considers linguistic structures grounded in their observation of actual language use.

Speakers' knowledge of a language, in terms of language processing or language acquisition is influenced by their categorization and conceptualization of experience. These assumptions stand in sharp opposition with the generativist and structural Saussurean tradition of *langue* and *parole* which distinguish between the level of the message structure (*langue*) and the level of language use (*parole*). Similarly, in the perspective of generative grammar (Chomsky, 1965), a distinction is made between the concept of *competence* versus *performance*; the latter being of little significance according to generativists. The usage-based model rejects that hierarchy, and views language as a dynamic system whereby linguistic units emerge from general cognitive processes. Bybee (2010) identified several cognitive processes influencing the use and development of linguistic structure (summarized by Ibbotson, 2013, p.2): (1) categorization; identifying tokens as instances of a particular type, (2) chunking; the formation of sequential units through repetition or practice, (3) rich memory; the storage of detailed information from experience; (4) analogy; mapping of an existing structural pattern onto a novel instance, and (5) cross-modal association; cognitive ability to form link and meaning. The first two processes (categorization and chunking) are particularly relevant to the study of (dis)fluency, and will be further developed in the following subsection. The notion of frequency plays a crucial role in the integration of usage-based processes, as the more frequently items consistently co-occur together, the more likely they will become automatized.

In sum, language is made of fluid categories and dynamic structures, altogether shaped by experience, usage, communication, and other cognitive abilities such as conceptualization or processing. Its acquisition and development rely on actual language use in intersubjective environments i.e., through interaction. When speakers interact with one another, they engage in two main activities, one which consists in conveying social intentions, and another establishing joint attention (Tomasello, 2003). While this perspective was developed mainly in terms of its implications for first language acquisition, it also has an effect on second language acquisition (e.g. Bybee, 2008; Segalowitz, 2016; Wulff & Ellis, 2018): second language learners acquire conventionalized constructions (i.e. form-function mappings, or syntactic frames, see Goldberg, 2006) in their target language through repeated exposure, but also through processes of abstraction (e.g. deriving a general rule from the usage of a prototypical construction such as -s + 3rd person singular). Bybee (2008) looked at the effect on token frequency (i.e. the number of times a unit appears in speech) in the process of SLA, and its "conserving effects" (e.g. how repetition strengthens memory representations for linguistic forms and make them more accessible (Bybee, 2008, p. 218). This plays a key role in the process of acquisition, as the more exposed a learner is to a given construction (such as irregular forms), the more likely they will produce the constructions correctly. In addition, L2 learners need to acquire the ability to take into account the social demands of communication (i.e. establishing joint attention and conveying social intentions) in order to communicate successfully, thus *fluently* (Segalowitz, 2016).

3.1.2   *Why study (dis)fluency in the framework of Cognitive Grammar?*

As Segalowitz (2016, p. 14) pointed out, the study of fluency has often been decontextualized from the social and communicative situations in which the target language is acquired. On that account, he argued that fluency should be regarded as "the outcome of a dynamical system where cognitive, social, sociolinguistic, pragmatic, and psycholinguistic considerations interact in complex ways" (Segalowitz, 2016, p. 18). This argument is in tune with the central assumptions of usage-based grammar. Similarly, Cienki (2012, 2015b) discussed several implications regarding the analysis of "usage events" (i.e. contextualized linguistic units) within the framework of Cognitive Grammar, and focused on the three following behaviors: (1) non-lexical sounds, (2) intonation, and (3) gesture.[16] He claimed that despite being nonlinguistic per se, these recurrent structures could gain symbolic status. This implies that some non-lexical sounds can gain a symbolic relation to certain meanings, with for example the association of "uhm" with uncertainty. However, this mapping can be done to varying degrees; filled pauses are not always related to feelings of uncertainty, and in some contexts, they may not have such a strong form-meaning correspondence. While Cienki's (2012, 2015b) arguments are only made on non-lexical sounds (i.e. "uh", "mm", "uh uh"), I will show how these claims can be applied to other fluencemes as well. The idea that non-lexical sounds, and hereby fluencemes, can be considered lexical (hence "fluent") in different degrees and according to their context of use is one of the main theoretical

---

16. See Section 3.3 for more details.

claims of the present study, based on Crible et al., (2019)'s functionally ambivalent approach to (dis)fluency.

In her corpus-based study of (dis)fluency and discourse markers, Crible (2018) described two of the major tenants of usage-based grammar (among others) which lie at the core of the study of (dis)fluency, mainly frequency and schematicity. Frequent combinations of fluencemes, such as filled pauses and unfilled pauses, can become conventional to a certain degree if they are exposed to highly repeated instances, and thus form recurrent patterns of combination, which can then be schematized (e.g. *filled pause+ unfilled pause*). This claim is based on the corpus-based and experimental evidence that fluencemes very often co-occur with one another rather than exclusively on their own (e.g. Benus et al., 2006; Betz & Lopez- Gambino, 2016; Duez, 1991; Grosjean & Deschamps, 1972; Shriberg, 1994). Therefore, Crible et al., (2017, p. 71) discussed the *sequential* aspects of (dis)fluency: the fact that fluencemes can form specific patterns of combination, known as "sequences". They are thus better understood as constructions, which can be either "simple" (isolated tokens) or "complex"[17] (combined tokens). The more frequent the combinations, the less cognitively demanding they will be perceived. Rare combinations on the other hand (e.g. *filled pause+repetition+unfilled pause+repair)*, will appear less automatic, thus more disfluent. One of Crible's (2018) major contributions was to treat sequence frequency as one factor of fluency in order to examine the extent in which rare and frequent combinations could reveal different degrees of (dis)fluency. This was done through systematic quantitative analyses which combined different variables, such as co-occurrence, position, and register variation. Additionally, Crible (2018) largely investigated the clustering of (dis)fluencies with discourse markers (e.g. coordinating conjunctions, adverbs, or interjections, all included in the fluenceme category)[18] which was also conducted in previous corpus-based studies in line with the usage-based framework (read Schneider, 2014).

In line with these frameworks, the concept of (dis)fluency has been redefined by Crible et al., (2017, p. 71) as being sequential, situational, and ambivalent. Three central assumptions thus emerge. First, fluencemes are better understood in terms of constructions, whose degree of entrenchment (i.e. the process whereby linguistic units become entrenched in speakers' memories) relies on the high frequency of specific patterns. Secondly, this degree of entrenchment and conventionality

---

17. The term "complex" is borrowed from Shriberg (1994, p. 58) which refers to disfluencies that overlap with one another.
18. Her typology of fluencemes (of which the present work is partly based) also includes discourse markers, but it should be noted that the latter are excluded from the present analysis for theoretical and methodological reasons.

is determined by social and contextual factors. Thirdly, the status of fluencemes is highly flexible and dynamic, showing either sides of fluency and/or disfluency depending on their context of use. These assumptions lie at the core of the present study which is also based on different cognitive and usage-based models of (dis)fluency, presented below.

3.1.3 *Cognitive and usage-based models of (dis)fluency: Towards a multi-dimensional model*

Segalowitz (2016, p. 5) distinguished between three different levels of fluency:

1. *Utterance fluency*: Fluidity of observable speech as characterized by measurable temporal features (e.g. syllable rate, duration, and rate of hesitations).
2. *Cognitive fluency*: Fluid operation (i.e. speed, efficiency) of the cognitive processes underlying L2 speech acts.
3. *Perceived fluency*: subjective judgments of L2 speakers' oral fluency.

In this framework, a distinction is made between the fluidity of observable speech at the level of the utterance, the cognitive processes underlying the production of utterances, and the perception of the final speech output. All of these dimensions are inter-related, as a disfluent execution of cognitive operations (i.e. semantic retrieval) can potentially result in a disfluent speech output, which will in turn be perceived and judged as disfluent.

Another relevant theoretical and methodological framework of L2 fluency was introduced by Götz (2013) in which she coined the term *fluenceme*. The latter was also categorized in three different types: fluencemes of production (similar to *utterance fluency*) which are related to temporal variables and fluency-enhancement strategies (e.g. filled and unfilled pauses, repeats, and repairs); perceptive fluency (similar to *perceived fluency*) based on the listener's attention; and nonverbal fluencemes which include aspects of non-verbal communication (e.g. hand gestures and facial expressions). Her three-fold typology of fluencemes is not quite the same as Segalowitz's model, as she mostly focused on a speaker-based approach which includes observable features of communication, while Segalowitz targeted a more abstract cognitive based approach (as pointed out by Crible, 2018, p. 21).

More in line with Cognitive Grammar theory, Grosman (2018) introduced a socio-cognitive framework of fluency, based on Schmid & Gunther's framework on salience (2016). In her model, three dimensions of fluency were also evaluated: the grammatical, the discourse-level, and socio-interpersonal dimension.[19] This

---

[19] These are translations made by Grosman and colleagues in their paper, but the original terms were "fluence componentielle linguistique-phrasique", "fluence socio-interpersonnelle",

tridimensional evaluation of fluency was used for experimental purposes (cf Grosman et al., 2019; Grosman, 2018), and was based on six assertions which corresponded to an evaluated dimension of fluency, presented below (Grosman et al., 2019, p. 24).

1. Grammatical
    - The sentence is well formed.
    - The sentence includes hesitations.
2. Discourse-level
    - The speech is fluid.
    - The speech is nice to listen to.
3. Socio-interpersonal
    - The speech in this context appeals to me.
    - The speech in this context is improper.

The first dimension, similar to the *utterance* and *productive* levels of fluency presented earlier, refers to decontextualized linguistic expectations, in relation to wellformedness and grammaticality judgments. The second dimension is based on the discourse flow with regards to social expectations. Lastly, the last dimension is related to interpersonal norms and expectations in a specific register.

The notable contribution of the fluency models presented above is their acknowledgement of the different dimensions of (dis)fluency (also proposed by Lickley, 2015 cf Section 2.1.1). While psycholinguistic and SLA research have mainly focused on the grammatical, utterance, or productive dimension of disfluency,[20] others, who disagreed with the term "disfluency" have rather focused on its pragmatic and socio-interpersonal dimension. The understanding of these different dimensions may thus further justify the multiple terminological backlashes found in the literature. Being disfluent at the level of the utterance is not quite the same as being disfluent at the level of the interaction, where social expectations differ greatly from grammaticality judgments. For instance, Grosman et al. (2019) found that speech samples which contained repetitions were found to be judged more disfluent by listeners when evaluating the socio-interpersonal dimension of fluency than the discursive or grammatical dimensions. However, this perception of fluency also strongly relies on the type of speech produced, in line with the social expectations of the situation.

---

and "fluence situationnelle" (same order, cf Grosman, 2018, p. 296). Their translation caused slight terminological changes, as "socio-interpersonnelle" (*socio-interpersonal*) became "discourse-level", and "situationnelle" (*situational*) became "socio-interpersonal".

20. A lot of psycholinguistic work has also been done on the perception of disfluencies, which is not the topic of this book.

In sum, the three proposals presented by Segalowitz, Götz, and Grosman are a valuable contribution to the present study of inter-(dis)fluency for two main reasons: first, their typology of (dis)fluency goes beyond the traditional definition of disfluency presented in Section I, as it integrates several central aspects of human communication beyond the level of speech production (e.g., social expectations, situational features, cognitive processes, aspects of nonverbal communication, etc.); secondly, their tridimensional account of (dis)fluency vouches for a multi-approach perspective on these phenomena, which further justifies the need to situate this study within a larger integrated theoretical framework. However, it should be noted that these models were used for different purposes, mostly experimental in the case of Grosman et al. (2019) and Götz (2013), with a strong focus on the hearer's perspective, which goes beyond the scope of this book. Moreover, as Crible (2018) pointed out, Götz only extracted several features from the data semi-automatically, but without annotating them systematically with an annotation scheme; Götz (2013)'s framework is thus mostly conceptual, and has not been formalized into an annotation scheme. This gave rise to a novel corpus-based annotation model of (dis)fluency, introduced by Crible et al. (2019).[21]

Borrowing from Shriberg's (1994) formal *disfluency classification*, and grounded in a functionally ambivalent view of (dis)fluency, the collaborative work of Crible et al. (2019)[22] combined a fine-grained identification of (dis)fluencies with a thorough and reliable technical format. Their typology of *fluencemes* (following Götz, 2013) offers a systematic and detailed annotation of ambivalent devices, which includes "typical" non-lexical (dis)fluencies (e.g. filled pauses, repeats, deletions, repairs etc.) and more lexical ones, such as discourse markers (e.g. *well, I mean, but*). Their annotation model was applied to spoken L1 and L2 speech (cf Dumont, 2018), as well as signed languages (with the cross-modal study of palm-up signs and filled pauses, cf Notarrigo, 2017). Their typology of fluencemes included the clustering of immediately adjacent fluencemes, which were called *sequences*, a term also adopted in this book. The internal structure of the sequences was analyzed, by taking into account their content (e.g. the number of markers found within a sequence and their combination pattern, such as

---

[21]. This research team was part of a five-year research project entitled "Fluency and disfluency markers. A multimodal contrastive perspective" conducted at the University of Louvain and Namur. They were involved in a large scale usage-based study of (dis)fluency markers in spoken French, L1 and L2 English, and French Belgian Sign Language. For more information go to *https://uclouvain.be/fr/instituts-recherche/ilc/fluency-and-disfluency-markers-a-multimodal-contrastive-perspective.html (last retrieved on August 26th 2021)*

[22]. This includes the work of Crible (2018); Dumont (2018); Grosman, (2018), and Notarrigo (2017).

FP+UP+TR) and their cluster (i.e. whether the markers occurred on their own or as part of a sequence, see Crible, 2017, p. 119).

To conclude, this section has outlined different theoretical and methodological frameworks of (dis)fluency situated within the scope of Cognitive Grammar and usage-based linguistics. These typologies altogether provided relevant analytical and methodological tools for the present study, which represents the first step toward the construction of the integrated multi-level and multi-modal approach to (dis)fluency.

3.2 Interactional linguistics and conversation analysis

Most studies conducted on (dis)fluency phenomena focus on *the utterance level* of fluencemes (cf Segalowitz, 2016) and the simultaneous cognitive, processing, and planning processes associated with their production.[23] Even though some researchers have highlighted their contextual, situational and interpersonal dimension, their qualitative examples are much too often based on isolated utterances which do not illustrate their sequential unfolding within the course of interaction (e.g. Kjellmer, 2003). As a matter of fact, a large number of studies on (dis)fluency tend not to illustrate their findings with qualitative examples, but exclusively rely on quantitative results. While it is true that quantitative findings can give a robust, representative, and statistically valid overview of the data, they fail to illuminate particular and complex instances within their context of use. This issue is even more relevant to the study of (dis)fluency which has shown to be functionally and interactionally ambivalent. I believe that this ambivalence can be further examined in detailed qualitative analyses, through the medium of conversation analytic tools, further grounded in the framework of interactional linguistics.

3.2.1 *Introduction to the interdisciplinary framework of Interactional Linguistics*

The interdisciplinary framework of Interactional Linguistics (IL)[24] emerged in the early 21st century, altogether with a growing community of linguists who were interested in studying grammar and prosody from a specific interactional approach. Couper-Kuhlen & Selting (2001) traced back three main theoretical influences (discourse-functional linguistics, Conversation Analysis, and anthropological linguistics) which represented major stepping stones towards establish-

---

23. Except for a few notable exceptions, such as Tottie (2011,2015,2016,2019), Clark & Fox Tree (2002); Bortfeld et al. (2001) among others.

24. There is another closely related research field dealing with aspects of social interaction known as *Language and Social Interaction* (LSI), see LeBaron et al., (2003) for review.

ing the Interactional Linguistics Framework. In particular, *Conversation Analysis* (CA; Sacks et al., 1974) introduced major analytic tools for the study of social interaction, through qualitative micro-analyses of *talk-in-interaction* (i.e. naturally occurring speech in every day conversation, cf Schegloff, 1991). CA regards interaction as "the home environment of language", (Sidnell, 2016, p. 2), an orderly, interactionally managed system, whereby norms and practices are shaped by speakers' *actions*. Actions refer to what the co-participants of a conversation are doing interactionally in relation to one another (Pomerantz & Fehr, 2011; Schegloff, 1996a). In other words, the act of speaking does not only involve the individual productions of one speaker, but its coordination and cooperation with other participants of a conversation within turns. This perspective is thus very different from the psycholinguistic assumptions that speech planning results from several cognitive operations that are mentally performed by an individual speaker without taking into account the co-speaker's contribution in the interaction.

Sacks et al., (1974)'s seminal paper, entitled *A simplest systematics for the organization of turn-taking for conversation* sketched out some of the fundamental aspects underlying the construction of talk-in-interaction, and demonstrated the way speakers, when engaged in ordinary, everyday practices, co-produce stretches of talk in orderly ways, which can be subject to detailed qualitative analyses. Sidnell (2016, p. 2) reviewed some the fundamental aspects regarding the orderliness of interaction, summarized in the following points:

1. *Distribution of turns.* Conversations are governed by turn-taking mechanisms which are organized in various ways by the participants (e.g. turn holding, turn yielding, turn allocation) through *turn constructional units* (i.e. lexical items, phrases or clauses which determine the shape of a speaker's possible turn).
2. *Addressing problems of hearing, speaking or understanding.* During the course of their talk, participants may need to signal speaking, hearing, or understanding troubles through repairs[25] which can be initiated by the speaker or another participant (Schegloff et al., 1977).
3. *The formation of actions.* Participants are able to project or recognize what type of action is being performed (e.g. responsive action, pre-sequence action, sequence-initial action) by adding stretches of talk.
4. *The sequential dimension of actions.* Actions are organized into sequences (e.g. *adjacency pairs*, sequences made of two turns, such as question-answer or request-accept) as a way to construct "an architecture of intersubjectivity–a basis for mutual understanding" (Sidnell, 2016, p. 2).

---

25. Note that the term "repair" does not have the same implications as Levelt's (1989) term (cf Section 1.2).

This area of research is thus in sharp contrast with the formalist approach to discourse and grammar which views language primarily as a mental and autonomous phenomenon, independent from human social or cognitive abilities. In this book, I will especially draw on the analytic tools provided by CA, as well as the *participation framework*.

A major contribution in the field of social interaction and linguistic anthropology is found in the work of C. Goodwin and M.H. Goodwin (Goodwin, 1981, 2003, 2007, 2010, 2017; Goodwin & Goodwin, 1996, 2004, 1986) who studied embodied *participation frameworks* (initially introduced by Goffman, 1981). Participation refers to "action demonstrating forms of involvement performed by parties within evolving structures of talk" (Goodwin & Goodwin, 2004, p. 222). Within this framework, the focus is essentially on two interactive practices, mainly (1) how participants orient themselves in ways relevant to the activities they are engaged in, and (2) how situated analysis of an emerging course of action shapes the further development of action (Goodwin & Heritage, 1990, p. 292). In this respect, participation is viewed as a "situated, multi-party accomplishment" (Goodwin & Goodwin, 2004, p. 231), in which the status of the participants (e.g. *speaker* or *hearer, addressee or recipient* etc. cf Goodwin & Heritage, 1990) can shift depending on the organization of particular situated activities (e.g. assessment, topic initiation, story preface). For instance, during a storytelling activity, a speaker may need to create a complex participation framework which will includes multiple participants, such as the hearers of the story, the character in the story who is doing its retelling, as well as the characters within the story who are absent from the telling (Goodwin & Goodwin, 2004).

To conclude, the interdisciplinary field of Interactional Linguistics, which includes multiple contributions from CA, anthropological linguistics, and discourse-functional linguistics, among other fields, altogether provides a relevant theoretical and methodological framework to the study of fluencemes, which leads us to the following subsection, focusing on the study of "repairs" in CA.

3.2.2 *The study of conversational repairs in talk-in-interaction*

Before addressing studies investigating (dis)fluency phenomena in the field of interactional linguistics, it should first be noted that the term *disfluency* is virtually excluded from all researchers' analyses. This is not surprising, given what the term *disfluency* entails (cf Section I), which is in sharp opposition with the central assumptions of Conversation Analysis and Interactional Linguistics. The latter used the label *repair* (Schegloff et al., 1977) instead, as well as other terms, such as *non-lexical sounds, vocalizations, uhm*, etc. The term *repair*, although homonymous with the one used by Levelt (1983), which presupposes that an item needs to be repaired, has different implications. In this section, I provide a brief overview of the study of repair within the framework of Interactional Linguistics.

Repair is a key area of research within Conversation Analysis. It refers to an organized system which is addressed to deal with recurrent problems in speaking, hearing, and understanding. Repairs can be distinguished between self-corrections and other-corrections, which is similar to the distinction presented by Levelt (1983), but this type of phenomena, unlike what Levelt addressed in his model, is "neither contingent upon error, nor limited to replacement" (Schegloff et al., 1977, p. 363). Repair mechanisms are in fact regarded as a sequential[26] phenomenon, which have a specific organization within the course of interaction. They include different segment parts, such as "initiation" and "outcome". Their initiation can be placed in three main positions, (1) within the same turn, (2) in a turn's transition space, and (3) in a subsequent turn. Self-initiations within the same turn are said to use "a variety of non-lexical speech perturbations, e.g. cut-offs, sound stretches, "uh" etc. to signal the possibility of repair-initiation immediately following" (Schegloff et al. 1977, p. 367). It is interesting to note that this comment on the repair structure is similar to the description of the interregnum region of the *disfluency surface structure* (cf Section I.1.2). This was also found in Goodwin & Goodwin (2004, p. 230) who illustrated the display of a repair structure, by taking into account the participants' gaze. Within a participation framework, repairs are said to occur when speakers "lack the visible orientation of a hearer" (Goodwin & Goodwin, 2004, p. 229). In other words, when the positioning of a hearer is not oriented to the ongoing talk, a speaker can modify stretches of their speech to repair the participation format. During face-to-face encounters, hearers may resort to a range of visual or vocal backchannels (i.e. head nods or vocal continuers, cf Stivers, 2008) to display their status as recipient, or listener. Hearers can also display that they are attending to the speakers' talk by gazing towards them (Goodwin, 1981). However, in some cases, hearers may not be fully oriented to the ongoing talk, which may invite speakers to interrupt and modify their utterance in order to secure the gaze of their addressee. Therefore, the grammatical structure of a sentence can be modified to adapt potential changes in the participants' status. During a word search for instance, repairs can be used to achieve a state of mutual orientation between speakers and hearers. Goodwin (1981) further explored similar types of repair phenomena, such as lengthening, additions, or phrasal breaks. He showed how speakers needed to delay the final

---

26. Note that the term "sequential" is different from the one mentioned in Section 3.1.3 when discussing fluenceme sequences. In this case, it refers to sequences of turns or of talk found within the interaction, while in Crible et al's. (2019) case, it refers to the combinatory patterns of adjacent fluencemes.

syllable of a word to coordinate its completion with the arrival of the hearer's gaze. This kind of coordination was also achieved by adding an "uh" in the utterance. In this sense, instances of repairs are not limited to contexts of speech error, as they can also function as requests to secure mutual gaze, and help to achieve a state of mutual orientation in the talk. Similarly, producing "uhm" at the beginning of a turn can signal a speaker's commitment and understanding towards an ongoing activity. In a study on phone conversations, Schegloff (2010) showed how turn-initial "uhms" could be used as a reason for calling, or for launching a new topic in the upcoming sequence.

Repair phenomena can also be associated to the *preference structure* of an interaction. The concept of preference refers to a "socially determined structural pattern" (Yule, 1996, p.76) which is expected in a speaker's next action. For instance, during a greeting sequence, the expected answer to a first greeting (e.g. *hello*) would be another greeting (e.g. *good morning*), which conforms to social norms. This illustrates a case of preferred action. A dispreferred action, on the other hand, would mark an unexpected structure (Yule, 1996, p.79), which does not meet the social requirements of the situation. Yule (1996, p.81) gave a list of common patterns associated with dispreferred responses, one of which includes the entry "delay/hesitate" with pauses and "uhm".

In sum, repair phenomena (which includes instances of restarts, "uhms", pauses, repeats, and self-breaks) have been subject to thorough investigation within CA and the framework of Interactional linguistics. These analyses were conducted through micro qualitative examples of the data, drawing on CA analytic tools such as turn-taking or preference structure. Despite a few similarities in the analysis of the repairs' underlying structure, the conversation-analytic and interactionist approach is in sharp opposition with the psycholinguistic ones presented in Section I.

3.2.3 *Contribution of the field to the study of inter-(dis)fluency*

It would seem, at first, that the terms *disfluency* and *talk-in-interaction* are incompatible, since the former focuses on the mental planning processes of an individual, while the latter deals with the social and cultural mechanisms shaping social interaction. However, the phenomena under study are analyzed in both fields (i.e. psycholinguistics and interactional linguistics), but with clearly different methodological tools and research purposes. As claimed earlier (Section 2.2.3 and 2.3) I believe that (dis)fluency phenomena should not be restricted to a single label nor a single model, but should instead integrate a variety of perspectives. I suggest that the study of fluency and disfluency could gain insight from CA and Interactional linguistics for a number of reasons, elaborated below.

First, the study of (dis)fluency has much too often been excluded from traditional formal linguistics (cf *performance* vs *competence* distinction) while they can actually represent meaningful aspects of speech production. However, their role is not only restricted to the level of verbal utterance production, but to the level of interaction as well. As we have seen, fluencemes can exhibit essential features of talk-in-interaction, shaping the course of the talk which is constantly adapted to the exigencies of the interaction. Fluencemes thus result from both cognitive and socio-interactional processes. This view is also in line with the perspective of usage-based grammar described earlier.

Second, within an Interactional Linguistics framework, fluencemes are seen as the byproducts of a dynamic and flexible grammar, shaped by conversational, social and discourse constraints (cf Mondada, 2001). This emphasizes the flexible and dynamic nature of fluencemes, whose status is determined by its context of production. This notion of flexibility was also presented within the scope of cognitive grammar.

Third, the notion of fluency, and its negative counterpart DISfluency, which have mainly been restricted to the flow of speech, can include other types of flow, such as the interactional flow. This could be applied to the principle of *progressivity* in CA (e.g., Schegloff, 2007; Sterponi & Fasulo, 2010; Stivers & Robinson, 2006) which refers to the smooth unfolding of interaction, based on the temporal development of the talk.

This third point is particularly relevant to the present study of ambivalent fluencemes. While in some contexts they can help speakers display their engagement to the ongoing activity (e.g. indicate mutual cooperation, display understanding, or yield a turn), they may also display a form of disengagement. For instance, during silences, speakers may choose not to cooperate with turn-allocation techniques (Hoey, 2015), or they can display their lack of involvement in the ongoing activity (Szymanski, 1999). In addition, when speakers make assessments (i.e. claim knowledge of what they are asserting, cf Pomerantz, 1984), they can be declined by second assessments (i.e. responses to the previous first assessment through agreement, or disagreement)[27] in the form of "delay devices" (Pomerantz, 1984, p.70) such as "uh" or "well", as a way to preface disagreement. This can also relate to notions of *alignment* and *affiliation*. In a storytelling context, for example, *alignment* indicates a speaker's aligning with the turn-taking principles of the storytelling activity (i.e. that the teller of the story has the floor until its completion), and *affiliation* refers to a hearer's display of support to the speaker's stance (cf Stivers, 2008). Examples of *disaligned actions* (during storytelling activities)

---

27. Pomerantz (1984) in fact distinguishes between upgrade agreement, same evaluation, and downgrade agreements.

can thus illustrate the hearer's failure to treat the story told by the speaker as either in progress or over.

To conclude, the overall construct of (dis)fluency can further be extended to general principles addressed in CA such as (des)alignment,[28] (dis)engagement, (dis)affiliation, (dis)preference and (dis)agreement. In this view, the process of *fluency*, understood as *flow*, or *continuity*, can refer to different types of flow at different levels of analysis (i.e. utterance, cognitive, interpersonal). This type of analysis is made possible with the combination of different methodological and theoretical approaches, which vouches for a multi-level and multi-approach study of inter-(dis)fluency.

3.3 Gesture studies and multimodal interaction

3.3.1 *Multimodality in the study of embodied interaction*

In the past few decades, the study of what has commonly been labeled "nonverbal" or "non-linguistic" communication has increasingly become a central interest of research among scholars in various disciplines (e.g. cognitive linguistics, psycholinguistics, linguistics anthropology, interactional linguistics). With the rise of interactionist approaches to social interaction who started working on video recordings of everyday interactions, new perspectives emerged for studying language practices as *embodied* within their social, material, and spatial environment. This includes the study of gesture, gaze, head movements, facial expressions, body movements, as well as the manipulation of external objects in the environment (cf Boutet, 2018; Goodwin, 2003; Streeck et al., 2011). In this respect, this perspective on *embodied interaction* regards cognition as not a separate mental action working in the brain, but as an "embodied action" (De Jaegher & Di Paolo, 2007, p. 486 in Streeck, 2015). This "embodied turn" in social sciences (cf Mondada, 2016, p. 338; Streeck, 2015), marked the conception of what has been termed *multimodal* communication. The term *multimodality*, which has become an overarching term in the field of interaction studies and gesture studies, refers to the plurality of communication channels and modalities deployed in interaction. It is defined as "the various resources mobilized by participants for organizing their action – such as gesture, gaze, facial expressions, body postures, body movements, and also prosody, lexis and grammar" (Mondada, 2016, p. 337). Similarly, Stivers & Sidnell, (2005, p. 1) claimed that:

---

28. Mondada & Traverso (2005) spoke of *(dés)alignements*.

> Face-to-face interaction is, by definition, multimodal interaction in which participants encounter a steady stream of meaningful facial expressions, gestures, body postures, head movements, words, grammatical constructions, and prosodic contours.[29]

In addition, Cienki (2017, 2015a) introduced the notion of "dynamic scope of relevant behaviors", (SRB) which takes into account the kinds of symbolic status gestures can have. He suggested that in a communicative context, speakers may be invited to choose among a "scope" of behaviors (i.e. gesture, speech, gaze, etc.), by focusing on the *vocal* modality of discourse (which is the "default focus", Cienki, 2015a, p. 628), or by including a set of behaviors (i.e. the combination of the vocal and visual-gestural features) in a specific context. Further in line with CG his claim is that repeated instances of gestures paired with certain functions are more likely to become entrenched linguistic signs. This theory thus further reflects the multimodality of discourse which includes a range of vocal and visual-gestural behaviors.

Stivers & Sidnell (2005), following Enfield (2005), further distinguished between the vocal-aural and the visual-spatial modalities of face-to-face multimodal communication, which will be further described below. This distinction does not only dwell on differences in modality, but also with respect to "semiotic ground" (cf Enfield, 2005, p. 52). In sum, the combination of different modalities and semiotic resources can further our understanding of the multiple processes underlying the organization of talk-in-interaction. The vocal modality of talk-in-interaction was investigated in the work of conversation analysts who focused on the organizations of shared practices in the course of social interaction. It includes the lexico-syntactic channel (e.g. work on lexical items such as "okay"), as well as the prosodic channel (e.g. upward or downward intonation, prosodic contour, see Selting et al., 2010 for review). For instance, Ogden (2013, 2018) studied the uses of tongue clicks. He combined phonetic, kinetic, and conversation-analytic methods to study speakers' stance-taking displays (further analyzed in Chapter 5).

The visuo-spatial modality of discourse has been examined by a number of researchers who were interested in the study of hand gestures specifically, but it also includes the study of other types of behavior, such as gaze, and body orientation within the spatial environment. As Mondada (2013) pointed out, the analysis of embodied interaction cannot solely focus on the speaker's body posture or orientation alone, but also with regard to the arrangement of other bodies within the spatial environment. She further suggested the term *interactional space* (Mondada, 2013, p. 248) which refers to the "situated, mutually adjusted changing

---

29. However, it should be noted that linguistic anthropologists take on a slightly different approach which does not dwell on the distinction between different modalities, but rather insist on the "abstraction of the interacting body from the material world", see Streeck et al., (2011, p. 9).

arrangements of the participants' bodies". Similarly, Sweetser & Sizemore (2008) distinguished between three types of space: (1) *the personal gesture space*; space in front of the speaker's trunk and head (McNeill, 1992); (2) *the inter-speaker space*; space between the two personal gesture space which can be reached by speakers to mark common ground; (3) *the unclaimed surrounding space*; an adjacent space away from the personal and interpersonal gesture space. When speakers are co-oriented towards each other around a central interpersonal space, they may rely on their body movement and gaze to display their engagement to one another or to the ongoing activity (illustrated in Figure 2, taken from Goodwin (1981, p. 96)

Figure 2. Engagement display (Goodwin, 1981, p. 96)

In a similar vein, another body of research (e.g., Debras, 2017; Debras & Cienki, 2012; Streeck, 2009b) studied the uses of head tilts and shrugs in relation to postures of disengagement more specifically, as well as stance (i.e. the expression of a speaker's feelings, attitudes and judgement, see Kärkkäinen, 2006). Shrugs, which are defined as a "compound enactment" (Streeck, 2009b, p. 189) involve a manifestation of the hands, combined with a movement of the shoulders, as well as a particular facial expression and a head movement.

Another way to convey disengagement from a situated language activity is through the display of a distinct *thinking face* (Goodwin & Goodwin, 1986). This very iconic thinking face, which depicts an individual in "deep thinking" (i.e. eyebrow raised looking upwards or frowning) is rather stereotypical and highly recognizable across situations (illustrated in Figure 3).[30]

---

30. These examples are taken from the data under scrutiny in the present study (the SITAF corpus and the DisReg corpus, cf Chapter 3). More examples of thinking faces will be provided across Chapters 4, 5 and 6. Special thanks to Violette Kosmala for the illustrations.

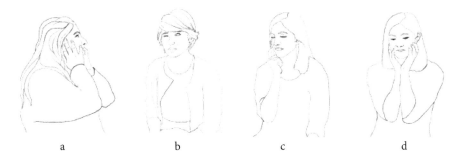

a   b   c   d

Figure 3. Embodied displays of thinking face (SITAF and DisReg)

In recordings of face-to-face conversations in natural settings, Goodwin & Goodwin (1986) explored the display of thinking faces and instances of gaze withdrawal during word searches. Such instances of visual display during word search can provide relevant information to the hearers, who are hereby informed that a change in the current activity has occurred. A change in participation status can also take place (i.e. from recipient to active participant) when the hearer's coparticipation in the search is appropriate.

To conclude, face-to-face interaction can be regarded as a joint and embodied manifestation of the vocal-aural and visual-spatial modalities of discourse, which continuously supplement one another through regulatory work. The present work mainly focuses on the visual-gestural actions deployed by gesturers, who make use of them respectively or conjointly to regulate interaction within their spatial environment. This enables them to regularly display their state of engagement or disengagement to the different activities they participate in. These central aspects of multimodal social interaction are highly relevant to the present study of embodied inter-(dis)fluency, as they serve as a basis for further development on the relationship between (dis)fluency and gesture.

3.3.2 *The different approaches to gesture*

As Harrison (2009, p.27) pointed out in his thesis work, gesture research can broadly be distinguished between two dominant approaches, the (1) *cognitive-psychological* approach (how gestures are related to the expression of thought), and (2) *the functional-communicative approach*[31] (how gestures function and are used by speakers to structure speech acts in interaction).

The cognitive-psychological approach was first reflected in the influential work of McNeill (1985, 1992) who viewed gesture as "a window onto the mind"

---

[31]. There are, of course, different existing approaches to gesture which will not be described in this book; see Beattie & Shovelton (1999); De Ruiter (2007) or Iverson & Thelen (1999) for review.

(also see Goldin-Meadow, 1999; Goldin-Meadow et al., 1993; Kita, 1993; Kita & Özyürek, 2003). In this view, gestures are said to share the same cognitive processes as speech, with the two being part of the same psychological structure. The combination of speech and gestures thus allows researchers to observe two simultaneous views of the same production process.

The functional-communicative approach to gesture is reflected in the pioneering work of Kendon (1980, 2004, 2014, 2017), Müller (1998, 2017) and Streeck (2009b, 2010, 2015), among others, who have documented their different forms and functions across languages and cultures within the study of social interaction.[32] Kendon's groundbreaking work on gesture, defined as the "utterance uses of visible bodily actions" (Kendon, 2004, pp. 1–2) regards it as an integral part of utterance construction. Kendon's approach to the gesture-speech relationship is slightly different from McNeill's in the sense that, while Kendon views gesture and speech as two different kinds of "expressive resources" available to speakers (Kendon, 2004, p. 111), McNeill views them as two separate channels of "observation of the psychological activities that take place during speech production" (McNeill, 1985, p. 350). Conversely, Kendon (2004, p. 111) does not believe that gesture and speech are part of the same production processes, but are rather "an integral part of what a speaker does in fashioning an object, the utterance, that is shaped to meet the expressive and communicative aims and requirements of a given interactional moment." In sum, the difference between McNeill and Kendon's approaches to gesture lies essentially in their contrasting views on language production: while McNeill considers language as the result of internal computations, Kendon regards it as a series of actions contributing to the utterance construction in interaction. The discourse-functional approach to gesture is thus further grounded in an "embodied, cultural sense-making praxis that draws on all the capacities of the human hand" (Streeck, 2009b, p. 30).

In sum, while the two contrasting views addressed above show some similarities with regard to the significant role gesture plays in speech, they are chiefly rooted in theoretical differences,[33] thus focusing on different types of gestures (e.g.

---

32. However, it should be noted that Kendon, Müller and Streeck's approaches have a few distinctions of their own. Kendon's work essentially focuses on gestures as an integral part of utterance construction, further shaped by their context of use, but Müller argues that the context-of-use alone is not enough to explain the meaning of certain specific gesture forms. She suggests that gestures are motivated by cognitive-semiotic techniques and different gestural modes of representation. Finally, Streeck's approach offers a view of gesture as "craft" (Streeck, 2009b) building on sensemaking practices and practical actions of the hands.

33. However, this does not imply that the two approaches presented here are strictly incompatible. They can also be complementary; see for instance *Metaphor and Gesture*, a multi-

Kendon focuses on pragmatic co-speech gestures, while McNeill focuses on iconic ones). While the psychological-cognitive view focuses on gestures working alongside speech to manage human thought processes, the functional-communicative view draws on speakers' abilities to build emerging utterances in different contexts of use through visible bodily action. Since the latter is more in line with some of the central topics addressed in interactional linguistics I will adopt a functional-communicative approach to gesture for the present study of inter-(dis)fluency, thus vouching for a *functional classification* of gesture (cf Section 3.3.3 and Chapter 3).

3.3.3 *Gesture classifications*

The present section is partly based on a selection of Kendon's (2004) review of gesture classifications, but it will also include other schemes not present in his book. One of the first influential gesture classifications was presented by Ekman & Friesen (1969), summarized as follows:

1. *Emblems*: highly conventionalized forms of manual gestures with a stable and shared semantic meaning which can be used as alternatives to speech (e.g. the thumbs up gesture, or waving goodbye)
2. *Illustrators*: manual gestures mainly used by speakers when speaking. This includes batons (used to emphasize a word or a phrase), and deictic gestures (used to point to an object).
3. *Affect displays*: displays of facial expressions and emotions
4. *Regulators*: gestures used to regulate speech
5. *Adaptors*: movements performed on the speaker's own body (self-adaptors), the body of others (alter-adaptors), or objects (object-adaptors).

As Kendon (2004) pointed out, Ekman & Friesen's classification, despite being highly influential, is difficult to apply into a gesture annotation scheme because it has not been established with a common set of criteria. Some categories, such as emblems, for instance, are identified based on their social and conventional significance, whereas illustrators are differentiated based on their connection to speech.

---

disciplinary volume on the use of metaphor in gesture, edited by Alan Cienki and Cornelia Müller.

(for more information, visit https://benjamins.com/catalog/gs.3) last retrieved on August 26th 2021.

Also see Rohrer et al., (2020) who offered a multimodal labeling manual which aimed to bridge the gap between the approaches used by Kendon and McNeill.

Another major well-known gesture classification is McNeill's which, as Kendon (2017) noted, was partly semiotic and semantic. His widely used categories include the following:

1. *Iconic gestures*: gestures which have a "formal relation to the semantic content of the linguistic unit" (McNeill, 1985, p. 354).
2. *Metaphoric gestures*: gestures that are related to abstract meanings.
3. *Beats*: "bi-phasic small low energy rapid flicks of the fingers or hand" (McNeill, 1992, p. 80) which serve punctual and discourse marking functions.
4. *Deictic gestures*: "pointing movements which are prototypically performed with the pointing finger" (McNeill, 1992; p. 80)

Several researchers have distinguished between different kinds of manual gestures based on whether they relate to the content of discourse or to its structure. For instance, McNeill's *beats* and Efron & Ekman's *batons* categories, as well as Austin's *non-significant gestures* refer to gestures that are related to the structuring of discourse, as opposed to *significant gestures, iconic* and *metaphoric gestures* which refer to the propositional content of discourse. However, the categories offered in these classifications are not exactly consistent with this distinction, given the confusion over formal, functional and semantic criteria. This was pointed out by Müller (1998) who criticized these classification systems (in Cienki, 2005, p. 425). For instance, in McNeill's classification, beat gestures are defined both on the basis of their form (i.e. rapid flicks of the finger) and their function (i.e. used to mark emphasis). Furthermore, iconic gestures and metaphoric gestures are distinguished on the grounds of different semiotic and conceptual criteria, which can be conflating (see Sweetser 1998 who reviewed a variety of gestures which *metaphorically* make use of the gesture space to mark discourse structure). The idea of metaphoricity is thus not restricted to referential gestures only, but can be applied to pragmatic gestures as well (cf Streeck, 2008c), so the distinction between "iconic" (concrete) and "metaphoric" (abstract) within the same referential gesture category is not entirely valid. Therefore, Müller (1998) offered a *functional classification* of gestures, which was later adapted by Cienki (2004, 2005). The different categories of gestures were determined based on their function in different speech situations. It distinguished between *referential gestures* (with concrete or abstract reference) and other types of *pragmatic gestures* which includes (1) *performative gestures* (gestures with an expressive function e.g hand clapping, or an appeal function such as requesting, or dismissing) and (2) *discursive gestures* (used for emphasis and discourse structuring).

In sum, several authors, such as Müller (1998), Kendon (1995, 2004, 2017) and others (Bavelas et al. 1995; Cienki, 2005; Lopez-Ozieblo, 2020 with differences in terminology) distinguished between two main classes of gestures: *referential ges-*

tures and *pragmatic gestures*. This distinction can be made on the basis of which aspect of the communicative situation they are about: whether they pertain to a specific thematic object in the content of discourse; or whether they relate to the interaction itself i.e., the expression of stance, an illocutionary force (the speaker's intention when producing the utterance), or the structuring of discourse.

According to Kendon (2004, 2017) referential gestures contribute to the propositional or referential meaning of utterances in two ways, (1) through pointing,[34] and (2) by performing actions which make a physical object or an action visible. In the same vein, Müller (1998, 2004) spoke of *representational* gestures which have two main modes of representation (acting and representing, cf Section 3.3.2), and Streeck (2008a) used the term *depictive gestures*. Bavelas et al., (1992, 1995) further distinguished between *topic gestures* and *interactional gestures*, which is another term for "pragmatic gesture". Topic gestures are defined as the depiction of "some aspect of the topical content of the conversation, such as the size of an object or (metaphorically) of a problem" (Bavelas et al., 1995, p. 397). Referential gestures can further fall into two different categories (see Cienki, 2004, 2005 based on Müller, 1998), those with concrete reference (objects, properties, actions, location) and those with abstract reference (entities, properties, events).

As Kendon (2017) pointed out, McNeill's classification mainly revolves around gestures that are used to represent objects or spatial relations, but lacks in the description of gestures' *pragmatic contribution to discourse* (except for beats). Pragmatic gestures, also known as *interactive gestures* (Bavelas et al., 1992, 1995), *speech-handling gestures* (Streeck, 2009a), *recurrent gestures* (Müller, 2017) or *performative gestures* (Cienki, 2004) draw attention to the pragmatic role of gestures in discourse and interaction, and how they may structure speech acts, indicate the relationship between different discourse segments, or "refer to some aspect of conversing with another person" (Bavelas et al., 1992, p. 473). Streeck (2009a) regarded *speech-handling gestures* as a variety of open-handed unilateral or bilateral gestures used by the speaker as manipulative actions to manipulate virtual objects (e.g. offer or receive an object of discourse and organize relationships between them). These pragmatic, *recurrent gestures* (Müller, 2017) comprise a number of highly common and recurrent gesture forms such as the palm-up-open hand, the palm-away-open-hand, the cyclic gesture (Figure 4).

In addition, pragmatic gestures can further be distinguished between different subcategories, suggested by Kendon (2017, pp. 170–172):

---

34. Deictic gestures can also be categorized in a different category, see for example Gullberg's (1995) category of deictic-anaphoric gestures.

Figure 4. Example of recurrent gestures (Müller, 2017, p.3)

- *Operational*: gestures that operate in relation to what is being expressed verbally (e.g. use of a headshake to express negation).
- *Modal*: gestures that give an interpretative frame for what the speaker is expressing (e.g. use of quotative mark gesture or finger bunch gesture).
- *Performative*: gestures that express the illocutionary force of an utterance (e.g. palm up used to give an example of something).
- *Parsing or punctual*: gestures used to make distinct segments of discourse, marking emphasis or contrast (e.g. beat gestures, or precision grip gesture to emphasize a stretch of speech).
- *Interactional regulation*: gestures used for waving, greeting, requesting, inviting someone to do something etc.

The terms used in these categories are also overlapping in other classifications (cf *performative gestures* in Cienki, 2004, 2005). For example, Bavelas et al.'s category of *interactive gestures* (1992, 1995) does not only include gestures used for interactional regulation, but all the gestures that are used to help maintain conversation as a social system. This includes four different aspects, such as (1) citing the interlocutor's previous contribution, (2) seeking agreement, understanding, help, (3) delivery of new versus shared information, (4) managing events around the turn. More recently, Lopez-Ozieblo (2020) offered a revised functional classification of pragmatic gestures, adapted from Kendon (2017), and further in line with a functional linguistic-based framework and a functional classification of discourse markers. It includes the following categories: (1) *cognitive gestures* (equivalent to modal gestures), (2) *metadiscursive* (equivalent to parsing), and (3) *interactive* (which includes performative, operational, and interactional regulators).

In sum, there are many different existing and overlapping gesture classifications which have been introduced in the field of gesture studies, and these categories can be distinguished with a different set of criteria (semiotic, semantic, functional, conceptual etc.). In this section, I mostly focused on two dominant trends in the field of gesture studies originally introduced by McNeill and Kendon, but as we have seen, gestures can be analyzed in different ways, on the basis of their form, their function, their iconicity, their relation to speech, to the material world (Streeck, 2009a), or to the affordances of the context. Indeed, another body of research largely focused on form-based approaches to gesture, with for instance the ToGoG group (*Towards a Grammar of Gesture*, cf Müller et al., (2013) and Boutet's kiniesological approach (Boutet, 2008, 2010, 2018).

Other gesture classifications, as we have seen, such as McNeill (1985)'s and Ekman & Friesen (1969) were criticized for mixing functional and formal criteria. Kendon (2017) and Cienki (2005; based on Müller (1998) thus offered a functional classification of gestures consistent with functional criteria, which can then be applied to larger annotation schemes (cf Graziano & Gullberg, 2018). The present work opts for a similar function-based approach, in line with the functional-communicative tradition. My identification and classification of gestures, which is partly based on Kendon (2004), Cienki (2004, 2005) and Bavelas et al.(1992,1995) thus rely on both formal and functional characteristics; but adopts a consistent function-based labeling system, avoiding terms such as "beats" or "metaphoric" for the reasons outlined above.

With this in view, gestures can thus fall into two main categories: (1) those that relate to the content of discourse, and depict "actual, imaginary, and abstract worlds" (Streeck, 2010, p. 27); and (2) gestures that relate to the interaction itself, and embody communicative acts and regulate interaction.[35] I discuss my choice of terminology in Chapter 3.

3.3.4 *(Dis)fluency and gesture*

While gestures are said to exclusively occur during speech (cf McNeill, 1985) and thus very rarely during disfluencies (observed by Akhavan et al., 2016; Christenfeld et al., 1991; Esposito et al., 2001; Graziano & Gullberg, 2013; Yasinnik et al., 2005), their relationship is still of interest for two reasons. First, it can shed light on the temporal coordination between gesture and speech production leading to the building of utterances; second, it further supports the view of (dis)fluency as an *embodied* phenomenon, made of a vocal and *gestural flow*, altogether shaped by the contingencies of social interaction.

Before reviewing some of the main studies that investigated the relationship between gesture and (dis)fluency[36] specifically, I shall first briefly introduce the concept of *gesture phrasing* and the *phases of gestural action*, offered by Kendon (2004, p. 111).[37] When a speaker engages in a gesturing activity, he or she will

---

[35]. Note that Streeck (2010, 2015) offered a more complex classification based on the ecologies of gesture i.e., their relation to their communicative intention within the environment (see Streeck, 2015, p. 426 for review).

[36]. It should be noted that all the studies described below used the term "disfluency" in their paper.

undertake a series of phases; first a phase of *preparation*, which leads to the core "expression" of the gesture, known as the *stroke*, which is then followed by a phase of relaxation, known as *recovery*. The stroke can also be followed by a phase in which the gestural movement is sustained, known as the *post-stroke hold* (Kita, 2003). Seyfeddinipur (2006), and Seyfeddinipur & Kita (2001) later used this model to investigate the coordination of disfluencies and gestures on a corpus of German semi spontaneous speech. They investigated the production of overt and covert repairs based on Levelt's (1983) *Repair Model* (cf Section I.1.1) in relation to the different phases of gesture (Seyfeddinipur, 2006, pp. 107–109), listed and illustrated in Figure 5:

- *Preparation*; a movement of the hands to a location where a stroke is deployed.
- *Hold*; when hands are in a static position, other than the rest position.
- *Stroke*; a phase which displays the core meaning of the gesture.
- *Retraction;* when hands move back into rest position (on the lap, arm rests, arms folded in front of the chest).
- *Interrupted preparation/stroke;* when a phase was abruptly ended.

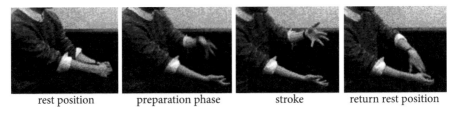

Figure 5. Phases of gestural movement (SITAF corpus)

Their results showed that many gestures tended to be suspended prior to the production of disfluencies: out of 432 speech suspensions, 306 were accompanied by gestures. Seyfeddinipur (2006) gave the example of a speaker who executed a deictic gesture, interrupted it midway, and returned to the starting position at the same time as he produced the repair. She also illustrated cases of gestural suspension (i.e. hands dropping back into rest position) temporally coordinated with a vocal speech suspension. These findings gave support to their *Delayed-Interruption-For-Planning* Hypothesis, a process whereby a speaker, as soon as he or she encounters an error in speech, will not interrupt his speech right away, but will start replanning first (through delaying). This hypothesis further accounted for the *Interruption-Upon-Detection Hypothesis* which predicts that when a speech

---

37. This is also found in McNeill (1992, p. 83) who spoke of "three phases of gesticulation", mainly "preparation", "stroke" and "retraction".

error is detected, a "stop signal" (Seyfeddinipur & Kita, 2001, p. 30) is sent to both modalities simultaneously. The fact that gestures were suspended prior to speech suspension further suggests that they could be seen as early indicators of upcoming interruption, which supports the view of speech and gesture as being part of the same planning process. In fact, in an earlier study conducted on hesitation and gesture, Butterworth & Beattie (1978) claimed that gestures could be seen as the product of *lexical preplanning processes*, indicating the onset of a lexical item currently unavailable in speech.

Similar results were reported in other studies. Esposito & Marinaro (2007) conducted a study on pauses and "gesture pauses" (i.e. holds) among adult and child speakers during an elicitation experiment, and showed a high frequency of overlaps between holds and speech pauses in both groups. This was also found in Yasinnik et al. (2005) who observed a high number of gestures which were temporarily held during disfluent speech in recordings of academic lectures. Similarly, Chui (2005) investigated the coordination of speech with the different phases of gesturing, and found that several gesture onsets occurred during *disfluent stretches of speech* (i.e. a self-repair accompanied by a hesitation pause). However, very few gestures were produced during speech, but the ones which occurred during *disfluent speech* were related to lexical problems or problems of planning. This last finding is also reflected in a different body of research who examined the role of gestures during lexical retrieval (e.g. Krauss & Hadar, 1999) in native and non-native speech, following the assumptions that gestures could help speakers compensate for their speech difficulties. I will address this issue more specifically in Chapter 4. In the same vein, Graziano & Gullberg (2013, 2018) investigated the temporal coordination of disfluencies and gesture, based on a corpus of retellings done by different groups of speakers (competent L1 speakers, adult and child L2 learners). They looked at the distribution of disfluencies in relation to the gestural phases, but they also coded the functions of gestures, i.e. *referential* and *pragmatic*, following Kendon (2004). Their findings yielded similar results as the ones reported above, mainly that gestures occurred significantly more during fluent stretches of speech and that gestures tended to be held during disfluent speech. However, their results also indicated that speakers (of all groups) produced a majority of pragmatic gestures during disfluencies, suggesting that the latter did not necessarily occur when speakers were trying to compensate for their expressive difficulties through referential gestures, but can also occur when speakers comment on their own utterance. Similarly, Akhavan et al. (2016) provided further evidence that the main role of gestures was *not* to remedy speech problems, with again the striking observation that a majority of gestures occurred when speech was fluent. They also found that several disfluencies were accompanied by iconic gestures related to the lexical-semantic system, but a number of disfluencies was also found to occur with beat gestures. The latter, the authors suggested, may have a more communicative role in communication.

Taken together, the findings summarized above provide evidence that processes of speech suspension can to some extent be synchronized with gesture suspension, with the observation that very few gestures accompany fluent speech, and a great deal of them tend to be suspended during disfluent speech. This was found to be true across speakers, languages, age groups, and task types, which further gives support to the notion that the visual-gestural and the verbal/vocal modalities reflect a unified planning process. In the same vein, the present study of inter-(dis)fluency will also investigate the temporal coordination of (dis)fluency and gesture production across languages, speech genres, and communicative tasks (see Chapter 6).

However, while the results found in the studies reviewed above acknowledge the importance of disfluency phenomena in relation to gesture, it still presents a number of limitations. First, these studies focus mostly on the lexical and planning processes associated with disfluency and gesture production, without much taking into account their potential pragmatic role in the interaction (except for Graziano & Gullberg, 2018 and Akhavan et al., 2016 who observed a co-occurrence between disfluencies and pragmatic gestures, but did not quite investigate it further). Their view of disfluency and gesture thus exclusively relies on the speaker's perspective and his or her own planning processes, without much taking into account the contribution of his or her interlocutor within the interaction. Conversely, Stam & Tellier (2017) and Tellier et al. (2013) investigated the functions of gestures during pauses in native and non-native interactions, and hypothesized that gestures produced during pauses could also be partner-oriented, and thus be used as a teaching strategy for the learners. They distinguished between gestures that were *production oriented* (e.g. word searching), *comprehension oriented* (e.g. introducing a concept, marking the word), and *interaction-oriented* (eliciting an answer, helping the interlocutor). Their results showed that, unlike previous work, a considerable number of gestures co-occurred with pauses, especially in non-native speech. But this result was not interpreted as a sign that gestures were used to reflect speakers' lexical difficulties, but were rather treated as strategies used by speakers to facilitate comprehension. Similarly, *fluencemes* can also positively contribute to the co-construction of meaning, for example through *embodied completions*. This practice can be defined as the completion of an action, previously initiated, through *gesture or embodied display* (Mori & Hayashi, 2006). In a study of interactions between non-native learners of Japanese, Mori & Hayashi (2006) demonstrated the way native and non-native speakers coordinate their talk through gesture and embodied completions in the context of L2 use. Although there is no overt mention of fluencemes in their paper, they are nonetheless present, specifically during *embodied word searching sequences* (Rydell, 2019). As Rydell (2019) argued, searching for a word is not only an internal process resulting from language difficulties, it is also an embodied visible activity (cf Goodwin & Goodwin, 1986) which can be collaboratively negotiated by two or more speakers through the mobilization of gaze and gesture.

Therefore, a second major limitation found in the studies addressed above is the fact that they have often been too restricted to a view of "disfluency" phenomena as speech error, affecting the speech (and hence gesture) production apparatus, while I have shown them to be a dynamic, functionally, and interactionally ambivalent system, further shaped by the social and interactional contingencies of talk-in-interaction.

To conclude, the present study of embodied inter-(dis)fluency draws on the different theoretical and methodological perspectives adopted by previous work on gesture and speech in different research fields (i.e. psycholinguistics, cognitive linguistics, interactional linguistics, linguistics anthropology etc.) which reflects the present interdisciplinary and integrated framework addressed in the following section.

IV. Summary of the approaches adopted in this book

In this chapter, I reviewed multiple theoretical frameworks which all had different (but sometimes interrelated) perspectives on (dis)fluency phenomena. I started with psycholinguistics, which was one of the first major field of research in the late 1950s to systematically investigate (dis)fluency, based on the earlier work conducted by clinical linguists on stuttering and verbal "dysfluency". Their approach to (dis)fluency was thus closely related to speech production models (e.g. Levelt, 1983, 1989) which investigated the different stages of speech production, from conceptualization of the main message to its articulation. This line of research provided several analyses of the *disfluency regions* and listed the major *disfluency types*, which altogether served as a basis for later work on (dis)fluency in other research fields such as corpus-based linguistics and second language acquisition. Psycholinguistics thus introduced the fundamental premises of *disfluency* as a legitimate topic of research, which had traditionally been excluded from "traditional" formal and generativist approaches to language.

However, as we have seen, there are a number of issues underlying the term "disfluency", as the latter presupposes a problem, or a deviation from ideally fluent speech. The term fluency, on the other hand, is traditionally found in second language acquisition research, and refers to aspects of L2 speech performance based on several temporal variables, which includes different "disfluency markers" such as pauses, repairs, etc. The notions of fluency versus disfluency have thus been consistently distinguished from one another, despite the constant overlap of terms found across theoretical research fields. Some researchers argued that disfluencies should be called markers of fluency instead of disfluency, as they have been shown to serve many positive structuring functions in discourse other than just signaling an interruption in the speech signal. This constant opposition between fluency and disfluency is reflected in two contrasting views of these phenomena, one that regards them as a cognitive burden, and another one which considers them as a communicative signal. It has come to my understanding that the real conflicting issue regarding the notions of fluency versus disfluency is not only terminological, but theoretical as well. The fact that these phenomena have been systematically analyzed from a strictly verbal and formal perspective (except for a few notable exceptions, e.g. Tottie, 2014; Allwood et al., 2015; McCarthy, 2009; Clark & Fox Tree, 2002 etc.) has hindered their evaluation on the basis of discourse, interaction, or even gesture. This led to a review of other theoretical fields which took on a new perspective to these phenomena, which are altogether relevant to the present study.

First, the framework of cognitive grammar and usage-based linguistics accounted for a dynamic approach to these phenomena which considers them as fluid categories whose degree of symbolic meaning, conventionalization, and entrenchment are shaped by repeated instances of specific patterns in different contexts of use. In light of this approach emerged different cognitive and usage-based frameworks on (dis)fluency (e.g. Crible et al. 2019; Grosman, 2018; Götz, 2013; Segalowitz, 2016) which serve as a basis for the present definition of (dis)fluency (cf Section 4.2). Secondly, the framework of interactional linguistics provided essential conversation-analytic tools to the study of inter-(dis)fluency based on their sequential development within talk-in-interaction, which considers their position within conversational turns, their relation to stance, intersubjectivity, or speakers' positioning in a *participation framework*. Interactionist approaches also rely on data-driven methods such as the *single case analysis*, which focuses on the analysis of a single episode with respect to a specific aspect, or a *collection study*, which generalizes the results of a cumulative series of single case analyses with regards to a relevant aspect (cf Mazeland, 2006). These types of analyses are rarely addressed in usage-based frameworks which rather focus on isolated utterances, or quantitative findings alone (cf Cienki, 2016). Thirdly, the field of gesture studies and multimodal interaction, which is further grounded in an interactional framework, accounted for a view of (dis)fluency as an embodied and multimodal phenomenon, tightly related to the deployment of visible bodily actions (e.g. manual gestures, gaze direction, body movement, facial expressions etc.) which altogether form an integral part of the utterance construction. Language is thus inherently embodied within its ecological and multimodal environment, which is comprised of our material, interactional, and cultural space. Additionally, the field of gesture studies provided relevant gesture classifications, grounded in a functional-communicative approach, which can be applied to the study of (dis)fluency through the analysis of its temporal coordination with gesture.

To conclude, the present study offers an integrated theoretical construction of inter-(dis)fluency, combining multiple approaches and perspectives, thus going beyond the first traditional psycholinguistic approach to disfluency. However, even though the present study is not exactly grounded in a psycholinguistic approach to (dis)fluency, it still borrows from its formal classification (i.e. the fluenceme classification, in line with Crible et al., 2019) for the purposes of corpus annotation. This has not been extensively done in other fields such as interactional linguistics which only focused on a selection of markers in specific interactional sequences. The integration of these different theoretical frameworks thus further reflects my mixed-method approach which relies on quantitative and qualitative methods (cf Chapter 3). In sum, the combination of the usage-based, interactional, and multimodal frameworks enables us to bridge the gap between large corpus-based quantitative studies and data-driven single case analyses or collection studies. While quantitative methods give a robust and statistically valid overview of the data, they fail to illuminate particular instances in a specific interactional sequence, whose complex information can never be truly conveyed in quantitative findings. On the other hand, single case analyses, although truly illuminating of all the ongoing relevant interactional and social processes shaping the course of the talk, only rely on a small selection of instances, thus disregarding all other instances of the same phenomena in the whole dataset. This is highly relevant to the present study of fluencemes which are highly frequent in speech, and which consequently do not systematically exhibit essential features of talk-in-interaction. Reciprocally, their use is not systematically restricted to contexts of speech error. This emphasizes their dynamic and fluid nature, whose degree of fluency, understood here as communicativeness, flow, or stream, depends on a number of contextual features.

V. Towards an integrated framework of inter-(dis)fluency

The aim of this chapter was to introduce different theoretical backgrounds in order to situate inter-(dis)fluency in a larger integrated framework, and thus bridge the gap between production-based psycholinguistic studies conducted on disfluency and usage-based, interactional, multimodal approaches to social interaction. This also invites us to consider (dis)fluency from multiple dimensions, based on Lickley (2015); Segalowitz (2016); Götz (2013), Candea (2000, 2017) and Grosman (2018).

5.1 Definition of inter-(dis)fluency

The present study adopts a definition of fluency as inherently multimodal, multidimensional, and multilevel. The notion of *fluency* is broadly understood in general terms such as "communicativeness" "smoothness" "fluidity" and "flow" which can all be applied respectively to: (1) speech production (i.e. flow of speech), (2) interaction (i.e. fluidity and progressivity of the exchanges), and (3) gestures (i.e. gestural and body flow). The *dis* in brackets is equally important, as it symbolizes the potential interruption or discontinuity of all these flows, e.g. the cut off of a speech segment, a communication breakdown, or the interruption of a gestural movement. This interruption further reflects the potential for the same forms to be either fluent and/or disfluent, self-oriented or other-directed, lexical or non-lexical, thus placing (dis)fluency phenomena in a multilevel continuum which considers a series of markers which can potentially gain symbolic status (in line with Cienki, 2015b). Lastly, *inter* views this multidimensional flow not as one way, but a *two-way-flow* influencing one another, in line with McCarthy's notion of *confluence*. I preferred to use the prefix "inter" here, as it also draws a parallel to notions of *intersubjectivity, interpersonal relations*, and *interaction*. My tripartite model of inter-(dis)fluency, whose dimensions are partly based on Grosman (2018), Segalowitz (2016), and Götz, (2013) is illustrated in Figure 6:

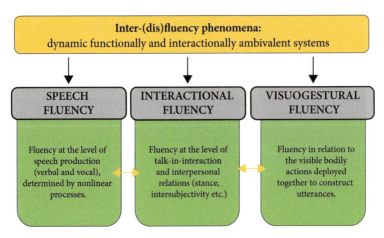

Figure 6. Multidimensional model of inter-(dis)fluency

The *speech dimension* is solely restricted to the level of speech (verbal and vocal) production which relies on multiple non-linear processes introduced in Section I.1.1. It also takes into account the combination level of fluencemes, whether they occur clustered with other markers, or isolated (cf Crible et al., 2019,

Section 3.1.3). The temporal features of fluencemes are also investigated within this dimension, which includes the duration of the vocal markers (e.g. filled and unfilled pauses, and prolongations). The second dimension, the *interactional dimension (inter-fluency)*, is similar to Grosman (2018)'s socio-interpersonal dimension (cf Section 3.1.3), but it further includes the situated conversational language practices shaping social interaction introduced in Section 3.2.1, which is also in line with French theories of *co-énonciation* reflected in the work of Candea (2000, 2017). Finally, the *visuogestural dimension*, which echoes Götz's (2013) *non-verbal fluency*, reflects the influential work of different gesture researchers, such as Cienki (2005); Kendon (2004), Morgenstern (2014, 2020), Müller (2017), and Streeck (2009b). The *cognitive* and *perceived* dimensions of fluency were excluded from the model (cf Segalowitz, 2016; Götz, 2013), as they cannot be as easily "measurable": *cognitive fluency* is rather an abstract construct, and *perception fluency* would require perception experiments, which goes beyond the scope of this study.

In sum, my definition of inter-(dis)fluency involves multiple dimensions which are not mutually exclusive, but interactively complementing one another in the course of the interaction (hence the term *inter-(dis)fluency*). In some contexts, a verbal utterance that is considered highly "disfluent" in the speech flow will not necessarily impede the interactional flow of the multimodal interaction; in other contexts, however, the presence of a single fluenceme could disrupt the progressivity of an interactional sequence. Once more, this view defends a dynamic approach to (dis)fluency, which includes different degrees of fluency and or/ disfluency.

5.2 Main theoretical assumptions

Starting with the analysis of typical "disfluency markers" which have traditionally been viewed as an interruption of the speech flow with no propositional content (Fox Tree, 2007), the present study aims to uncover the different discursive and interactional roles the same *a priori disfluent forms* can serve in different situations by taking into account different levels of analysis (speech, gesture, and interaction). Following Götz (2013) and Crible et al., (2019) I will speak of *fluencemes*, which are better understood in terms of constructions, whose degree of conventionality and entrenchment may rely on their frequency, position, and combinatory patterns. Highly frequent clusters (e.g. *filled pause + unfilled pause*) can show a high degree of automaticity, while highly complex combinations show greater disruption in the speech signal. This is one way to reflect the two sides of (dis)fluency, which is the starting point of this book.

- In this sense, inter-(dis)fluency phenomena should not be regarded in terms of binary opposition between fluency and disfluency, but rather as a multi-level embodiment of the notion of fluidity and flow (fluency) with its potential interruption (disfluency).
- The notion of interruption is to be understood on the basis of different levels: (1) *the disruption of the verbal flow and the acoustic signal*; or an interruption in the speaking activity; (2) *the interruption of the interactional flow* through postures of disengagement, disalignment, or disagreement; and (3) *the suspension or interruption of a gestural activity*.
- In line with Allwood (2017) the present study considers fluency as resulting from two systems of communication, mainly interactive communication management (ICM) and own communication management (OCM). In this sense, inter-(dis)fluency phenomena do not only deal with internal cognitive processes (OCM), but also exhibit essential features of talk-in-interaction (ICM).
- Fluencemes are thus highly flexible and dynamic categories which display different degrees of convention and different sets of meanings which are altogether shaped by their context of use. Context is understood here in terms of (1) the immediate neighboring environment of the fluencemes at the combination level (e.g. fluenceme sequence) (2) the syntactic position of fluencemes within the verbal utterance, (3) their sequential position within a turn (e.g. turn transitional place); (4) their co-occurrence with bodily actions; (5) the situated language activity speakers are currently engaged in (e.g. storytelling activity) and (6) their overall material environment (e.g. the objects they are manipulating).

To conclude, many of the assumptions addressed above follow assumptions from the different theoretical frameworks discussed in this chapter, mainly *cognitive grammar, interactional linguistics*, and *gesture studies*. The notion of fluidity and dynamicity, for instance, are found both in interactional linguistics (cf Mondada, 2007) and cognitive linguistics (cf Cienki, 2005), and the notions of embodied cognition, embodied experience and embodied interaction resulting in the situatedness of gesture and language are found across the three frameworks.

CHAPTER 2

Inter-(dis)fluency across languages and settings

The present chapter reviews a collection of studies in L1 and L2 fluency and gesture research. It explores the different variables affecting (dis)fluency and gesture use across languages and settings in order to formulate research questions for my two empirical studies (cf Chapters 4 and 5). I begin with a review of a collection of studies in Second Language Acquisition to better understand differences between L1 and L2 fluency and their relation to proficiency, then present other factors that may have an effect on (dis)fluency and gesture such as setting or language style, based on a review of the literature in different disciplines (psycholinguistics, second language acquisition, gesture studies, and conversation analysis).

I. Research on L2 fluency and gesture

1.1 L2 fluency, accuracy, and proficiency

Previous research in SLA has investigated how L1 and L2 fluency may differ, and which temporal aspects of speech may determine overall perceptions of fluency. For instance, pausing phenomena in non-native speech is more likely to be related to vocabulary than other linguistic problems, suggesting that lexical retrieval is one of the biggest "obstacles" of L2 speech fluency (De Jong, 2016a; Witton-Davies, 2014). In line with previous research (e.g. Hilton, 2009; Witton-Davies, 2014), Eguchi (2016) conducted a longitudinal study on three EFL learners in a Japanese university, and investigated the relationship between "breakdown fluency" (i.e. rate of filled and unfilled pauses, see Skehan, 2003)[38] and vocabulary, by paying specific attention to "lexical pauses" (see Cenoz, 1998 below), i.e. pauses related to lexical retrieval, which were found to be the most frequent, as opposed to other types of breakdown associated with syntactic or morphological errors.

---

38. Skehan (2003) and Tavakoli & Skehan (2005) distinguished between three aspects of fluency, "speed fluency" (rate of speech), "breakdown fluency", and "repair fluency" (repairs, repetitions, reformulations, substitutions etc.)

However, while some researchers have noted language-specific features of (dis)fluency (e.g. Clark & Fox Tree, 2002; Maclay & Osgood, 1959), there are, to my knowledge, few empirical crosslinguistic studies on fluencemes which compared fluency rates in native and non-native productions *across languages*, except for Grosjean & Deschamps (1975); De Leeuw, (2007); Candea et al. (2005); Hai, (2017), and Peltonen (2020). For instance, De Leeuw (2007) compared the duration and frequency of vocalic hesitation markers in English, German, and Dutch, and found differences across language groups, with Dutch speakers who produced 10.1 hesitations per minute, versus Germans who produced an average of 6.3 per minute. German speakers also produced more nasal hesitations than English and Dutch speakers. In another study, Candea et al. (2005) compared the production of vocalic fillers in eight languages (Arabic, Mandarin Chinese, French, German, Italian, European Portuguese, American English and Latin American Spanish), and looked at three acoustic parameters (duration, pitch, and timbre). Their results showed timbre differences across languages, with for example Spanish which used a mid-closed vowel, while English used low-central vowels. Similarly, Hai (2017) found differences between Russian native speakers and Chinese non-native speakers with respect to vowel quality. In addition, Grosjean & Deschamps (1975) observed differences between French and English with regard to speech rate (i.e. French speakers spoke faster than English speakers) but also fluenceme distribution (e.g. more lexical repairs produced by English speakers than French speakers). However, none of these studies (except for Hai, 2017) have compared the rate of fluencemes produced by the same native and non-native speakers in different languages. The present study (cf Chapter 4) thus aims to bridge this gap by comparing native and non-native productions of fluencemes both in French and English.

A larger number of studies in SLA have reported differences in fluency rates in native versus non-native speech. For instance, Tavakoli (2011) conducted a study on oral narrative tasks performed by English native speakers and L2 speakers of English, and found differences in the distribution of pauses, as L2 learners tended to produce more pauses in the middle of clauses and fewer end-clause pauses than the native speakers. The author thus suggested that it was not the frequency of pauses that distinguished L1 from L2 speech, but rather their position in the utterance. In a similar vein, Rasier & Hiligsmann (2007) emphasized the "erroneous" use of pauses in L2 speech, as L2 speakers were more likely to produce pauses between words in the utterance, i.e. between the adjective and the noun, than native speakers. Moreover, Cenoz (1998) found that L2 speakers produced non-juncture pauses very frequently, which suggested planning problems. She explained that L2 speakers were more likely to use non-juncture pauses because they had to look for words "in a language in which they present limited proficiency" (1998, p. 03). She categorized three types of pauses: (1) lexical pauses– indicating problems in lexical retrieval; (2) morphological pauses–pauses followed by repetitions and self-corrections indicating problems at the morphological level; (3) planning pauses. Their results indicated that a majority of pauses produced by the L2 speakers served planning functions.

Another body of research has provided evidence of a higher rate of pausing, "hesitation", or "error" phenomena in L2 than L1 productions (see Brand & Götz, 2013; Deschamps, 1980; Fehringer & Fry, 2007; Matzinger et al., 2020; Riggenbach, 1991). Fehringer & Fry (2007) have found significant differences in the number of hesitation markers produced by bilingual speakers of German and English, with higher rates in their second language. De Jong (2016b) further showed that high-proficiency Dutch learners produced fewer pauses than low-proficiency ones. Similarly, Riazantseva (2001) found that Russian learners paused more frequently in their L2 than in their L1, and their pauses were also found to be significantly longer in their second language. This was also the case in Kahng's (2014) study of Korean learners, who produced pauses which were almost twice as long as the ones produced by the English native speakers. These studies have shown a strong relation between fluenceme rate/duration and proficiency (cf Riazantseva, 2001). In sum, non-native speakers are said to produce more pauses of longer duration and in mid-clause position before low-frequency words, and this can be explained by their limited proficiency of the language (Cenoz, 1998).

In addition, specific emphasis is laid on temporal aspects of spoken fluency, in other words, how fluency fits into models of spoken production, which includes, in parts, a semantic system and a phonological system (Levelt, 1999, cf Chapter 1, Section I). As Hilton (2009) argued, many speech processes revolving around lexical retrieval, morphosyntactic encoding or phonological planning are carried out in L1 "without the need of attentional effort in the executive component of working memory" (Hilton, 2009, p. 645). Therefore, instances of retracing, repetitions, reformulations, pauses, and the like are often interpreted as a sign of encoding difficulties in the speech production process. In L2 production, the "network of automatically available lexical and morphophonological representations" is said to be "limited", as Hilton (2009, p. 646) argued.

Similarly, Dörnyei & Kormos (1998) claimed that many of the problem-solving processes emerging in L2 productions were the result of a *resource deficit*. This refers to the inability to retrieve the right lemma during a lexical search, difficulties in phonological encoding, or incomplete knowledge of the L2. Learners may thus resort to a series of "stalling mechanisms" e.g. "uh"/"um", lengthening, discourse markers (Dornyei & Kormos, 1998) to buy more time in speech, in order to deal with processing time pressure. Once more, the constructs of fluency and disfluency in SLA are deeply grounded in theories of language production, by relating to "breakdowns", "processing time pressure" or "encoding difficulties" in the L2 speech production apparatus. However, it has been emphasized multiple times throughout this book that this *cognitive-burden* view of (dis)fluency (cf Chapter 1 Section II.2.2.1) only gives a partial picture of the phenomena under study. While previous research in SLA has given evidence that (dis)fluency rates could relate to perceived fluency and language proficiency (except for Brand & Götz, 2013 who did not detect any clear correlation), this kind of analysis should not be restricted to error and accuracy measures, but should include other crucial components of L2 performance phenomena, such as the interactive nature of face-to-face interaction. In addition, the correlation between (dis)fluency rates and proficiency has also been criticized (e.g. Simpson et al., 2013) and it has been hypothesized that fluencemes in the L2 may mirror those produced in the L1, as they could be the result of similar cognitive processes (Zuniga & Simard, 2019). In this view, L1 and L2 fluency are said to be closely related (Derwing et al., 2009). In conclusion, the relationship between fluency, accuracy, and proficiency is not straightforward, and may also be related to other phenomena outside general cognitive processes. While these last aspects (proficiency and accuracy) are not central to the present research, the analysis of fluencemes and their distribution in L1 and L2 discourse may still contribute to the existing field of research in L2 fluency, by examining whether L1 and L2 (dis)fluency patterns strongly differ, and how they may do so, or whether they are closely related, not only on cognitive grounds, but on interactional ones as well.

1.2   L2 fluency, interactional competence, and "CA-for-SLA"

Additional research in SLA has examined fluency in second language learning, but without focusing on processing difficulties, in line with psycholinguistic-cognitive approaches, but further grounded in an interactional framework, as to identify the different strategies used by learners to deal with problems in interaction (Gullberg, 2011; Tarone, 1980). As Gullberg (2011) pointed out, fluencemes may also relate to interaction-related difficulties, with for example the potential loss of face and floor, which puts learners at an interactional risk. This may prompt learners to engage in multimodal word searching practices, which involve the display of a thinking face (Goodwin & Goodwin, 1986, see Chapter 1, Section III.3.3.1) accompanied by a thinking gesture (see Chapter 3, Section II.2.2.3). Specific attention is also paid to individual differences, which show how learners turn to a number of strategies that are very speaker-specific, reflecting their own communicative style, and which appears to determine L2 fluency behavior. Gullberg (2011) gave the example of a learner who had an issue with the term "prescription" and who produced a high rate of fluencemes, but without exploiting her multimodal resources. Her behavior was in fact found to be quite identical in her native speech. This may indicate that her L2 performance was not a necessarily a sign of limited L2 proficiency skills, but rather a reflection of her own individual preferences. This further justifies the need to conduct qualitative analyses in complement with quantitative observations of the data (see Peltonen, 2020). In addition, the analysis of L2 fluency is not only restricted to temporal variables, but includes other phenomena such as discourse markers, back-channeling and turn-taking. As Gürbüz (2017) argued, while the overuse of such phenomena (even in a native language) may be perceived as "disfluent" or inarticulate, no occurrence of them at all may be perceived as unnatural. Similarly, Gilquin (2008) conducted a corpus study on hesitation markers and "smallwords" (e.g. kind of, well, I mean) produced by French learners of English and native English speakers in interviews. Her study showed that pauses were very frequent among both native speakers and learners, but that the latter produced pauses more frequently overall. One interesting finding is that, while French-speaking learners overused pauses (both filled and unfilled), they did not make use of the full range of smallwords. In fact, they were extremely underused. She gave the example of "like", which was very common in native English speech, but almost absent in French learner speech. She added that filled pauses were crucial to non-native speakers as a conversational strategy, as they could be used to signal production difficulties to their conversational partner, but also to keep the floor or to be more polite, functions that also exist in native use. This functional approach to discourse markers, and more specifically (dis)fluency, which lies at the core of most corpus-based studies, aims to support the *ambivalent* view of fluencemes, and regards them as conversational tools. This ambivalence is also reflected in the work conducted on word searches in L2. On the one hand, word searches and their solutions are associated with communication strategies used to solve interactional difficulties (Kasper & Færch, 1983; Rydell, 2019); on the other hand, they are associated with "disfluency", which are treated as a deficit in the L2 (Dörnyei & Kormos, 1998).

A number of studies have also examined the way L2 learners may use fluencemes and *gestures* to deal with interactional related difficulties, with for instance the use of "uh" to start the conversation, or answer a question with the correct words (Azi, 2018), or the use of gestures as a communicative resource during repair practices in ESL conversational tutoring (see Seo & Koshik, 2010). In addition, micro analyses of interactional practices in L2 learning situations further shed light on the intersubjective role of gestures; they may be used to exhibit the learner's active co-participation in the language activity, or display alignment and achieve intersubjectivity through gesture replication or gesture co-production (see Belhiah, 2013). In sum, more and more studies in ESL and SLA have (re)considered the concept of L2 fluency, and now view it as a multimodal resource, or a strategy, rather than a cognitive deficit, with a strong focus on interactional data and collaborative aspects of fluency, or "confluence" (cf McCarthy, 2009; Chapter 1, Section II.2.2). In line with this concept of confluence, Peltonen (2017, 2019, 2020) offered a *Fluency Resources Framework*, which links L2 fluency analysis to a broader perspective of communication, rather than solely from the perspective of temporal speech fluency. She also incorporated the analysis of gestures to study the way speakers make use of them to maintain fluency in interaction. More and more studies in L2 language testing have foregrounded the concept of *interactional competence* (e.g. Galaczi, 2014; Galaczi & Taylor, 2018) in line with CA and interaction research. The construct of interactional competence is defined as the following (Galaczi & Taylor, 2018, p. 226):

> The ability to co-construct interaction in a purposeful and meaningful way, taking into account sociocultural and pragmatic dimensions of the speech situation and event. This ability is supported by the linguistic and other resources that speakers and listeners leverage at a microlevel of the interaction, namely, aspects of topic management, turn management, interactive listening, break down repair and non-verbal or visual behaviours.

As Pekarek-Doehler (2018, 2006) further argued, the notion of L2 competence needs to acknowledge the dynamic and adaptive nature of the linguistic system. She criticized the notion of competence as individualistic, mentalist, or monologic, and decontextualized from practical actions and concrete situations. The notion of competence is much too often based on the perception of the ideal native speaker from the point of view of his or her production, but without taking into account the co-participant of the interaction. By adopting a conversation-analytic and interactional approach to L2 learning, hence *CA-SLA* (Pekarek Doehler & Pochon-Berger, 2011; Pekarek Doehler, 2006), the notion of L2 competence and fluency are thus "anchored in language use, that is, embedded in the moment unfolding of talk-in-interaction" (Pekarek Doehler & Pochon-Berger, 2011, p. 1). *CA-SLA* thus offers a "socially situated" view of learning (Mondada & Pekarek Doehler, 2004), which implies that the processes of L2 learning are only fully understood when "abstracted from their natural ecology, that is, the practices the learner engages in" (Pekarek Doehler & Pochon-Berger, 2011, p. 3). In sum, the analysis of L2 fluency does not only revolve around internal language processes or linguistic structures alone, but their intricate relation to the organization of actions during language practices. Pekarek Doehler & Pochon-Berger (2011) applied this method to their micro analyses of (dis)agreement sequences in French foreign language classroom interactions in German-speaking Switzerland. Their study identified different features of disagreement with regard to preference structure, turn allocation, but also linguistic properties, and they presented quantitative findings which provided a general picture of the techniques used for doing disagreement, as well as qualitative analyses which illustrated the specific turn construction methods adopted by learners to display disagreement. The present integrated theoretical model of inter-(dis)fluency is very much in line with this body of research which offers a valuable contribution to the field of SLA.

To conclude, the present study follows the approaches adopted by researchers in different disciplines from various research fields, from applied linguistics to conversation analysis, which bring together valuable insights on L2 fluency, proficiency, second language testing, and interaction. This combination of studies invites us to (re)consider the construct of L2 fluency without solely focusing on temporal variables or general accuracy rates. As De Jong (2018, p. 14) further argued, fluency behavior is "in part dependent on personal speaking style". In addition, fluencemes are not only signals of trouble in processing and formulating, but can be "part of communicatively effective speech" (De Jong, 2018, p. 14). Once more, this notion of ambivalence is one of the most central aspects of this book, and will be explored in both quantitative and qualitative analyses.

1.3 Gesture production in Second Language Acquisition

In Chapter 1, I reviewed a number of studies which looked at the relationship between (dis)fluency and gesture (cf Chapter 1, Section III.3.3.4). This section focuses more specifically on the role of gestures in L2 discourse, by drawing on a number of studies in psycholinguistics, second language testing, and interactional linguistics.

It has been proposed that iconic and deictic gestures are very often produced when speakers experience lexical problems, and that these gestures may help facilitate word finding (Beattie & Butterworth, 1979; Krauss & Hadar, 1999). Further in line with models of speech production (e.g. Levelt, 1989, 1999) a number of authors, such as Krauss & Hadar (1999) and Krauss et al., (1995) proposed that gestures are triggered by the activation of the spatial representation in the *conceptualizer* (one of the mental procedures involved in the planning of messages, see Levelt & Schriefers, 1987). This body of research is in line with the *cognitive-psychological* approach to gesture presented in Chapter 1 (see Chapter 1, Section 3.3.2), and follows the assumption that gestures serve a *compensatory* role in speech production. Krauss et al., (2000) offered the *Lexical Retrieval Hypothesis* (henceforth LHR), further in support of this model. According to this hypothesis, word findings are said to be more successful when accompanied by iconic gestures, as they facilitate access to lexical memory. In the field of SLA, one related question regarding gesture use is whether it can help learners resolve speech difficulties. Studies have reported a tendency for L2 learners to produce more gestures in their L2 than in their L1 to overcome language difficulties in their target language (e.g. Gullberg, 1998; Kita, 1993; Stam, 2006). Stam (2006, 2008, 2018) further demonstrated that the gestures produced by L2 learners provided an "enhanced window onto their mind through which we can view their thinking and mental representations" (Stam, 2018, p.165). In this view, speech and gesture are viewed as a single-integrated system (cf Chapter 1, Section 3.3.2) reflecting processes of L2 speaking, thinking, and learning. In line with Slobin's (1987) theory of *thinking for speaking* McCafferty (1998) investigated the gesture production of Japanese learners of English during a picture narration task. His findings showed that L2 learners predominantly co-produced gestures with speech when engaged in problem solving activities. He also looked at cases of pausing and repairs (labelled "self-regulation"), and observed an absence of gestures during these instances. He concluded that speakers seemed to "look within themselves" (McCafferty, 1998, p.88) and thus did not "externalize" their thinking processes, as opposed to when they were gesturing. In another paper, following Kita's (2000)'s *Information Packaging Hypothesis* which claims that referential and deictic gestures constitute a spatio-motoric mode of thinking, McCafferty (2004) explored the way L2 learners used gestures to solve intrapersonal problems. He conducted another study based on interactions between Taiwanese learners of English in the United States, and argued that speakers used referential gestures (i.e. deictics and representational gestures) to provide "a greater degree of spatial exactness" (McCafferty, 2004, p.163): because the learners experienced difficulties when speaking their L2, they resorted to the *spatio-motoric channel for thinking* (Kita, 2000), i.e. representational gestures which activate spatio-dynamic information (Krauss et al., 2000). This helped them to "orchestrate speech production in the L2 and to actionally structure the discourse" (McCafferty, 2004, p.161). In sum, a large number of studies in SLA research have focused on the *intrapersonal* functions of gestures, as well as their cognitive aspects (read Gullberg & McCafferty, 2008, for extensive review), and the role gestures play in L2 developmental processes, leading to a number of linguistic difficulties.[39]

However, as Lopez-Ozieblo (2019) pointed out, gestures used by L2 speakers do not only relate to lexical related problems, but can be used for turn-taking, repair, or discourse management, among other intersubjective actions (also see Chapter 1, Section 3.3.4). In fact, a number of studies on gestures in SLA reject the assumption that L2 learners' gestures are used to overcome lexical shortcomings.

---

39. A large body of research has also examined the facilitative role of gestures in L2 learning, with for instance the acquistion of L2 vocabulary for children and adults (e.g. Kelly et al., 2009; Tellier, 2008b) or L2 phoneme acquisition (e.g. (Hoetjes & Van Maastricht, 2020; Zhang et al., 2020). Read Hoetjes & Van Maastricht (2020) for an extensive review.

For instance, Gullberg (1998, 2011) studied interactions of Swedish and Dutch learners of French and French learners of Swedish, and found that while learners did produce gestures to resolve lexical difficulties in their L2, they were also used to elicit help from the interlocutor, and thus relied on multimodal communication strategies to manage the interaction. Solutions to such difficulties were characterized by "active co-constructions in which both participants jointly deploy speech, gaze, and representational gestures in a highly structured fashion" (Gullberg, 2011, p. 141). More recently, Graziano & Gullberg (2013, 2018) supported evidence against the LHR by examining the types of gestures that frequently occurred during fluencemes (cf Chapter 1, Section 3.3.4). As we have seen, their study reported a high number of pragmatic gestures during fluencemes, which suggests that gestures produced in L2 were not necessarily related to lexical difficulties but rather to difficult aspects of interaction.[40] This does not support the LHR which expects referential gestures to predominantly occur during fluencemes, as to activate lexical items in the conceptualizer. In addition, for gestures to be truly compensatory, it would mean that they would have to occur *during* speech difficulties (i.e. during fluencemes), but as Graziano & Gullberg (2018) argued, the observation that gestures are more likely to occur with "fluent" rather than "disfluent" stretches of speech makes it difficult to assess theories such as the LHR. Once again, this "internalized" and production-based view of gestures only gives a partial picture of the phenomena. As emphasized throughout this book, the present work adopts an *integrated* approach to gesture and inter-(dis)fluency, which focuses on situated language use and interactional dynamics, (see Gullberg & McCafferty, 2008) and views gesture as integral to human communication, both with regard to *intrapersonal* and *interpersonal* processes.

To conclude, we can find a large body of research on gesture and SLA across disciplines and theoretical frameworks, and the studies presented here largely reflect the two dominant views presented earlier, mainly the *psychological-cognitive* and the *functional-communicative* view (cf Chapter 1, Section 3.3.2). The present study on fluencemes and gestures in L2 discourse largely follows Graziano & Gullberg's work (2013, 2018) which rejects the compensatory role of gestures in L2 discourse.

---

40. These findings were also found in Akhavan et al. (2016), among others (cf Chapter 1, Section 3.3.4).

II. Effects of task type, discourse domain, and style

In the previous section, I presented a large existing body of research in Second Language Acquisition, gesture studies, and corpus linguistics, to better understand differences between L1 and L2. Language proficiency (i.e. native versus non-native speech) was thus the primary avariable that was used systematically in the analyses to compare other sets of variables (i.e. position, duration, gesture production etc.). The present section identifies other factors, such as type of delivery, setting, style, or task type, as potentially affecting (dis)fluency and gesture rate.

2.1 Type of delivery and speech mode

As Witton-Davies (2014) pointed out, speech samples can be categorized in various ways, depending on the means of elicitation (naturalistic or experimental), the mode (monologue or dialogue), the interface (face-to-face, computer, or laboratory), and the type of task and condition. He elaborated on the degree of preparation time required by different speaking tasks, by identifying three types: (1) scripted– read aloud or memorized speech; (2) prepared – speech prepared beforehand, and (3) spontaneous – no preparation at all. As a lot of researchers have shown (e.g. Feirrera & Bailey, 2004, Lickley, 2015; Goldman-Eisler, 1958; Shriberg, 1994, among others, see section Chapter 1, Section I. 1.2) unplanned, unprepared, and spontaneous speech deliveries necessarily give rise to many disfluencies. For instance, Silverman et al., (1992) examined prosodic characteristics of over a hundred utterances, and compared spontaneous and read versions of it. Half of the utterances were taken from a corpus of spontaneous answers to request the name of a city, and the others were the same word strings read by subjects who tried to model authentic dialogue. In their analysis of silent pauses, they found differences between spontaneous and read segments, with 45% of pauses that were "ungrammatical" in spontaneous speech (i.e. not located at grammatical boundaries) whereas only 11% were ungrammatical in read speech. In a similar vein, Deese (1984, in O'Shaughnessy, 1992) found that planned speech contained fewer restarts (3.8 phw) than unplanned speech (5 phw). In a more recent study conducted on different speech samples (e.g. reading, conference, news broadcast etc.) for the purposes of developing prosodic detection tools, Goldman et al., (2010) also found that spontaneous speech samples contained a higher amount of hesitations than in read or prepared speech. However, the distinction between "spontaneous" and "read" speech remains restricted to the domain of speech analysis, and is thus not suited to the present study. In addition, it is not only the type of delivery that distinguishes these two conditions, but to a larger extent the overall setting: in one case speakers are usually interacting face-to-face, while in another they are most often reading from a text in front of an experimenter (or alone).

In addition, previous research on (dis)fluency in monologue and dialogue have led to contradictory results (read Witton-Davies, 2014, pp. 62–66 for an extensive review). One the one hand, a number of papers have shown that fluency correlates with dialogues, with a faster speech rate, shorter utterances, and a fewer number of pauses in dialogic situations (e.g. Kowal et al., 1983; Michel, 2011); while others have found evidence that speakers tend to be more fluent during monologic tasks than dialogic ones (e.g. Skehan, 2001). However, it should be noted that all these studies were conducted on non-native speakers and examined temporal characteristics of L2 fluency specifically (cf Section I of this chapter) which adds another crosslinguistic variable. As Witton-Davies (2014) observed, other effects may have an impact on (dis)fluency rates such as task complexity, or topic. In sum, mode of speech alone (i.e. dialogue versus monologue) is not enough to compare differences between speech samples, and calls for further discussion.

2.2 Evidence from experimental and corpus-based studies

In order to understand the different processes associated with (dis)fluency and identify the different causes underlying their production, several researchers have conducted experimental and corpus-based studies which manipulated task type, discourse domain, utterance complexity, or topic. In addition to the type of delivery or speech mode, other factors, such as discourse domain or familiarity may thus also come into play. For instance, Schatcher et al., (1991) conducted a study on the production of disfluencies in different academic disciplines, based on lectures in the humanities and natural sciences. They argued that undergraduate students were less required to choose among options to structural, "formal" and "factual" lectures like pure sciences, as opposed to humanities lectures, and thus predicted that lecturers in the humanities and social sciences would produce more disfluencies[41] (and more specifically filled pauses) than those in natural sciences. Their results showed indeed a higher number of filled pauses during lectures in humanities (6.46 per minute) than during natural sciences (1.39 per minute), which supported their prediction. They further designed an interview to all the lecturers during which they were asked to talk about graduate training procedures and practices, and also found significant differences in the rate of disflu-

---

41. Note that the terms "disfluency" and "hesitation" are mostly used in this section to reflect the authors' terminology, even though I do not adopt these terms.

encies between lectures and interviews, with a higher rate of disfluencies during interviews (5.28) than during lectures (4.85).

Similarly, Bortfeld et al. (2001) found that speakers produced a higher rate of disfluencies when discussing unfamiliar topics than familiar ones. Based on a large corpus of English conversations, they investigated the different processes associated with the different types of disfluency. They found that disfluency rates increased when speakers were faced with "heavier cognitive demands" (Bortfeld et al. 2001, p.135), in other words, when the topic was unfamiliar (e.g. discussing tangrams versus discussing children), or when speakers produced longer turns (in line with Oviatt, 1995, Shriberg, 1996, and Beattie, 1979, who found that high disfluency rates were associated with longer utterances). This last effect could be explained by the difficulty of planning longer utterances. However, it should be noted that while this was true for most disfluency types, there was quite a different pattern for filled pauses which were not correlated with utterance length, and were found to serve interpersonal functions. This evidence was also supported by Tottie (2011, 2014, 2015, 2016, 2019) who, as we have seen earlier (cf Chapter 1, sections II.2.2.1 and III.3.1.2), argued that filled pauses could be used intentionally for a stylistic purpose, and thus belonged to the same category of "planners" along with discourse markers such as "and" or "but". Filled pauses were found to be more frequent during task-related interactions taking place in non-private settings than during conversations between family and friends. She hypothesized that long narrative turns or a thoughtful presentation of evidence required more planning than a conversation among relatives and friends, which may indicate that filled pauses were linked to the demands of planning what to say.

More in line with the notion of style and register, Duez (1982) conducted a study on the distribution of filled and unfilled pauses in the speech of French politicians across three different contexts (political speech, political interviews, and casual interviews) in order to investigate their possible stylistic function. She found that pauses were much more frequent in interviews than in political speeches, but were strikingly longer in the latter. She suggested that the high rate of pauses found in interviews may relate to the fact that the politicians were focusing on planning and production issues when producing spontaneous speech, while the long duration of pauses in political (prepared) speeches reflected a stylistic function, namely to emphasize what was being said. This is in contradiction with Tottie (2016) who claimed that long narrative turns required more planning than conversations, hence more pauses. It would appear that, in Duez's case, the effect of register and formality (which she called "political power", Duez, 1997) was much stronger than the effect of speech mode and turn-taking, since French politicians (unlike common speakers) are trained oral performers who are expected to deliver convincing speeches with very few hesitation marks. Conversely, Moniz (2019) and Moniz et al., (2014) found that lectures contained more disfluencies than conversations. They conducted a corpus-based study based on two speech samples, one which includes recordings of university courses in the presence of the lecturer and the students, and another one which contains map-task dialogues between two participants. While they found a considerable range of speaker variation within both dialogues and academic presentations, their results showed significant differences in the distribution of disfluency types overall: dialogues showed twice as much fragments as lectures but fewer additions, and filled pauses were the most frequent ones in both corpora. They also found more instances of silent pauses in lectures than in dialogues, and more complex sequences made of repetitions and substitutions used for lexical searches. These findings are thus not consistent with Schachter et al., (1991) who found a higher rate of disfluencies during interviews than during lectures. This lack of consistency in the literature can be explained by the different types of speech samples used: while Schatcher et al., (1991) worked on interviews, Tottie's (2016) work was based on casual conversations between friends and family members, and Moniz et al., (2014) conducted their study on map-task dialogues. While these three speaking tasks are all "dialogic" ones (as opposed to lectures and narratives), they exhibit substantial differences in style and setting, which makes it difficult to compare their findings.

Taken together, these corpus studies have shown the impact of degree of preparation and formality on the distribution of fluencemes. Other factors, such as anxiety, may also come into play. For instance, Christenfeld and Creager (1996) investigated the relationship between filled pauses and anxiety in a production experiment with undergraduate students. They found significant differences between the low anxiety and high anxiety conditions, with an average of 7 filled pauses per minute in the latter and 4 in the former. They concluded that the use of filled pauses was *not* necessarily a by- product of anxiety, but a sign that students were more self-conscious of their speech (cf. Broen & Siegel, 1972). The role of such self-monitoring can also explain Tottie's (2014) corpus findings that showed a higher frequency of filled pauses in task-oriented contexts (deliberation, presentation of evidence), where there can be more instances of professional pressure and/or important outcomes at stake than in casual conversation, where speakers might not be very self-conscious.

In sum, these experimental and corpus-based studies on (dis)fluency have shown that different variables, such as topic of conversation, anxiety, degree of formality, mode of speech, etc. all seem to have an effect on the distribution and frequency of fluencemes. However, the relationship between these variables is not a simple one, as it involves multiple factors and processes (cognitive, interpersonal, social, etc.), which have led to contradictory results in the literature.

The present study is motivated by the assumption that cognitive, social, and situational factors may all interact to affect speech and gesture production. As Bortfeld et al., (2001) further criticized, the issue with a majority of the past studies conducted on (dis)fluency is that fluenceme rates have often been compared in different corpora which were collected under very different conditions with different tasks and different samples of speakers. This is not the case of DisReg (see Chapters 3 and 5), which includes samples of the same speakers engaged in two distinct speaking tasks.

2.3   Effect of style and setting on gestures: A gap in the literature

While a considerable amount of research has been conducted on the different effects influencing (dis)fluency rates, very few studies have targeted these aspects specifically in gesture research. There have not been, to my knowledge, many studies that investigated the effect of setting or style on the production of gestures, except perhaps for Bavelas et al. (2008, 2014) who studied the independent effects of dialogue on gestures, drawing on a number of papers in experimental research. These papers (read Bavelas et al., 2008, p. 497 for review), described different visibility experiments in which speakers were asked to perform a task in two different conditions, (i) visible, i.e., face-to-face and (ii) not visible, telephone conversation, or listening to a tape-recorder. The aim of these studies was to measure the effect of visibility on gesture rates. However, the task was the same one in both conditions (i.e. giving directions to a location, giving an opinion, retelling a cartoon, etc.), and the only difference was whether the addressee was visible or not. As Bavelas et al., (2008) noted, these experimental studies have often overlooked the possibility that dialogue itself could have an effect on gesture. In order to measure the effect of dialogue on gesture independent from visibility, they designed an experiment which consisted in describing the picture of an 18th century dress, in three different conditions: (1) two participants talking face-to-face (dialogue/visibility), (2) two participants on the phone (dialogue/ no visibility), (3) one participant talking to a tape recorder (monologue/ no visibility). Their findings showed that dialogue had a significant effect on the speakers' rate of gesturing, which was independent of the effect of visibility, as it was consistently higher in the telephone condition than the tape recorder. A majority of these gestures were referential,[42] and they were much more frequent in the dialogue condition overall (13.9 phw in the visible dialogue condition, 10.3 in the dialogue not-visible condition, and 3.77 in the not-visible monologue condition). Interactive gestures, although less frequent than referential ones, were also found to be more frequent in the dialogue

---

42. "Topic gesture" in their terms, see Chapter 1, Section III.3.3.3.

condition (0.77 phw in the visible dialogue condition, 0.26 phw in the not-visible dialogue condition, and 0.36 phw in the not-visible monologue condition). This confirmed their prediction that visibility was not the only variable affecting gesture rates, and that gestures were highly sensitive to situational and social factors, regardless of whether they were seen or not. However, it should be noted that the gestures analyzed in their study were elicited in a controlled setting, i.e. as part of an experiment, so it does not truly reflect the situated ecology of gestures and the context in which they occur (e.g. Goodwin, 2000; Mondada, 2018). In line with previous experimental studies, it was again the same task which was performed in the three conditions, so their study only targeted differences in speech mode (i.e. monologue vs dialogue) and visibility, but it did not account for differences in style or setting.

In addition, we can find several papers in the gesture literature that focus on the analysis of gesturing behavior in specific contexts, such as during lectures (Sweetser & Sizemore, 2008) in political communication (Streeck, 2008b), or during auctions of fine arts (Heath & Luff, 2011), among others; but the gestures analyzed in these institutional settings have not been systematically compared to other conversational ones. For instance, Sweetser & Sizemore (2008) noted that lecturers would most likely use gestures differently from conversational participants as they would often take up a larger personal gesture space to keep the attention of an audience who is sitting further away. However, they also found that some kinds of gestures, such as deictic or interactive ones, could show very similar patterns in the two situations. In their paper on gestural space, they analyzed a few instances of a lecturer's gestures during a lecture at a Colloquium, and described the way he directly addressed the audience by pointing towards them. Even though the lecturer was somewhat engaged in a "monologue", he was in fact "addressing their silent partners in the exchange" (Sweetser & Sizemore, 2008, p. 48) which accounts for the dialogic dimension of the lecture. This example shows that the line between "monologue" and "dialogue" is not so clear, and should thus include other parameters. Sweetser (1998) also documented the use of two specific hand gestures (the B "barrier hand" and the Palm-Up gesture) used by lecturers, but did not offer a systematic comparison of these gestures produced in different communication settings. This limitation was pointed out in Sweetser & Sizemore's paper (2008) in which they strongly suggested to conduct more comparative analyses.

Lastly, we can also find a number of studies specialized in teachers' gestures in classroom environments (to name but a few: Alibali & Nathan, 2007; Azaoui, 2015; Holt et al., 2015; Moro et al., 2020; Tellier, 2008a) in which they stressed the importance of gestures to increase learning and understanding. We can also find papers on students' gestures recorded in the classroom when trying to understand algebraic concepts (e.g. Dwijayanti et al., 2019) or negotiating schemas when learning mathematics (e.g. Abrahamson & Bakker, 2016). These papers, however, which are more pedagogical-oriented, do not systematically compare the types of gestures produced by students in the classroom with the ones produced in a conversation. I believe that the field of gesture research could benefit from the present corpus-based study in order to understand more precisely how speakers differ across situations, and how they adapt their gestures to the audience, by taking into account the social environment in which they interact, as well as other parameters such as style and register. These differences can both be measured quantitatively and qualitatively by drawing on statistical evidence, coupled with micro-analyses of the data.

CHAPTER 3

Corpus and method

The present interdisciplinary and integrated approach to inter-(dis)fluency, which draws on a multilevel fluency-disfluency continuum, aims to analyze the distribution and behavior of ambivalent fluencemes in multimodal discourse. Fluencemes are highly flexible and dynamic, and their ambivalence can be evaluated by looking at several variables, such as language proficiency, register variation, or task type, among others. These findings can be yielded using a corpus-based methodology, which relies on quantitative treatments (e.g. frequency measures, percentages, average values etc.), in line with corpus-based approaches to cognitive linguistics and pragmatics (e.g. Crible, 2018; Crible et al., 2019; Schneider, 2014; Tottie, 2014, 2015). Furthermore, the degree of fluency and/or disfluency of fluencemes can be evaluated qualitatively at the interactional level, by integrating the social, sequential, and bodily actions participants may turn to when engaged in specific interactional practices (e.g. Kendon, 2004; Mondada, 2013; Sacks et al., 1974). Therefore, this study relies on a *mixed-method* approach (cf Morgenstern et al., 2021; Stivers, 2015; Tashakkori & Creswell, 2007) which includes quantitative and qualitative analyses of the data. Quantitative analyses rely on the treatment of dependent and independent variables in the whole dataset using statistical tools, while qualitative analyses rely on a close observation of specific occurrences in the data, examined within their ecological environment.

The present chapter is structured as follows: First, I explain my motivations for working on a videotaped dataset which comprises two corpora, the SITAF corpus and the DisReg corpus. I then describe the annotation protocol used for quantitative annotation analyses, using a specific annotation scheme. Lastly, I end this chapter with the description of the methods used to conduct the qualitative analyses.

I. Data

The present study of inter-(dis)fluency is conducted on a video-recorded dataset comprised of two different corpora in semi-spontaneous, semi-naturalistic settings, reflecting different degrees of language proficiency (L1 and L2) and speech preparation (prepared versus spontaneous). This dataset was deliberately compiled to obtain different discourse characteristics and genres. The data therefore exhibits differences in language, setting, genre, and register, which will further account for contextual and situational differences found in the distribution of ambivalent fluencemes across data types (cf Chapter 4 and 5). In addition, the use of semi-guided interactions has also been adopted in previous work on multimodality (e.g. Boutet et al., 2016; Debras, 2013; Cienki & Irishkhanova, 2018), which further justifies my choice of data.

1.1 The SITAF corpus

The SITAF corpus (*Spécificités des Interactions Verbales dans le Cadre de Tandems Linguistique*) was collected at Sorbonne Nouvelle University between 2012 and 2014 (Horgues & Scheuer, 2015). It was collected within the framework of the SITAF project, a research project funded by Sorbonne Nouvelle University, which aimed to gather various semi-spontaneous tandem exchanges in English and in French.

The data consists of a 25-hour video recorded corpus, comprising 21 pairs of undergraduate students. It includes 21 native French participants, all female, and 21 native English participants, 16 female and 5 male, all aged from 17 to 22. The participants were recruited on a voluntary basis, and the members of the SITAF team selected the pairs using an online questionnaire which had previously been answered by the participants. The questionnaire addressed: (1) their linguistic background, (2) their level of proficiency in their second language, (i.e. English for the French speakers and French for the English speakers), by rating it on a scale from 1 to 10; and (3) their personal interests, e.g. favorite conversation topics.

A majority of the French students were enrolled in an English major (i.e. English as a foreign language) as part of their undergraduate program. Their average score in L2 oral expression was 6.8 out of 10. The average score for the English native speakers in their L2 (French) was 6.6 (see Table 5 in Section 1.2.3). The English native speakers came from a variety of language backgrounds: American English, Canadian English, British English, Irish, and Australian. English-French bilinguals were excluded from the corpus. The latter include speakers whose parent is a native speaker of the target language, speakers who started learning their L2 before the age of 5, and speakers who attended L2-medium school for a long period of time.

1.1.1 *Methods and data collection procedure*

All the video recordings were made in a sound studio at Sorbonne Nouvelle university. The paired participants (who were tandem partners as part of the tandem project at university) were video recorded twice using three cameras – two filming each participant individually, and one recording the whole interaction, as shown in Figure 7. The participants were recorded twice; the first time in February 2013, several days following their first encounter, and the second time in May 2013. They were encouraged to meet regularly between the recording sessions (e.g. once a week). By the end of the experiment, they had met about twelve times on average during the three-month interval.

The experiment was conducted in two different settings: the L1-L1 "control" settings (English-English or French-French) and L1-L2 "tandem" settings (English-French, French-English). The participants first interacted in L1-L1 settings during the first recording session in February, then in L1-L2 settings during the second one in May. Before the experiment, the instructors emphasized on the notions of "solidarity" and "mutual assistance", as well as the need to separate English and French when performing the tasks. During the recording sessions, each pair was asked to perform three communicative tasks, first in English, and then in French.

Figure 7. Camera configurations (SITAF corpus)

The first task, entitled "Liar, Liar" is a storytelling task in which one participant had to talk about his/her last vacation and insert three lies in the story, which was later identified by the tandem partner. The participants who told the story were allowed to prepare their narrative before the recording session, but they were not allowed to write anything down, except for a few key words to help them as they went along. The instructions given to the partners (who were not doing the retelling) were to carefully listen to the story, and only take part in the interaction when they needed to ask for clarification, or to assist their interlocutor with language difficulties. At the end of the narrative, the partner had to guess the three lies, and if they failed to identify them, the participant who had initially told the story would reveal them.

The second task, entitled "Like Mind" required no preparation beforehand, and is a more collaborative argumentative task. It consists in discussing a relatively controversial topic, such as "the best years of your life are teenage years", "prisoners should have the right to vote", or "a good friend should always take your side, whatever happens." For this task, the participants were asked to respectively give their opinion on the topic, and later justify their position. At the end of the debate, they would both decide on their level of agreement on the topic, rating it on a scale from 0 (complete agreement) to 10 (complete agreement).

The third task was a reading task; the participants were instructed to read a small text written in their second language (i.e. in French for the English speakers, and in English for the French speakers), first with the help of their tandem partners, and a second time on their own. At the end of the two sessions, the participants filled in two questionnaires, and talked about their learning experience within the tandem setting to a member of the SITAF team and an expert in L2 pedagogy.

All the participants had to read and sign a consent form in order to take part in the study. All their faces are blurred or hidden in this book in order to preserve their anonymity (Horgues & Scheuer, 2015). They were also assigned labels (e.g. F07, A07, A03, F03 etc.) as well as pseudonyms to protect their identity.

1.1.2 *Why the SITAF corpus?*

The first motivation for selecting the SITAF corpus was for its sound and video quality; the use of three cameras is particularly helpful for analyzing each participant's facial expressions, as well as their body movement and hand gestures. While more and more videorecorded corpora are being documented and shared on open resources in English and in French (e.g. the Talkbank database, the ORTOLANG repository, or the ColaJE corpus, among others),[43] it is still difficult to find multimodal data in two languages within the same groups of speakers. Several researchers have already explored the multimodal quality of the SITAF corpus and worked on various topics, such as corrective feedback (Debras et al., 2015, 2020; Scheuer & Horgues, 2020) miscommunication (Horgues & Scheuer, 2017) and chains of reference (Debras & Beaupoil-Hourdel, 2019). The present study, which is based on an earlier preliminary study conducted on the same data (Kosmala, 2021; Kosmala & Morgenstern, 2017) offers another contribution to this corpus, following the multimodal approach adopted from past studies.

Another motivation for choosing the SITAF corpus is that it provides a scope for comparative analysis of L1 and L2 productions of the same speakers both in

---

43. For more information, visit https://www.ortolang.fr, https://www.talkbank.org, and http://colaje.scicog.fr/index.php/corpus (last retrieved on August 26th 2021)

French and in English, and in similar contexts. While a considerable amount of research has been conducted on EFL learners (English as a Foreign Language, or English as lingua franca), such as Spanish, Turkish, or French learners of English (e.g. de Jong, 2016a; Gilquin, 2008; Stam, 2001, among others), these groups of speakers have systematically been compared to different groups of native English speakers. To my knowledge, less work has been done on fluency rates in L1 and L2 productions within the same speaker groups. This is the case with the SITAF corpus, where each speaker alternated between their native and their non-native language, which allows for the analysis of intra-speaker variation.

1.1.3   *Selected sample under scrutiny*

In order to treat task type and language proficiency separately and avoid crossing too many variables within the same investigation, I only selected L1-L2 settings (and not L1-L1) in the present data sample to compare the same participants' L1 and L2 productions in the same tandem settings. In addition, the present study does not target aspects of sociolinguistic variation such as age, gender, or language variety; in this respect, only American speakers from the corpus were selected to create a homogenous sample. All the participants of the study were roughly the same age, i.e., in their early twenties. In addition, this sample only includes Task 2 which exhibits more interactional features than Task 1 and Task 3.

11 pairs from Task 2 in L1-L2 settings were selected from the data. This includes 22 speakers in 22 video recordings. The interactions lasted on average 3:40 minutes. The total duration of the selected data is approximately 1h21. More information regarding sample size is provided in Table 2.

Table 3 includes the self-assessment scores made by the participants when they evaluated their level of L2 oral proficiency. While these numbers do not officially assess the students' proficiency levels within a framework of reference such as the CEFR (*Common European Framework of Reference for Languages: Learning, Teaching, Assessment*),[44] they still give an approximate idea of the L2 learner's oral skills with some accuracy (cf Ma & Winke, 2019). Unlike previous work on Fluency in SLA, the primary focus of the present work is *not* to assess proficiency through (dis)fluency rates; however, the relationship between proficiency and fluency is still discussed in Chapter 4.

---

44. For more information visit https://www.coe.int/en/web/portal/home (last retrieved on August 25th 2021)

Table 2. Selected sample size of the SITAF corpus

	L1-L2 English		L1-L2 French	
	Duration (min)	Number of words	Duration (min)	Number of words
Pair 02	02:36	394	03:24	527
Pair 03	04:40	888	05:07	820
Pair 07	04:44	796	04:58	999
Pair 09	05:57	919	05:44	1153
Pair 10	02:00	267	01:31	239
Pair 11	05:30	1112	03:06	571
Pair 13	04:40	673	03:26	506
Pair 15	03:35	617	02:50	487
Pair 16	03:04	560	01:56	560
Pair 17	02:32	432	05:03	866
Pair 18	02:15	358	02:25	377
Total	41:33 min	7016 words	39:30 min	7105 words

Table 3. Students' self-evaluation scores

	Listening comp.	Oral prod.		Listening comp.	Oral prod.
	French participants			American participants	
F02 (Maria)	8/10	7/10	A02 (Haley)	7/10	6/10
F03 (Marina)	7/10	7/10	A03 (Julia)	7/10	6/10
F07 (Julie)	7/10	7/10	A07 (Amber)	8/10	6/10
F09 (Emilie)	7/10	7/10	A09 (Arthur)	8/10	7/10
F10 (Juliette)	5/10	5/10	A10 (Betty)	6/10	6/10
F11 (Sally)	6/10	6/10	A11 (Harry)	8/10	6/10
F13 (Elena)	7/10	8/10	A13 (Francis)	7/10	7/10
F15 (Melissa)	7/10	7/10	A15 (Simon)	8/10	7/10
F16 (Elisa)	7/10	8/10	A16 (Beth)	8/10	4/10
F17 (Lola)	7/10	8/10	A17 (Ruth)	7/10	6/10
F18 (Sophie)	7/10	6/10	A18 (Rosie)	7/10	5/10

1.2 The DisReg corpus

The DisReg corpus (DISfluency across REGisters) was collected as part of my 3-year PhD project supervised by Professors Aliyah Morgenstern and Maria Candea at Sorbonne Nouvelle University. This corpus comprises 18 video recordings of 12 undergraduate French students enrolled in a French literature class held at Sorbonne Nouvelle University. The corpus is twofold: the first part includes recordings of the students giving an oral presentation in front of the whole class and their teacher. Their presentation was part of an evaluation which counted for approximately 50% of their overall grade. The presentation consisted in analyzing a sonnet or an excerpt taken from a novel, essay, or play, using French dissertation methods (i.e. introduction, three-part presentation and analysis, and conclusion). The presentations lasted 29.5 minutes on average. The second part includes video recordings of the same students who were filmed in pairs when engaged in semi-guided conversations. The interactions lasted 22.6 minutes on average.

1.2.1 *Methods and data collection procedure*

All students were recruited on a voluntary basis. They were given a consent form for the presentation and conversation sessions. During the presentations, the students were recorded individually as they sat or stood by the teacher's desk while they were delivering their presentation. Sometimes the presentations were also made in pairs (cf Figure 8). The camera filmed the upper part of the participant's body (face, shoulders, and arms, see Figure 8). During the conversations, two chairs were arranged so that the two students would sit face to face during the exchange (cf Figure 9). Unlike the oral presentation in class, which was prepared at home in advance, and involved a certain degree of stress, this part was much more relaxed and spontaneous. The students were given a sheet of paper which included a few topics that could help start the conversation; the topics included: (1) last film/ TV show you have seen; (2) last novel/article you've really liked; (3) last trip, and (4) funny anecdote at university. The participants did not have to go through all the topics, and they were free to talk about anything else if they wanted. Unlike the participants from SITAF, all the subjects accepted to have their faces shown, so they did not have to be blurred. They were also assigned code names (A1, A2, B1, B2, etc.) as well as pseudonyms to protect their identity.

Figure 8. Participants in class during their oral presentation

Figure 9. Participants in pairs during the conversation-session

1.2.2 Why the DisReg corpus?

The primary objective was to collect data that had a comparable corpus design with the SITAF corpus. In addition, it includes video recordings, which, as emphasized earlier, are fundamental to the study of multimodal face-to-face spoken communication. Most importantly, the video recordings include productions of the same students engaged in different practices and in different communication settings.

1.2.3 Selected sample under scrutiny

The initial objective of the present empirical and corpus-based study is to triangulate evidence from two different corpora with a comparable corpus design, and this also includes sample size.

Table 4. DisReg corpus sample size duration (number of words)

	Conversation	Class presentation	
Pair A	04:56 (1048)	A1 (David)	02:08 (324)
		A2 (Jessica)	04:11 (590)
Pair B	03:53 (766)	B1 (Paul)	03:00 (431)
		B2 (Paula)	02:54 (402)
Pair C	05:53 (1295)	C1 (Dan)	02:44 (389)
		C2 (Laura)	03:06 (513)
Pair D	05:56 (1140)	D1 (Alex)	02:33 (559)
		D2 (Jenny)	03:36 (489)
Pair E	06:26 (1385)	E1 (Lea)	02:30 (306)
		E2 (Tina)	02:43 (391)
Pair F	06:20 (1347)	F1 (Linda)	02:42 (352)
		F2 (Matt)	03:23 (863)
Total	33:24 min	35:30 min	
	(5609 words)	(5609 words)	

The video recordings from the SITAF corpus last on average 3:40 minutes (cf Section 1.2.3), while the ones from DisReg are significantly longer (over 20 minutes, cf Section 1.3). Therefore, since the latter comprises video recordings of considerably longer duration than SITAF, I randomly extracted 2–6 minutes from each video file from the DisReg corpus (equally representing all participants) to approximately match the size of SITAF. The total duration of the selected sample is 1h08. The exact duration of the selected recordings is found in Table 4.

1.3 Motivations for working on a "small" corpus

The selected sample (2h30) is relatively small compared to the actual size of the whole dataset (25 hours for SITAF and 8 hours for DisReg), but also compared to most corpus-based studies in linguistics, which are very often associated with large-scale collections of spoken or written corpora. Conversely, I argue in favor of "small" and context-specific corpora, and emphasize their benefits for both quantitative and qualitative treatments, in line with Vaughan & Clancy (2013); Danino (2018) and Debras (2018). Table 5 summarizes the total corpus size in number of words (26,000) and total duration (2h30), broken down by speaker group and setting in the two corpora under scrutiny.

Table 5. Total corpus size

	SITAF corpus	DisReg corpus
Number of words	Tandem interactions (Task 2 EN): 7016 Tandem interactions (Task 2 FR): 7105	Class presentations: 5609 Conversations: 6981
Duration (min)	Tandem interactions (Task 2 EN): 41:33 Tandem interactions (Task 2 FR): 39:30	Class presentations: 34:30 Conversations: 31:30
Participants	22 participants 11 American speakers 11 French speakers	12 participants French speakers

Despite the relatively "small" size of the corpus, it should be noted that the data still yielded a rather high number of tokens overall: 6042 fluencemes (3172 in SITAF and 2870 in DisReg) and 2381 hand gestures (1362 in SITAF and 1019 in DisReg) in total, which can still be used efficiently for quantitative treatments. Moreover, my findings do not solely rely on quantitative treatments, but also draw on qualitative analyses, which focus on several case studies of local pragmatic patterns. This further reflects my mixed-methods approach to corpus linguistics and conversation analysis (cf Hashemi & Babaii, 2013; Johnson et al., 2007; Stivers, 2015; Tashakkori & Creswell, 2007), which can be defined as the following (Tashakkori & Creswell, 2007, p. 4):[45]

> Research in which the investigator collects and analyzes data, integrates the findings, and draws inferences using both qualitative and quantitative approaches in a single study or program of inquiry.

---

45. Read Candea (2017); Hashemi & Babaii (2013), and Johnson et al. (2007) for a more detailed review and definition.

As Stivers (2015) noted, there has recently been an increase in the use of a mixed methods approach combining CA methods with quantitative treatments. She argued that this combination of methods enabled CA research to target a broader audience. This kind of approach is not only beneficial to CA research, but to (dis)fluency research too. For instance, Peltonen (2020) further argued in favor of mixed-methods in L2 fluency research, and criticized studies for being mostly quantitatively oriented, involving frequency-based analyses of fluency, without paying attention to their functions or the contexts in which they occurred. She thus promoted the use of a qualitative approach to provide "a more comprehensive picture of fluency, enabling detailed analyses of fluency-related features in their immediate contexts" (Peltonen, 2020, p. 23).

1.3.1 *The benefits of using "small" corpora*

As Vaughan & Clancy (2013) pointed out, significant value has been given to the study of considerably large corpora, with the emergence of modern corpus-based linguistics. Large corpora have successfully been exploited in many corpus-based studies to explore different aspects of language, such as language variation, historical linguistics, or language pedagogy. The larger the data sample, the more reliable it becomes for efficient quantitative treatments. However, as Vaughan & Clancy argued, there are equally many benefits to studying smaller corpora which do not only rely on generalized findings of frequency measures. Their arguments are presented below.

First, relevance to corpus size is relative, as it depends on the language modality. Spoken corpora often tend to be smaller than written corpora, as the data needs to be collected, transcribed as adequately as possible using transcription conventions (cf Appendix 1), and then manually annotated by researchers, which can be a long and difficult enterprise. When it comes to videotaped corpora, which are often collected by researchers in CA, language acquisition, and ethnomethodology, their analysis can be even more challenging and time consuming, as they rely on careful manual annotations of the observed phenomena (e.g. gestural actions and contextual features) at several levels of analysis (e.g. prosody, phonology, syntax and gesture, see Debras, 2018, p. 9). Therefore, what is traditionally considered a "small" corpus, in fact comprises a multiplicity of richly annotated multimodal features, carried out manually by one or several members of a research team. When the annotation is carried out alone, which is often the case with researchers who are limited by time constraints within a Ph.D project (e.g. Debras, 2013, who collected a 2-hour videotaped corpus during her Ph.D), it is often virtually impossible to build a very large corpus, for practical reasons.

There are, however, other advantages to working on smaller corpora that are not necessarily motivated by time limitations. In the field of pragmatics, one of the central benefits of working on a small corpus is that it enables researchers to "access authentic, naturally occurring language and to maintain a close connection between language and context." (Vaughan & Clancy, 2013, p.6). Smaller corpora thus give easier access to contextualized findings which further illustrate specific instances of a given phenomenon. In addition, a majority of small corpora were compiled by the researchers themselves, which reflects a close relationship between corpus and researcher (cf the mention of investigators as social actors, Section 1.1). As pointed out by Koester (2010) researchers often have a close proximity and a high degree of familiarity with the data they compiled, as they are more aware of the contexts in which it was collected. This better ensures that the generated quantitative findings are also complemented with qualitative contextual analyses. For instance, Cutting (2001, 2002) deliberately chose to work on a small corpus (26,000 words) which includes casual conversations of six students who took part in a Master's course in Applied Linguistics. The deliberate choice of working on a "small" sample can thus be motivated by the wish to produce a specialized corpus delimited by register, setting, speaker idiosyncrasy and discourse domain. One key consideration regarding corpus design is that it should be suitable for specific research purposes; while larger corpora tend to be built for "general" linguistic phenomena, specialized corpora often target more specific research questions (Koester, 2010). This is also the case with the two corpora under study. The SITAF corpus was originally collected to address research questions related to pronunciation and phonetic features, linguistic transfer, and L2 acquisition processes (Horgues & Scheuer, 2015). The present study targets more specifically multimodal inter-(dis)fluency phenomena in semi-spontaneous tandem settings, which motivated my choice to work on a smaller specialized sample. Similarly, the DisReg corpus was collected for the purposes of studying inter-(dis)fluency across communication settings and language styles, and the selected sample was motivated by the wish to approximately match the size of the existing SITAF sample.

1.3.2 *Comparable corpus design*

Even though (dis)fluency rates will not be compared statistically in the two different datasets, it was still deemed important to work on similar corpora, as to ensure continuity between the two investigations. In this section, I describe the commonalities between the SITAF corpus and the DisReg corpus.

First, the two corpora comprise similar speaker profiles. All of them are students studying at the same university, or who at least had some experience when staying at this university (i.e. the American students who only stayed for a semester or a year). All of them are also undergraduate students, studying social sciences (i.e. with an English or French major), and they all know each other from university. Their relationship is, in fact, bound to the university, to a certain extent: In SITAF, the participants are tandem partners who met through the tandem exchange program, and in DisReg, the participants are classmates, who spent a considerable amount of time together at the university.

Secondly, the students were also recorded in a relatively familiar institutional setting, i.e. on campus: in a sound studio for SITAF, and in an actual classroom for DisReg. In both corpora, all the participants had access to some kind of material object, most oftentimes a piece of paper; whether it was the instructions for the argumentative task (SITAF), the lists of different topics of conversation, or the students' notes (DisReg).

One last point to consider is the nature of the data. The two studies are neither fundamentally experimental nor naturalistic, but rather rely on semi-structured elicitation techniques (Eisenbeiss, 2010). The latter refer to techniques that "keep the communicative situation as natural as possible, but use interviewing techniques, videos or games to encourage the production of rich and comparable speech samples" (Eisenbess, 2010, p.1). This is particularly relevant to SITAF, which involved speaking tasks, or games to encourage participants to interact in their first and second language. The nature of the data in DisReg is slightly different, since the participants did not have to perform a specific task, and were simply "guided" by a list of topics to start the conversation. It still involved semi-structured elicitation techniques on the part of the investigator (i.e. eliciting productions on a given topic), but to a lesser extent than in SITAF. As to the recordings of students in class, the latter are perhaps closer to naturalistic techniques, since the recording situations are very close to a real-life situation (i.e. a student giving an oral presentation at the university), despite being in a highly institutional and nonpersonal setting.

To conclude, despite some differences regarding the nature of the data, the two corpora under study share a set of similar features. They both involve a certain degree of researcher control over the data, but still offer ecological validity in the sense that they include semi-naturalistic real-life situations of students interacting within a shared institutional and social environment, the university. Additionally, given the semi-controlled and semi-structured design of the data, the present contextual and multimodal analysis of inter-(dis)fluency phenomena can be conducted on relatively comparable speakers who were subjected to the same semi-structured elicitation tasks. This allows for an efficient and reliable quantitative treatment of the corpus sample, despite its relatively "small" size.

II. Annotation protocol for the quantitative analyses

2.1 (Dis)fluency annotation

2.1.1 *Fluenceme level*

The present fluenceme classification is adapted from the ones used by number of experts in the field, such as Shriberg (1994); Crible et al. (2019); Lickley (2015); Candea (2000); Ginzburg et al. (2014); Eklund (2004); Pallaud et al. (2019), Götz (2013), Meteer et al. (1995) among others. However, unlike most previous work on disfluency phenomena, I did not make any *a priori* judgement on the potential "disfluent" functions of fluencemes to annotate them (i.e. distinguish between "significant" and "non-significant" repetitions, cf Maclay & Osgood, 1959), and I mostly used acoustic (i.e. duration) and morpho-syntactic criteria for their identification. Therefore, their annotation was initially made on formal grounds, i.e., by relying exclusively on their form, from a production perspective. This is the first step of the analysis (fluenceme level). In line with Guaïtella (1993) who spoke of "vocal hesitations", and Pallaud et al. (2019) who studied "morpho-syntactic markers", I distinguished between *vocal fluencemes*, which have perceptible vocal and acoustic features (e.g. decreasing of pitch, diminution of glottal pressure, lengthening of a vowel), and *morpho-syntactic fluencemes*, which mark a break or an interruption in the syntagmatic channel. I also annotated non-lexical vocalizations, also known as *non-lexical sounds*, or *liminal signs*, (e.g. tongue clicks, inbreath, laughter, creaky voice, sigh) in line with Ginzburg et al., (2014), Wright (2011); Ogden (2018); Ward (2006), and Dingemanse (2020).[46] These markers, which have not typically been categorized as "disfluency" markers in the disfluency literature, were annotated whenever they appeared within a fluenceme sequence,[47] in the exception of inbreaths and tongue clicks, which were also annotated outside sequences. For this reason, non-lexical sounds were included in the *peripheral marker* category (in line with Crible, 2018), which refers to markers that very often occur within the vicinity of fluencemes. In this category are also

---

46. Filled pauses are also typically included in the category of non-lexical sounds, but since they are also widely known as vocal hesitations, I preferred to include them in the vocal fluenceme category. Non-lexical sounds are, to a larger extent, vocal markers too; but they are not generally recognized as typical "disfluency" markers, and I wanted to remain consistent with previous classifications in disfluency research.

47. I chose to annotate them only within fluenceme sequences as they are very frequent in speech and their analysis would require a different type of investigation. I made an exception with clicks and inbreaths because they co-occur very frequently together, so I conducted a study that targeted these markers specifically (Kosmala, 2020b).

included *explicit editing terms* (Shriberg, 1994). A total of 9 different fluencemes were identified, which are all listed below. They are marked in bold in the examples provided within the list, and their transcription follow the CHAT convention format (cf *Transcription Conventions* in *Appendix 1*).

VOCAL MARKERS (VOC) (Guaïtella, 1993)
The duration of each vocal marker was annotated in milliseconds. In addition, filled pauses were distinguished on the basis of their form, whether they were realized with a central vowel ("uh"/"euh") or with a nasal consonant ("um"/"eum").[48]

1. **Filled pause (FP)** (Clark & Fox Tree, 2002; Candea et al., 2005; Rose, 1998; Vasilescu & Adda-Decker, 2007) also known as "autonomous fillers", they are defined as "the insertion at any moment within spontaneous speech of a long and stable vocalic segment, defined as a type of filler" (Candea et al., 2005, p. 10). They have also been called "filled pauses" in contrast to "silent pauses" (Goldman-Eisler, 1968; Maclay & Osgood, 1959). They usually consist of a centralized schwa vowel [ə] and a nasal variant [əm] in English (Clark & Fox Tree, 2002). In French, they mainly consist of a central vowel [ø] (Duez, 2001a), but the nasal variant can also be realized [øm]. Back-channeling, such as "uh-uh" or "mhm" is not included in this category. The term *filled pause* is adopted in this book, to avoid ambiguity with the term *filler* that can also refer to filler syllables in language acquisition (cf Peters, 2001).

   ```
   like when I was a teenager my life was very um (1.429) +//.
   (SITAF corpus, speaker A18)
   ```

2. **Prolongations (PR):** also known as lengthening, or drawl (Betz & Wagner, 2016; Clark, 2006; Eklund, 2001; Lickley, 2001; Merlo & Barbosa, 2010; Rohr, 2016; Fox Tree & Clark, 1997). Instances of syllable or word prolongations, resulting in above-average syllable and word duration (Betz & Wagner, 2016, p. 1). *Disfluent lengthening* is often distinguished from *phrase-final lengthening* which is used as a cue for perceiving phrase boundaries (Betz & Wagner, 2016), while disfluent lengthening is said to be used with no prosodic intention (Merlo & Mansur, 2004). These types of lengthening can also modify the pronunciation of certain items, such as "the" pronounced with a non-reduced vowel [i] (Fox Tree & Clark, 1997). In line with Rohr (2016), and

---

48. It should be noted that no phonological distinction was made between English-sounding *uh/um* and French-sounding *euh/eum*, even though some speakers transferred their own pronunciation of *(e)uh/m* in their second language. The goal here was simply to distinguish between the two variants, but not to elaborate on pronunciational features. The distinction between *uh* and *euh* is only used for transcription clarity and coherence (i.e. one is more specific to English and the other one to French).

Eklund (2001) I adopt the term *prolongation* in this book. No minimum duration threshold was adopted for the identification of prolongations, and they were identified entirely based on my own auditory judgment, without making an a priori distinction between "disfluent" and "phrase-final".[49]

```
becaus:se if they (a)re going towards the teacher:rs which I am assuming is what
they mean.
(SITAF corpus, speaker A02)
```

3. **Unfilled pauses (UP)**, also known as silences or silent pauses (Campione & Véronis, 2002; Cenoz, 1998; De Jong, 2016b; Duez, 1982; Eklund, 2004; Maclay & Osgood, 1959; Nicholson, 2007),[50] they are defined as "silent periods between vocalizations" (Cenoz, 1998). "Hesitation" pauses are often distinguished from "articulatory" pauses (Goldman-Eisler, 1968) e.g. physiological micro-pauses occurring before plosives (De Jong & Bosker, 2013). Researchers have opted for different minimum duration thresholds to exclude articulatory pauses from their analyses, ranging from 180 ms (Duez, 1982), 200 ms (Candea, 2000; Kormos & Denès, Candea) to 400 ms (Derwing et al., 2009; Tavakoli, 2011). Others, on the other hand, such as Campione & Véronis (2002) chose not to use a threshold at all. In this book, I adopt Kaghn's (2014) and De Jong & Bosker's (2013) minimum threshold of 250 ms, which is a popular choice in L2 fluency studies, and is considered an optimal cut-off point for L2 research (see De Jong & Bosker, 2013). This threshold avoids missing too many pauses and losing potentially key information.

```
I thought I just had that at the (0.750) [/] the French speaker.
(SITAF corpus, speaker F13)
```

---

49. I am aware that my method for identifying prolongations (i.e. purely based on perception) is limited to a certain extent, as it can be very difficult to tell exactly when a segment is prolonged (see Eklund, 2001). However, this subjective identification can still be effective as Rohr (2016) argued: the human ear is in fact said to be quite efficient at making predictions based on a speech performance (read Rohr, 2016, p. 72 for more details).

50. This category is particularly difficult to define, because there are many issues concerning the detection and classification of silences, see Betz (2020, p. 15) for review. Pauses can also serve many different functions, such as marking a syntactic boundary, or gaining time during planning etc. (cf Cenoz, 1998; Nicholson, 2007). It is thus very difficult to tell whether pauses reflect "disfluency" or not (Eklund, 2004). For this reason, I preferred to label all of them "unfilled/silent pauses" without making any a priori judgment on the basis of their duration or function. I still wanted to use a minimum duration threshold, in line with L2 fluency research.

MORPHO-SYNTACTIC MARKERS (MS) (Pallaud et al., 2019)

4. *Self-repairs, (SR),* also known as self-corrections, or substitutions (Eklund, 2004; Fox et al., 2013; Levelt, 1983, 1989) self-repairs refer to corrections (when a string of words is replaced by another) made by the speaker and not the interlocutor. Self-repairs are further distinguished between several subcategories, based on Levelt (1983): (a) syntactic repairs (change in the syntax) (b) morphological repairs (change of morpheme), and (c) lexical repairs (change of lexical term). Repaired elements further include (d) additions (added lexical elements or phrases i.e,. Shriberg, 1994; Crible et al., 2019; Eklund, 2004).

    ```
    [!] so to me [//] for me it's free. (syntactic repair)
    (SITAF corpus, speaker F13)
    ```

5. *Self-interruptions (SI)* also known as false-starts, self-breaks, or deletions (Maclay & Osgood, 1959; Pallaud et al., 2013, 2019; Shriberg, 1996), they refer to syntactically or semantically incomplete utterances. This applies to cases when a speaker interrupts their own utterance mid-way, and formulates a new one that shares no syntactic nor semantic link with the previous one. In this book, I adopt the term *self-interruption*.

    ```
    A13: and good professors are not necessarily:y +//.
    A13: if you pay more you don't necessarily get better professors.
    (SITAF corpus)
    ```

6. *Truncated words, (TR)* (Eklund, 2004; Crible, 2017; Shriberg, 1994) Truncation or cut-off of a word before completing its articulation, defined as "linguistic items that are not fully executed/finished, whether or not they are finished later" (Eklund, 2004, p. 164). These items very often co-occur with morphological repairs.

    ```
    you [/] you (a)re growing hu [//] you'(a)re growing up.
    (SITAF corpus, speaker F07)
    ```

7. *Identical Repetitions (IR)* (Candea, 2000; Clark & Wasow, 1998; Crible et al., 2019; Foster et al., 2000; Lickley, 2015; Maclay & Osgood, 1959; Shriberg, 1995). Identical repetitions of a word, a phrase or a clause that was previously uttered in the speech channel. "Disfluent" repetitions (Shriberg, 1995) are often considered "non-significant", as they have no emphatic stress. In fact, Dumont (2018, p. 47) noted the distinction between language-based repetitions and speech-related repetitions, following Candea (2000). Language-based repetitions, such as oratory repetitions, are often excluded from disfluency analysis because they are commonly used for rhetorical purposes (e.g. marking emphasis) and are thus said to be produced voluntarily by speakers. Just like unfilled pauses, filled pauses, and prolongations, I did not make an a priori judgement

on their function, and thus annotated all instances of identical repetitions in the data. Such repetitions can be made more than two times, but they were still annotated as a single repetition of the same item.

I [/] I can't say ok let's see tomorrow.
(SITAF corpus, speaker F09)

PERIPHERAL MARKERS (Crible, 2018)

8. *Explicit Editing Terms (EDT)* (Crible, 2017; Eklund, 2004; Meteer et al., 1995; Shriberg, 1994); words and expressions used by speakers to "compose, and edit and prompt themselves for their verbal behavior" (Shames & Sherrick, 1963, p. 8); this includes words such as "oops", "sorry", "wrong", but also any lexical expression "by which the speaker signals some production trouble" (Crible, 2017, p. 108) such as "I don't know", or "what's the word".

but I think um (1.460) **how do I say it** yes it's the same person.
(SITAF corpus, speaker A03)

9. *Non-lexical sounds* (NL) also known as vocalizations, sound objects, or liminal signs (Dingemanse, 2020; Hoey, 2020; Keevallik & Ogden, 2020; Ogden, 2018; Ward, 2006; Wright, 2011). Sounds that have typically been consigned to "the margins of language" (Dingemanse, 2020, p. 191), but which can nonetheless display interactional work. They are described as non-lexical vocalizations,[51] but some of their meaning is conveyed by prosody (e.g. a sigh is typically associated with relief or tiredness). Their category includes respiratory conduct, such as inbreaths, sighs, and laughter, as well as vocalizations (*mm*, and tongue clicks).

[!] so does more money mean a better education?
(SITAF corpus, speaker A13)

2.1.2 *Sequence level*

As the examples have shown above, fluencemes very often appear in combination, so they are better understood in terms of sequences, or units, constituting simple or complex constructions (Crible et al., 2019; Shriberg, 1994). For instance, truncated words tend to gravitate around morphological repairs, and filled pauses very often cluster with unfilled pauses (Benus et al., 2006; Betz & Kosmala, 2019; Candea, 2000; De Leeuw, 2007; Grosjean & Deschamps, 1972). Once the first level of analysis is completed (i.e. identification of individual fluencemes), the

---

51. However, the prefix "non" has been criticized by Dingemanse (2020) who suggested the term "liminal sign" instead.

Chapter 3. Corpus and method 91

goal is to study their pattern of co-occurrence more closely. This second level of analysis can shed light on their potentially fluent or disfluent contribution at the utterance level, in line with studies in SLA, in psycholinguistics, computational linguistics, and corpus-based linguistics. The description of my annotation scheme is provided in Table 6.

Table 6. Annotation scheme (sequence level)

Tag	Tier definition/description	Entry	Example
Type	Type of sequence, whether it is made of a single fluenceme (simple) or a cluster (complex). Complex sequences only apply to immediately adjacent fluencemes.	"simple"	**euh** la legitimite de leur technique et de leur style (A1, DisReg)
		"complex"	donne je te le lis et puis après si tu veux **le:e (0.580) [/] si tu veux le** lire. (F13, SITAF)
Sequence list	List of all the fluencemes found within the sequence.	"FP" "UP+NL" "FP+MR+UP+TR" etc.	and you're always you know **um (0.689) um (1.290)** being careful ("FP+UP+FP+UP") (F07, SITAF)
			things like that **it is [//] I still** have time ("SR") (F07, SITAF)
Sequence length	Number of markers combined within a complex sequence.	"2" "3" "4" "5" "6" etc.	**I was um (1.201) [!] [/] I was** walking with a friend ("4") (A18, SITAF)
			on est pas **&ob [//] obligé de:e (1.099) [!] [//] pas vraiment de:e (1.138) [/] de** défendre ("10") (A13, SITAF)
Sequence configuration	Pattern of co-occurrence between the different kinds of fluencemes (in no specific order). Includes the combination of two, or three different kinds, or of the same one.	"VOC+VOC" (two or more vocal markers)	**(0.659) um (0.758)** well I've only not been a teenager for one year (A18, SITAF)
		"MS+MS" (two or more morpho-syntactic markers)	et ouais le **&pr le [/] le [//] celui** qui a gagné (A2, DisReg)
		"NL+NL" (two or more non-lexical sounds)	donc **[!] hhh.** en tant que suivante (C2, DisReg)
		"VOC+MS" (one or more vocal marker and a morpho-syntactic marker)	that's **like (2.082) [/] like** seven thousands dollars right there (A13, SITAF)

Table 6. *(continued)*

Tag	Tier definition/description	Entry	Example
		"MS+NL"(one or more morpho-syntactic markers and non-lexical sounds)	hhh. &no &n [//] **not** large but significant (F10, SITAF)
		VOC+NL (one or more vocal markers with morpho-syntactic markers)	en effet **eum** [!] le premier mot du poème était une aphostrophe (A1, DisReg)
		VOC+MS+NL (one or more of the three kinds)	au début je trouvais ga **un peu:u** ((sighs)) [/] **un peu** gros (F2, DisReg)
		MIX (any other configuration; contains an EDT)	(0.742) [!] **euh qu'est ce que je voulais dire hhh.** oui donc l'anecdote (D1, DisReg)
Sequence position	Position of the fluenceme sequence within the utterance.	"initial" (near the beginning of the utterance)	**euh** mais tu les vois pas (A7, SITAF)
		"medial" (in the middle of the utterance)	and one day **(0.420)** maybe if they're not **(0.850)** killed there (F03, SITAF)
		"final" (near the end of the utterance)	mais c'est un **peu:u euh** +//. (A09, SITAF)
		"standalone" (constitutes an utterance on its own)	**o:or** +//. (A02, SITAF)
		"interrupted" by other participant, so their position is unclear)	en faisant le mort tu sais **euh** +/. (C1, DisReg)
Communication management (Allwood et al. 1990)	Level of communicativeness of the fluenceme sequences, whether they are used to manage the production of a speaker's own production (Own communication management) or to manage the interaction (ICM)	"OCM" (own communication management)	(0.573) [/] **o:on** on savoure toute la sonorité du nom Ronsard (A1, DisReg)
		"ICM" (interactive communication management)	C1: tu trouves? C2: **ba:ah** elle est très maternelle avec lui. (C2, DisReg)

This table contains the name tag of the categories, the different entries, their description, and an example from the data. The present model is largely adapted from Crible et al., (2019), but also borrows from Allwood et al. (1990)'s categories. The table contains 6 different categories.

The first one (*Type*) gives information about the type of sequence (isolated versus combined), and the second (*Seq. List*) gives information about which individual fluenceme is found within a sequence; it provides a list (in the order in which they appeared) to get a precise idea of their combination pattern. A unit composed of different fluencemes (e.g. FP+UP+TR+MR) can be abstracted into a recurring structure (e.g. VOC+MS). Because a considerable number of different combinations are possible (depending on their order, the fluenceme used, the number of markers within the same sequence etc.), it was necessary to first distinguish between the length of a sequence and its pattern, but also to narrow the number of sequence configurations to only 8 possible configurations. The latter were determined by grouping formally and conceptually similar types of markers (vocal markers, morpho-syntactic markers, and non-lexical markers),[52] in order to get a clearer idea of the most frequent and recurrent patterns.[53] In addition, the position of the sequences was annotated (similar to Shriberg, 1994) based on their location in the utterance (but without using syntactic criteria). The final category (*communication management*) lies at the frontier between quantitative production-based methods and qualitative conversation-analytic analyses. I first looked at speech processes related to verbal planning, lexical search, repairs etc., to identify cases in which speakers worked on their own production (OCM) while producing fluencemes. In addition, I relied on conversation-analytic methods (cf Section III) to find whether fluencemes were more other-oriented and pertained to the development of the interactional exchange (ICM), by looking at cases of adjacency pairs, intersubjectivity, stance taking, progressivity, preference structure, and the like.

---

52. Explicit editing phrases are not included in this list because they are very rare, which is why they belong to the MIX entry. I also did not want to mix EDTs with NLs, despite being in the same "peripheral marker" category in the previous section. Non-lexical sounds were distinguished from vocal markers (even though they both rely on vocal features), for reasons already described above, mainly that they behave quite differently in discourse.

53. This type of analysis is inspired by the work of Crible (2017, p. 119) who identified a limited number of possible configurations by focusing on discourse markers and their neighboring fluencemes, following a hierarchical system.

2.1.3 *Visuo-gestural level*

At the visuo-gestural level, three specific aspects are targeted, mainly (1) gesture phrase, (2) gesture functional type, and (3) gaze direction. Other instances of bodily behavior, such as facial expressions, body movement, body orientation, and the like, were examined in the qualitative analyses. It should be noted that only (2) and (3) were annotated in all the data (i.e. during fluencemes and outside fluencemes), while information contained in (1) was only annotated during fluenceme sequences.

1. *Gesture phase*

This annotation is based on the analysis of phases of gestural movement within gesture units (cf Kendon, 2004, Chapter 1, Section III.3.3.4), and adopts similar categories used by Seyfeddinipur (2006) and Graziano & Gullberg (2018), which are listed below:

Rest position	Preparation phase	Stroke	Hold	Retraction

15% of the data was annotated by a second annotator to measure inter-coder reliability on the recognition of gesture phrases, and received a Kappa score of 0.84.

2. *Gesture type*

Gesture types were annnotated based on a functional classification of gestures (cf Chapter 1, Section 3.3.3). Even though functional gesture classifications can be relatively subjective, and miss out on other central aspects of gesture production such as shape, configuration, direction, and movement, they rely on a limited number of well-defined categories, which can in turn be used efficiently for quantitative treatments. Additionally, it was essential to choose a consistent gesture classification that did not conflate formal and functional categories (cf Chapter 1, Section 3.3.3) as to provide a reliable overview of gesture distribution across the data.

I first distinguished between two general classes of gestures, mainly (a) referential gestures and (b) pragmatic gestures (in line with Kendon, 2004). Referential gestures comprise two subtypes: representational, and deictic-anaphoric gestures. Pragmatic gestures fall into 3 subcategories: (1) parsing/discursive, (2) interactive/performative, and (3) thinking gestures. My classification system is largely adapted from Kendon (2004); Cienki (2004); Müller (1998), Streeck (2008b), and Bavelas et al., (1992).

Referential gestures refer to gestures that convey meaning related to the referential content of discourse. Representational and deictic-anaphoric gestures are similar conceptually, in the sense that they both relate to the content of discourse, but they behave differently, and perform slightly different functions, as **represen-**

tational gestures rely on depictive methods that draw on practical abilities of the human hand (cf Müller, 1998, Streeck, 2008b) to depict an object or event, real or imagined, abstract, or concrete; while **deictic-anaphoric gestures** make use of space to point (with finger, hand, palm, head, or foot etc.) to a location, person, or event, to draw potential relationships between referents, or to place events and objects of imaginary discourse in the gestural space.

Pragmatic gestures, on the other hand, do not pertain to the propositional content of discourse, but rather enact pragmatic actions. **Interactive/performative** gestures have expressive features (e.g. *quotation marks, finger bunch, grapollo,* etc., Kendon, 2004), and enact interactional moves, or actions (dismissing, turning down, requesting etc.). This subcategory can be distinguished from other gestures with regard to the orientation and direction of the hand – if it is oriented towards the interlocutor, then it is considered interactive (as opposed to when it is oriented to the left or right) as it is directly addressed to the interlocutor (see Bavelas et al., 1992). These kinds of gestures convey information about "the process of conversing with another person" (Bavelas et al., 1992: 473). Gestures associated with these functions are included in Kendon's (2017) categories of *interactional regulators, performative*, and *operational* (cf Chapter 1, Section 3.3.3).

Parsing/discursive gestures are used to mark discourse segments, present an idea or an argument, or emphasize parts of discourse; they thus serve typical discursive functions in discourse such as emphasis, structuring, linking, and the like (Cienki, 2004). They are not directly oriented towards the interlocutor, but they can still be used to facilitate comprehension or capture the interlocutor's attention (cf *comprehension-oriented* gestures, Stam & Tellier, 2017).

Lastly, **thinking gestures**, also known as *word searching* gestures (Stam & Tellier, 2017) or "*Butterworth*"[54] (Tellier & Stam, 2012), enact a planning, thinking, or word searching activity. This category is not traditionally labelled under the category of pragmatic gestures, although it has been mentioned by a number of authors, such as Ladewig (2014) in her paper on cyclic gestures, or Goodwin & Goodwin (1986) in their paper on co-participation within a word searching activ-

---

54. This gesture was named after the author Brian Butterworth.

ity. Gullberg (2011, p.143) labels them *thinking gestures*, and they are described as metapragmatic gestures produced during communicative breakdowns as a comment on the silence. These types of gestures are very often accompanied with a salient thinking face, and overt verbal manifestations of lexical search ("oh what's the word"). They can also be manifested through finger snaps (cf first picture below Chapter 6).

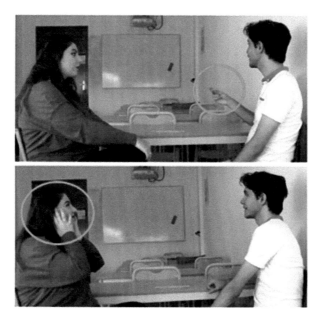

While these gestures share recurrent structural, formational, and conventional features (cf Müller et al. 2013), some of which can help with the disambiguation of different categories (e.g. a pointing gesture directed towards the interlocutor versus towards the left or right; shrugs, finger bunch, and palm-up open hands gestures are typically recognized as conventionalized pragmatic gestures), specific attention was especially paid to the **ecology** of the gestures, and the **context of use** in which they appeared (in line with Kendon, 2004, 2017). This type of identification is very context-specific and thus relies on subjective judgements, so 15% of the whole data was subjected to a second annotation by a different annotator, to measure inter-coder reliability. The Kappa score obtained was κ = 0.85 for the gesture types, and κ = 0.78 for gesture subtypes.

3. *Gaze direction*

Each change of gaze direction was annotated as either "towards interlocutor", "away" (from the interlocutor), "towards paper" (i.e. the students' notes, books, laptop; the piece of paper with the instructions, etc.), "in different directions", and a few times "towards camera" (only in DisReg).

2.2 Tools

2.2.1 *Statistical tests*

The annotation scheme includes both numerical variables (i.e. any value with a finite or infinite interval, e.g. length, duration) and nominal variables (i.e. categorical variables that can take only a limited number of values, e.g. "simple" and "complex") so different types of statistical tests were used to analyze the data. The tests, which are summarized in the list below, were conducted with various online calculators.[55]

---

55. All the tests were performed using the following links: (last retrieved on August 26th 2021) https://biostatgv.sentiweb.fr/?module=tests (t-test, Pearson, and Wilcoxon)

– I ran **log-likelihood tests** to measure frequency differences across corpora (e.g. rate of fluencemes per hundred words in L1 versus L2, or in class versus conversation).
– In order to check whether the numerical variables were normally distributed, a **Shapiro-Wilk Test** was first performed, obtaining a W value. A small W value (i.e. below the accepted range 0.99–1.00) indicates that the sample is not normally distributed. If the data is normally distributed, **T-tests** can be used to compare means of numerical variables (e.g. duration, number of markers within a sequence) to examine whether there are significant differences between the two populations.. If the data is not normally distributed, then a non-parametric test is used (**the Wilcoxon Signed-Ranks test**), to evaluate the differences between the two treatments.
– I also computed **Z-scores** to assess the significance of differences between proportions (e.g. proportion of fluencemes in complex versus simple sequences, proportion of gestures in "fluent" versus "disfluent" stretches of speech, etc.).
– I performed a **chi-square test** of independence to measure the association between two categorical variables, whether the values of one variable relates in some way to the values of others, e.g. whether gesture types relate to speech type, or whether communication management is associated with sequence type.
– I ran **Pearson's correlation coefficient** to measure the statistical relationship between two numerical variables, mainly between language proficiency score and (dis)fluency rate in SITAF, and mean length of utterance and (dis)fluency rate in DisReg.
– Lastly, I measured inter-rater and intra-rater reliability for the annotation of some of my qualitative categories, i.c., *gesture phrase, gesture type,* and *gesture subtype* with **Cohen's Kappa**. Kappa scores are interpreted on a scale from 0 to 1.00, in which values between 0 and 0.20 indicate non to slight agreement, 0.21 to 0.40 indicate fair, 0.41 to 0.60, moderate, 0.60, 0.61 to 0.80 indicate substantial, and values between 0.81 and 1.00 show almost perfect agreement (Landis & Koch, 1977a, 1977b).

---

http://vassarstats.net/propdiff_ind.html (z statistic)
http://ucrel.lancs.ac.uk/llwizard.html (log-likelihood) https://www.graphpad.com/quickcalcs/kappa1/(kappa)
https://www.socscistatistics.com/tests/(chi square)
https://www.statskingdom.com/320ShapiroWilk.html(Shapiro-Wilk)

2.2.2   ELAN Software

The video recordings were transcribed and annotated with the software **ELAN** (EUDICO Linguistic Annotator) (Sloetjes & Wittenburg, 2008). ELAN is a multipurpose and multilayer annotation tool which was developed at the Max Planck Institute for Psycholinguistics to provide a technological basis for the annotation of multi-media recordings. It allows for multi-level annotations, aligning speech and gesture. All the fluencemes and gestures were therefore manually annotated directly on ELAN and then exported to Excel to run statistical analyses.

III.   Methods for qualitative analyses

Qualitative analyses were carried out on a selection of excerpts from all the data, which were chosen to highlight several instances of the same phenomena, or similar phenomena in different contexts, to provide an interactive multimodal frame of analysis, in line with interactional and conversation-analytic methods.

3.1   Conversation-analytic methods

I paid specific attention to the following practices in relation to inter-(dis)fluency behavior, which are typical of social interactions (cf Chapter 1, Section III.3.2 and 3.3.3):

- *Turn-taking mechanisms*; how fluencemes are organized within turns, if they occur at a turn transition place (TRP), if they project upcoming talk, allocate or yield a turn, etc.
- *Episodes of repair*; when they are co-achieved, and not only self-initiated.
- *Preference structure*; if the fluenceme sequence prefaces or delays talk to embody a disaffiliative or dispreferred action.
- *Adjacency pairs*; whether fluencemes occur during adjacent actions, ordered as a first part and a second part (i.e. greeting sequence, question/answer, etc.), or within insertion sequences (i.e. a sequence of turns that intervenes between the first and second parts of an adjacency pair).
- *Alignment*; how fluencemes may be used to anticipate misunderstanding or disagreement, or on the other hand to restore alignment and mutual understanding.
- *Participation Framework*; the status of participants in the interaction (e.g. speaker versus recipient), and the different interactional roles they may play, whether they engage or disengage from the interaction.

3.2 Multimodal analysis: Use of PRAAT for the vocal dimension

The PRAAT acoustic software (Boersma, 2001) was designed by Paul Boersma and David Weenink from the University of Amsterdam. It comprises a wide range of features, such as spectral analysis, pitch analysis, formant analysis, intensity analysis, etc., and can be used for labelling, segmentation, filtering, and speech synthesis. Just like ELAN, it allows for multi-level analyses, by aligning audio data with textual or phonetical tiers. While the present work does not linger on phonetic and acoustic aspects of (dis)fluency, the vocal dimension of these phenomena can be further illustrated in the qualitative analyses with regard to pitch and duration. These two features are part of a larger set of measures that can be carried out thanks to PRAAT, and are found on a spectrogram. A spectrogram is a visual way of representing three main dimensions of speech and prosody, mainly, *fundamental frequency* (i.e., f0, or pitch curve on the vertical axis), *duration* (i.e., period of time, shown on the horizontal axis), and *energy* (using dark bands to stand for formants on the vertical slice). These specific features can contribute to the present analysis of inter-(dis)fluency as a *multimodal flow*. For instance, they can illustrate how the acoustic signal is momentarily *suspended* or *interrupted*, and how this suspension may synchronize with sudden shifts in eye gaze or head movement.

Conclusion to the chapter

This chapter presented various aspects of my methodology, which includes the choice of data, the development of my annotation grid, and the application of interactionist and conversation-analytic methods for multimodal qualitative analyses. While I selected a relatively "small" video corpus to conduct my analyses (26,000 words, 2h30), I made sure that the choice of my sample was relevant for the implementation of my annotation scheme (i.e. similar corpus design and size between DisReg and SITAF). I further argued in favor of "small" corpora, which, I believe, can legitimately be thoroughly exploited for both quantitative and qualitative analyses in the field of multimodal and pragmatic research, in line with Vaughan & Clancy (2013).

In line with previous work on disfluency research (e.g. Shriberg, 1994; Pallaud et al., 2019; Ginzburg et al., 2014; Crible et al., 2019; Candea, 2000) I implemented a multi-level annotation scheme of inter-(dis)fluency. This model reflects different levels of analysis (i.e. individual marker, fluenceme sequence, and visual-gestural level), which were carried out with different tools (e.g. ELAN, PRAAT and statistical tools). They were further completed with qualitative analyses of the data, which rely on a careful observation of the timely social and institutional practices embedded within talk-in-interaction, in line with conversation-analytic methods.

CHAPTER 4

Inter-(dis)fluency in native and non-native discourse

The present chapter deals with the analysis of inter-(dis)fluency[56] and the distribution of fluencemes in native and non-native discourse, based on the SITAF corpus, thus targeting aspects of L1 versus L2 uses in French and English. While a lot of research in L2[57] fluency has focused on the relationship between fluency and proficiency by examining the frequency of temporal variables in L2 versus L1 speech, the present study does not linger on proficiency measures specifically, but rather pays attention to the interplay of the different prominent features surrounding the construct of fluency, mainly gesture, gaze, and interactional dynamics. The general aim of this chapter is to introduce new methods for evaluating the degree of inter-(dis)fluency, with respect to fluenceme rate, visual-gestural behavior, and interactional dynamics.

This chapter is structured as follows: I first present my research questions and hypotheses, then report on my corpus-based findings regarding the distribution of fluencemes in native and non-native discourse, by integrating different levels of analysis (fluenceme, sequence, and gesture/gaze), extracted from my annotations. These findings are then further exploited with fine-grained qualitative analyses of the data. Lastly, I end this section with a discussion of my findings.

I. Research questions and hypotheses

The present research questions stem from the large body of research conducted in L2 fluency (see Chapter 2, Section I). They aim to address the specificities of native versus non-native fluency by situating them in a larger interactive and multimodal framework. The main issue with a number of studies conducted in SLA is the tendency to systematically associate L2 fluency to proficiency and language difficulties solely on the basis of production, without necessarily relating it

---

56. While the term *inter-(dis)fluency* covers all the main aspects of this study (with the notion of interactional, gestural and functional ambivalence) the core term *fluency* will often be used in this chapter with respect to the field of L2 fluency research in SLA.

57. *L1/L2* and *native/non-native* are interchangeable terms, as both of them are used very frequently in the literature.

to interactional dynamics. Three central research questions thus emerge, which comprise a series of subquestions, listed below. My hypotheses are also based on assumptions following cognitive grammar and usage-based linguistics introduced earlier (cf Chapter 1, Section III.3.1).

RQ1: Are L1 and L2 fluency closely related? If not, how does L2 fluency differ from L1 fluency, and how would these differences be characterized?
RQ2: Is L2 fluency necessarily associated to the learners' proficiency levels?
RQ3: How do L2 learners make use of fluencemes to overcome language difficulties? Do they use gestures to "compensate" for lexical shortcomings?

To answer these questions, I present the following assumptions and hypotheses:

RQ1:
- Several differences between L1 and L2 fluency behavior are expected, mainly differences in frequency, duration, position (in line with De Jong, 2016b; Fehringer & Fry, 2007, Gilquin, 2008, Tavakoli, 2011, among others), but also sequence complexity (i.e. sequence configuration and number of markers combined within a sequence).
- Crosslinguistic differences between French and English are also expected, following the assumption that (dis)fluency is language-specific (Grosjean & Deschamps, 1975; De Leeuw, 2007; Candea et al., 2005).
- I also hypothesize that L2 learners will produce fewer recurrent patterns of combination, and more complex fluenceme sequences. In line with Crible (2018), rare combinations are less automatic, less entrenched in speakers' memories, and may therefore be one characteristic of L2 fluency.
- I also expect differences in gestural behavior, with a higher rate of gestures produced in L2 than in L1 both during fluencemes and outside fluencemes. However, contrary to the LHR (Krauss et al., 2000) I do not expect L2 learners to produce more referential gestures than L1 speakers.

RQ2:
- In line with Brand & Götz (2013), I do not expect a clear correlation between fluency and proficiency, but rather expect a high number of individual differences (De Jong, 2018; Gullberg, 2011).
- In addition, while L1 and L2 fluency may show overall differences (in line with RQ1) it does not mean that a higher rate of fluencemes in L2 is systematically associated with limited proficiency. These differences may also reflect individual strategies (Gullberg, 2011), or language specificities (Grosjean & Deschamps, 1975). These differences thus need to take into account not only temporal variables and frequency measures, but interactional factors as well, in line with the notion of *interactional competence* (Galaczi & Taylor, 2018) and *CA-SLA* (Pekarek-Doehler, 2006).

RQ3:
- In line with Cienki's (2015) dynamic *scope of relevant behavior* theory, I expect speakers to use the spoken modality as a default mode for dealing with language difficulties, but there can also be specific instances during which they make use of visible bodily behavior to act on their multimodal communication strategies (Gullberg, 2011, 2014). In sum, I expect L2 learners to mobilize all available relevant resources (i.e. speech, manual gesture, gaze, body movement) along with fluencemes to deal with language difficulties.
- Contrary to the LHR, I also expect L2 speakers to use more pragmatic gestures than referential gestures during fluencemes, either to seek help from their interlocutor, to enact a speech act, to embody a word search activity, or to mark distinct aspects of discourse, depending on the context.

II. Quantitative findings

This section presents the quantitative findings extracted from the annotations, which were obtained through several statistical treatments. Results are provided in raw values[58] and relative/normalized frequency (i.e. a frequency relative to some other value as a proportion of the whole, such as the number of words in the corpus, or a total number of tokens). The basis of normalization for the rate of fluencemes and gestures is *per hundred words* (henceforth phw) due to the small size of the data (i.e. 141,121 words, see Chapter 3, Section I.1.4).

2.1 Marker level: Rate, form, and duration of individual fluencemes

A total of 3172 fluencemes were annotated and extracted from the SITAF corpus, with 1173 tokens found in L1 (English and French) and 1999 in L2 (English and French). Figure 10[59] reports the distribution of fluencemes in relative frequency per participant (American and French) and per language proficiency (L1 versus L2). A test of log-likelihood (henceforth LL) was conducted to measure these differences statistically. Results indicate that American speakers produced significantly more fluencemes in their L2 (49.2 phw) than in their L1 (16.1 phw) ($LL = 495.45$, $p < 0.0001$), and this was also the case of French speakers who produced 23 fluencemes phw in their L1 as opposed to 33.1 phw in their L2 ($LL = 48.69$; $p < 0.0001$). We can also observe differences between American and

---

[58]. All the statistical analyses were run on raw numbers, but most of the tables and figures provide relative values, for ease of exposition. Raw values can be found in Appendix 2.
[59]. The exact values (relative and raw) are found in Table 35 in Appendix 2.

French speakers, with the American speakers who produced significantly more fluencemes in their L2 (49.2 phw) than French speakers (33.1 phw) (*LL*=77.24; *p*>0.001), while they produced fewer ones in their L1 (16.1 phw) compared to French speakers (23 phw) (*LL*=104. 88; *p*>0.001).

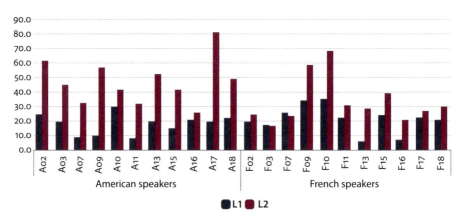

Figure 10. Rate of individual fluencemes per hundred words

Overall, results show high differences in frequency between native and non-native productions, as well as between speaker groups. We can note, however, a number of individual differences and instances of speaker variability within the two groups. For instance, A07 produced 32.6 fluencemes phw in her L2, as opposed to A17, who produced significantly more tokens (81.6 phw). Similarly, F13 only produced 5.9 fluencemes phw in her L1, while F10 produced 35.2.

Tables 7 and 8 identify all the fluencemes that were annotated in the data (excluding EDTs and additions which were extremely rare overall).

Results show that, for the American speakers, differences were found in the proportion of certain fluencemes in their L1 and L2, especially morpho-syntactic and vocal markers. They produced more identical repetitions in their L2 (18.2%) than in their L1 (11.7%), but more self-interruptions in their L1 (4.7%) than in their L2 (1.7%). In addition, they produced more filled pauses in their L2 (19.4%) than in their L1 (9.6%) as well as more prolongations (28.4% versus 14%). However, they produced more unfilled pauses in their L1 (37.9%) than in their L2 (26.1%). No significant differences were found for the rest of the markers.

For the French speakers, on the other hand, fewer significant differences were found. As Table 8 reports, French speakers produced slightly more self-interruptions in their L1 (3.6%) than in their L2 (1.8%), but contrary to the American speakers, they produced more prolongations in their L1 (18.6%) than in their L2 (12.1%), and fewer unfilled pauses in their L1 (23%) than in their L2 (29.1%).

Table 7. Proportion of fluencemes in L1 and L2 (American speakers)[*]

	L1 % (raw)		L2 % (raw)		Z score	P value
	Morpho-syntactic markers					
lexical repair	1.7%	(9)	0.9%	(9)	1.43	0.1
morphological repair	2.5%	(13)	2.5%	(25)	0.02	0.9
syntactic repair	2.7%	(14)	4.8%	(48)	−1.94	0.05
identical repetition	11.7%	(60)	18.2%	(181)	−3.27	0.001*
self-interruption	4.7%	(24)	1.7%	(17)	3.35	0.0008*
truncated word	5.7%	(29)	4.9%	(49)	0.59	0.5
	Vocal markers					
filled pause	9.6%	(49)	19.4%	(193)	−4.94	< 0.002*
prolongation	14%	(72)	28.4%	(283)	−6.25	< 0.002*
unfilled pause	37.9%	(193)	26.1%	(260)	−4.58	< 0.002*
	Peripheral markers					
NL sound	9.4%	(48)	11.4%	(114)	−1.26	0.2

[*] Rates per hundred words can be found in Appendix 2, Table 35 for the French speakers, and Table 52 for the American speakers. Tables 13 and 14 of this section look at the proportion of fluencemes, to get an idea of their frequency relative to one another in a specific language.

They also produced more NL sounds in their L2 (11.6%) than in their L1 (7.3%). We can thus find a number of crosslinguistic differences between the two groups: while American speakers produced a relatively high proportion of unfilled pauses in their L1 (37.9%) it was not the case for French speakers (21.6%) ($z=5.48$; $p<0.002$); on the other hand, French speakers produced significantly more filled pauses in their L1 (21.6%) than American speakers (9.6%) ($z=-5.50$; $p<0.002$).

The duration of the vocal markers was also analyzed for all speakers of both groups. Results show that, despite differences between the two groups on average, a great number of individual differences prevented the former from being statistically significant (cf Table 38, 39, and 40 in Appendix 2 for more details). For the American speakers, filled pauses were on average longer in their L1 ($M=658$ ms; $SD=238$ ms) than in their L2 ($M=514$ ms; $SD=192,3$ ms; $p=0.1$), as well as unfilled pauses which had a longer duration on average in their L1 ($M=754$ ms; $SD=444$ ms) than in their L2 ($M=683$ ms; $SD=300$ ms; $p=0.2$). For the French speakers, it was quite the opposite: their filled pauses were longer in L2 ($M=465$ ms; $SD=190$ ms) than in L1 ($M=371$ ms; $SD=214$ ms; $p=0.1$), and this was also the case for their prolongations ($M=383$ ms; $SD=122$ ms in

Table 8. Proportion of fluencemes in L1 and L2 (French speakers)

	L1 % (raw)		L2 % (raw)		Z score	P value
	Morpho-syntactic markers					
lexical repair	1.6%	(11)	0.6%	(5)	1.94	0.05
morphological repair	1.6%	(11)	3.1%	(25)	−1.72	0.08
syntactic repair	4.1%	(27)	2.4%	(20)	−1.79	0.07
identical repetition	13.5%	(88)	11.8%	(95)	0.99	0.3
self-interruption	3.6%	(24)	1.8%	(15)	2.14	0.03*
truncated word	4.4%	(29)	4.4%	(36)	−0.01	0.9
	Vocal markers					
filled pause	21.6%	(141)	22.6%	(182)	−0.41	0.6
prolongation	18.6%	(121)	12.1%	(98)	3.41	0.0006*
unfilled pause	23%	(150)	29.1%	(235)	−2.62	0.008*
	Peripheral markers					
NL sound	7.3%	(48)	11.6%	(94)	−2.74	0.006*

L1; $M = 459$ ms; $SD = 187$ ms in L2; $p = 0.01$) and unfilled pauses ($M = 629$ ms; $SD = 292$ ms in L1; $M = 717$ ms; $SD = 443$ ms in L2; $p = 0.4$).

As the Shapiro-Wilk test revealed, neither filled pause, prolongation, nor unfilled pause duration were normally distributed ($W = 0.97$; $W = 0.80$; $W = 0.86$), so the duration values (aggregated per speaker) were submitted to a Wilcoxon test for comparison of means. Given the lack of statistical evidence (except for prolongations in French), hardly any conclusion regarding duration can be reached at this point. This may suggest that duration is not necessarily a reliable indicator of (dis)fluency, contrary to what previous studies have shown (e.g. Kahng, 2014; Riazantseva, 2001). This is more in line with Cucchiarini et al. (2000) who found that the difference between native and non-native speakers was more determined by a greater number of pauses than a longer duration. These findings also further suggest high individual variation, as shown in the boxplots in Figures 11 and 12 which give information about the variability and dispersion of the data. The lower part of the box displays the first quartile, the higher part shows the third quartile, and the line dividing them is the median (the middle value of the dataset). The upper and lower whiskers represent scores outside the middle 50%, and the data points that are located outside the whiskers show observations that are distant from the rest of the data. In this case, the data shows a skewed distribution (where the median cuts the box into two unequal pieces, e.g. prolongations in the French group), with some data points that are located further outside the upper quartiles (e.g. for the unfilled pauses for the French and American group).

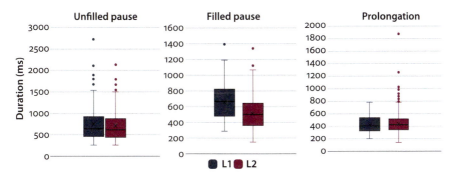

Figure 11. Duration of vocal markers in L1 and L2 (American group)

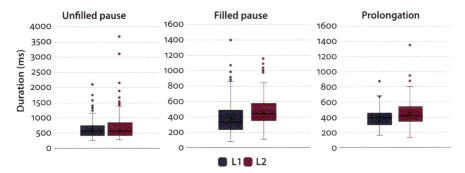

Figure 12. Duration of vocal markers in L1 and L2 (French group)

Turning now to the form of the filled pauses (see Figure 13), as either produced with a central vowel *(e)uh)* or a nasalized one *(e)um)*,[60] results show that American speakers produced more instances of "ums" in their L1 ($N=43/49$) than in their L2 ($N=62/193$) ($z=7.017$; $p=<.0002$), but more "uhs" in their L2 (131/193) than in their L1 (6/49) ($z=-7.017$; $p=<.0002$). The French speakers, however, showed an opposite trend: they produced more "euhs" in their L1 ($N=125/141$) than in their L2 ($N=115/182$) ($z=5.195$; $p<.0002$), but more "eums" in their L2 ($N=67/182$) than in their L1 ($N=16/141$) ($z=-5.195$; $p<.0002$). We may wonder whether this result may be linked to language-specific features; while American speakers used "um" a lot in their first language (88%), French people rarely did (11%), so the latter may have produced more "ums" in their L2 to adapt their speech to "sound" more like the Americans, and the other way around (i.e. Americans may have produced more "euhs" in their L2 to adapt it to the French). This

---

60. As explained in Chapter 3, no acoustic differences were made between English-sounding *uh/ums* and French-sounding *euh/eums*, so a bracket is used to avoid making a distinction in writing.

kind of phenomenon is known as *phonetic adaptation* (Hwang et al., 2015), and refers to the production of L2-like sounds that are missing in the L1 in order to adapt it to the target language. While this kind of hypothesis needs to be further investigated by running a thorough acoustic and phonetic analysis of filled pauses (which calls for a different type of investigation), it is still interesting to note significant differences in form distribution between the two groups and between L1 and L2.

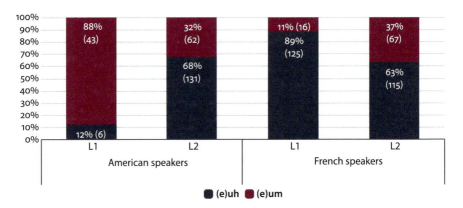

Figure 13. Proportion of filled pause types in L1 and L2

As to the types of non-lexical sounds, three main categories emerged: (1) clicks, (2) inbreaths, and (3) other. The latter includes various sounds and sound objects, i.e. sigh, nasal vocalizations, laughter, coughs, creaks and the like. They were grouped together because they did not often co-occur with fluencemes, as opposed to clicks and inbreaths, but their exact distribution can be found in Tables 41 and 42 in Appendix 2. Figure 14 shows the proportion of non-lexical sounds in L1 and in L2. While numerical values seem to suggest some differences (e.g. 27% of clicks in L1 versus 39% in L2 for the Americans), none of them actually reached statistical significance, as reported in Table 43 in Appendix 2 which shows the scores obtained with the z tests.

Unlike filled pauses, the differences between the two means in L1 and L2 were not significant, and this may be interpreted as a sign that non-lexical sounds are not necessarily language-specific, as opposed to filled pauses. However, we should be cautious when making this assumption, given the lack of statistical evidence. Once more, these kinds of results call for further investigation in phonetic research, which goes beyond the scope of the present study.

Before moving on to the *sequence* level of analysis in the following section, let us briefly investigate the possible relationship between fluenceme rates and proficiency levels, in line with previous research in SLA on fluency (see Section 1.2).

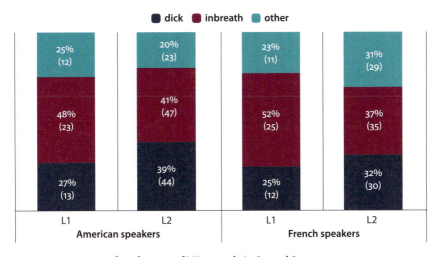

Figure 14. Percentage distribution of NL sounds in L1 and L2

As explained in Chapter 2 (cf Chapter 2, Section I.1.2.3) the students who took part in the study assessed their own level of proficiency, by rating it on a scale from 0 to 10. Even though these scores are very subjective and by no means provide a reliable measure of L2 proficiency, it is still interesting to enquire into a potential relationship between perceived proficiency and fluency.

Table 10. Pearson R scores and p values for the correlation tests

	American speakers	French speakers
Oral prod. score and L2 rate	$r=0.1315$; $p=0.2$	$r=0.5779$; $p=0.04$
Listening comp. score and L2 rate	$r=-0.3956$; $p=0.2$	$r=-.0626$; $p=0.05$

To that aim, a Pearson's correlation (cf Chapter 2, Section II.2.3.2) was conducted to measure a possible correlation between fluenceme rates and self-assessed evaluation scores (cf Table 10). These values are given in Table 9, as a reminder. It is interesting to note, at first glance, that the American speaker (A16) who was attributed the lowest self-evaluation score for oral production (4/10) actually produced the lowest rate of fluencemes in her group (25.5 phw). In the French group, on the other hand, the French speaker (F10) who was attributed the lowest self-evaluation score for oral production (5/10) produced the highest rate of fluencemes in her group (68.2 phw). This brief look at the data already suggests individual and/or language-specific differences. Indeed, none of the scores found in Table 10 yielded a substantial significant correlation between the two means, according to the Pearson's correlation test.

Table 9. Self-evaluation scores and L2 fluenceme rate

	Self-evaluation score (oral production)	Self-evaluation score (listening comprehension)	L2 rate (phw)
A02	6/10	7/10	61.7
A03	6/10	7/10	45
A07	6/10	8/10	32.6
A09	7/10	8/10	56.8
A10	6/10	6/10	41.7
A11	6/10	8/10	32.2
A13	7/10	7/10	52.6
A15	7/10	8/10	41.7
A16	4/10	8/10	25.5
A17	6/10	7/10	81.6
A18	5/10	7/10	48.9
F02	7/10	8/10	24.8
F03	7/10	7/10	16.5
F07	7/10	7/10	23.3
F09	7/10	7/10	58.7
F10	5/10	5/10	68.2
F11	6/10	6/10	31
F13	8/10	7/10	28.8
F15	7/10	7/10	39.4
F16	8/10	7/10	20.9
F17	8/10	7/10	26.9
F18	6/10	7/10	30.4

So far, the findings reviewed above suggest that the most striking difference regarding fluenceme distribution in native versus non-native productions is *frequency*, as all the speakers from the two groups showed a tendency to produce considerably more fluencemes in their L2 than in their L1, which was found to be statistically significant. When it comes to the other features (i.e. duration, form, proficiency), the differences between L1 and L2 patterns of behavior are not so straightforward, as they largely depended on other variables, such as language (English versus French) and individual variation.

2.2 Sequence level: Type, length, position, and patterns of co-occurrence

1567 sequences (i.e. isolated or combined markers) were identified in total, with 821 for the American speakers, and 746 for the French speakers. Figure 15 reports the proportion of *simple* (isolated tokens) and *complex* (combined markers) sequences in L1 and L2 for the two groups. Numbers show that the American speakers produced more complex sequences in their L2 ($N=302/512$) than in their L1 ($N=133/309$), which was found to be statistically significant ($z=-4.435; p<.0.0002$).

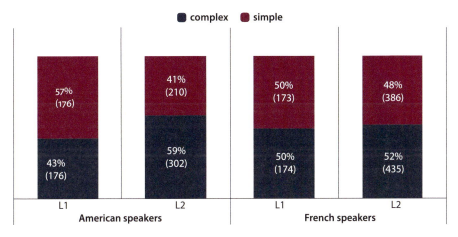

Figure 15. Proportion of complex and simple sequences in L1 and L2

For the French speakers, however, no significant difference was found between the proportion of complex sequences in their L1 ($N=173/347$) and in L2 ($N=206/399$) ($z=-0.0177; p=0.6$). Once again, these results may indicate that (dis)fluency behavior is not necessarily determined by differences in proficiency, but may also be influenced by language differences and/or individual preferences.

Turning now to the length of sequences, i.e. the number of markers found within a complex sequence, Table 44 (in Appendix 2) gives information about sequence length, i.e. average number of markers combined within a sequence. As the Shapiro-Wilk test revealed, the values were not normally distributed, so a Wilcoxon test was performed to measure differences between L1 and L2. American speakers combined 1.7 markers on average in their L1, versus 2.4 in their L2, which was statistically significant ($p=0.005$), but French speakers produced 1.9 markers per sequence in their L1 versus 2 in their L2 on average, which does not show significance ($p=0.5$). However, the standard deviation values are rather high in L2 for both the American and French speakers, which suggests a large amount of variation within the two groups. This is further illustrated in Figure 16.

114   Beyond Disfluency

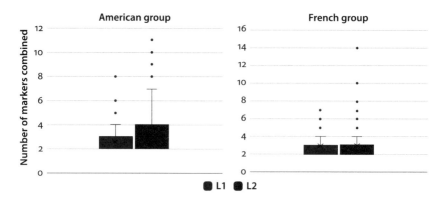

Figure 16. Range of markers combined in L1 and L2

The number of markers combined ranged from 2 to 8 in L1 versus 2 to 11 for the Americans, and from 2 to 7 in L1 versus 2 to 14 for the French. Some speakers, such as F13, combined up to 3 markers in her L1, versus 14 in her L2, and on average combined a higher number in her L2 as well (1.6 in L1 versus 2.2 in L2), others, such as F11, combined up to 5 markers in her L1, as opposed to 10 in her L2, but combined roughly the same amount on average (2.3 in L1 vs 2.4 in L2). Similarly, A17 combined up to 10 different markers in her L2, as opposed to 3 in her L1, while A03 combined up to 8 markers in her L1, and 10 in her L2. These different patterns of behavior largely reflect how spread out the data is, but it may also suggest individual preferences, which are not directly observable in overall measures of frequency or tendency. This further justifies the need to illustrate specific instances of the data through qualitative analyses (see Section III).

Tables 11 and 12 show the different sequence configurations and their distribution in L1 and L2 for the American and French speakers. Once more, the differences are more significant within the American group, as nearly half of their sequences (48%) are made of vocal markers and morphosyntactic markers (VOC+MS) in their L2 as opposed to 29% in their L1. By contrast, 35% of their sequences consisted in combinations of vocal markers (VOC+VOC) in their L1, as opposed to 20% in their L2. In short, these findings suggest that the American speakers made use of mainly two different patterns of co-occurrence in their L1 and their L2, with a slight preference for stalling strategies in their L1 (VOC+VOC) as opposed to a mixture of stalling and repair mechanisms (VOC+MS) in their L2.

For the French speakers, however, the differences are not so clear-cut, given the lack of statistical significance between the two proportions. Only one pattern (VOC+MS) reached a significant statistical score ($p = 0.01$), and shows differences between L1 and L2, with a higher rate in L1 (49%) than in L2 (36%).

Table 11. Sequence configurations (American group)

Seq. conf.	L1 % (raw)		L2 % (raw)		Z score	P value
MIX	2%	(2)	2%	(6)	N/A	
MS+MS	14%	(18)	4%	(11)	3.821	< 0.0002*
MS+NL	1%	(1)	1%	(3)	N/A	
VOC+MS	29%	(38)	48%	(145)	−3.757	< 0.002*
VOC+MS+NL	7%	(9)	9%	(27)	−0.749	0.4
VOC+NL	14%	(19)	17%	(50)	−0.584	0.5
VOC+VOC	35%	(46)	20%	(61)	3.229	0.001*

Table 12. Sequence configurations (French group)

Seq. conf.	L1 % (raw)		L2 % (raw)		Z score	P value
MIX	1%	(2)	3%	(7)	N/A	
MS+MS	10%	(18)	9%	(19)	0.432	0.6
MS+NL	1%	(1)	2%	(5)	N/A	
NL+NL	1%	(1)	1%	(3)	N/A	
VOC+MS	49%	(85)	36%	(76)	2.516	0.01*
VOC+MS+NL	8%	(13)	6%	(12)	0.697	0.4
VOC+NL	10%	(18)	17%	(36)	−0.06	0.05
VOC+VOC	20%	(35)	24%	(51)	−0.9	0.3

One major difference is also found between the French and American groups. While the French group used the VOC+MS pattern 49% of the time in their L1, the American group only produced it 29% ($z=-3.637$; $p<0.0002$), and the two groups showed an opposite tendency in their L2 (fewer VOC+MS combinations in the L2 for the French, as opposed to a higher proportion in the L2 for the Americans). Lastly, the American speakers used the VOC+VOC pattern in their L1 more frequently (35%) than the French speakers (20%), although this difference did not reach much significance ($z=-2.822$; $p=0.04$).

The last variable analyzed at the sequence level is utterance position, and this time the two groups showed similar patterns of behavior. Results are reported in Tables 13 and 14. Not many differences were found between L1 and L2 in both groups, except for medial and final positions: American speakers produced more fluenceme sequences in medial position in their L2 (57%) than in their L1 (48%), and French speakers produced slightly more fluencemes in final position in their L1 (12%) than in their L2 (9%).

Table 13. Sequence position (American group)

Seq. position	L1 % (raw)		L2% (raw)		Z score	P value
final	12%	(38)	10%	(50)	1.136	0.2
interrupted	2%	(5)	3%	(13)	−0.873	0.3
initial	37%	(115)	30%	(155)	2.052	0.04*
medial	48%	(147)	57%	(290)	−2.253	0.01*
standalone	1%	(4)	1%	(4)	N/A	

Table 14. Sequence position (French group)

Seq. position	L1 % (raw)		L2 % (raw)		Z score	P value
final	14%	(48)	9%	(34)	2.313	0.02*
interrupted	1%	(5)	2%	(7)	−0.339	0.7
initial	30%	(105)	33%	(131)	−0.025	0.4
medial	53%	(185)	54%	(216)	−0.0082	0.8
standalone	1%	(4)	3%	(11)	N/A	

Overall, the distributions appear to be largely similar in the two speaker groups and in the two languages, which may suggest that language proficiency has little effect on the position of fluencemes in the data.

So far, the findings have exclusively focused on the verbal and vocal level of native and non-native fluency, analyzing different temporal variables, such as rate, distribution, sequence configuration, position, among others. We shall now move to the third level of analysis (above fluenceme and sequence) involving visible bodily behavior.

2.3 Visuo-gestural level: Gesture production and gaze behavior

Tables 15 and 16 report the proportion of the different gesture phases during fluenceme sequences in L1 and in L2, for the American and French groups. Two main differences can be observed between L1 and L2 in the two groups.

First, both American and French speakers kept their hands in rest position more frequently in their L1 (64% for the Americans, and 62% for the French) than in their L2 (48% for the Americans and 46% for the French). This suggests a higher gestural activity in L2 than in L1, but these findings will be further confirmed when I compare gestural rates during fluent and disfluent stretches of speech. Interestingly, the two groups also showed a tendency to hold their hands in a static position

Table 15. Proportion of gesture phases during fluenceme sequences (American group)

	L1 % (raw)		L2 % (raw)		Z score	P value
stroke	18%	(55)	21%	(107)	−1.081	0.2
hold	9%	(28)	18%	(92)	−3.5	0.0005*
preparation	5%	(15)	8%	(40)	−1.643	0.1
rest position	64%	(197)	48%	(244)	4.482	< 0.0002*
retraction	5%	(14)	6%	(29)	−0.706	0.4

Table 16. Proportion of gesture phases during fluenceme sequences (French group)

	L1 % (raw)		L2 % (raw)		Z score	P value
stroke	16%	(57)	24%	(94)	−2.418	0.01*
hold	9%	(32)	15%	(61)	−2.502	0.01*
preparation	6%	(20)	8%	(31)	−1.1083	0.2
rest position	62%	(216)	46%	(185)	4.34	< 0.0002*
retraction	6%	(22)	7%	(28)	−0.369	0.7

more frequently during fluencemes in L2 (18% for the Americans, 15% for the French) than in L1 (9% for the Americans and the French). This finding is further elaborated in Chapter 6. Overall, these results show that gestures rarely co-occur with fluencemes, in line with previous work (cf Chapter 1 and 2), but a larger proportion of them are produced in non-native productions. This leads us to the analysis of gesture production during fluent and disfluent cycles of speech.

Figure 17 reports the rate of gesture strokes per hundred words in native and non-native productions for the American and French speakers.[61] Numbers indicate that American speakers produced 16 gestures phw in their L2 ($N=376$), versus 11 in their L1 ($N=336$), which was found to be statistically significant ($LL=27.91$; $p<0.0001$). The same applies to the French speakers, who produced 10 gestures phw in their L1 ($N=375$), as opposed to 15 in their L2 ($N=275$; $LL=34.34$; $p<0.0001$). These findings confirm my earlier prediction that speakers produce more gestures in their L2 than in their L1 overall. Despite significant differences between L1 and L2 overall, a few exceptions can be noted. For instance, A03 produced more gestures in her L1 (21) than in her L2 (15), as well as F11 (24 in her L1 and 18 in her L2). Some speakers also showed a tendency to gesture a lot in their L2 (e.g. A10 and F11) while others gestured very little in comparison (e.g. A15 and F18).

---

61. Raw values can be found in Appendix 2, Table 47.

118   Beyond Disfluency

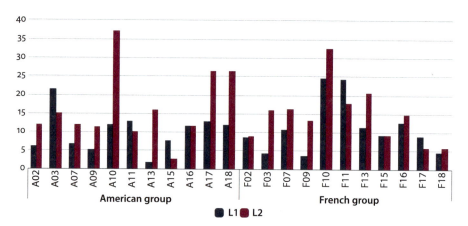

Figure 17. Rate of gestures (phw) in L1 and L2

Figure 18 shows the proportion of gestures in fluent versus disfluent stretches of speech (during fluencemes and outside fluencemes). Results show that gestures predominantly occurred without fluencemes, which supports previous work (cf Chapter 1, Section III.3.3.4). This was found to be true for the two groups and in L1 and L2, as the American speakers produced 84% of their gestures ($N=282/336$) during fluent stretches of speech, as opposed to 16% ($N=54/336$) during disfluent ones ($z=-14.59$; $p<0.0002$) in their L1. This was also the case in their L2, with a lower rate of gestures during fluencemes ($N=105/376$) than outside fluencemes ($N=271/376$) ($z=-12.10$; $p<0.0002$). Similarly, the French speakers produced significantly more gestures in their L1 during fluent ($N=218/275$) than disfluent stretches of speech ($N=57/275$) ($z=-13.73$; $p<0.0002$), as well as in their L2, with a lower rate of gestures during fluencemes ($N=94/375$) than without them ($N=281/375$) ($z=-13.65$; $p<0.0002$).

Moving now to the distribution of gesture types and subtypes in L1 and L2 (Tables 17 and 18). Speakers from both groups produced a higher proportion of referential gestures in their L1 (28% for the Americans and for the French) than in their L2 (21% for the Americans, 20% for the French), and American speakers produced more pragmatic gestures in their L2 (80%) than in their L1 (72%). As to the subtypes, the differences were not statistically significant in L1 and L2 in the two groups, except for thinking gestures, which were used slightly more frequently in L2 (5% for the Americans, 6% for the French) than in L1 (2% for the Americans and the French). This is an interesting point to consider, and it could indicate that speakers may need to "flag the fact of an ongoing word search" (Gullberg, 2001, p.143) more frequently in their L2 than in their L1 as a result of interactional difficulties. A more detailed typology of thinking gestures is provided in Chapter 6.

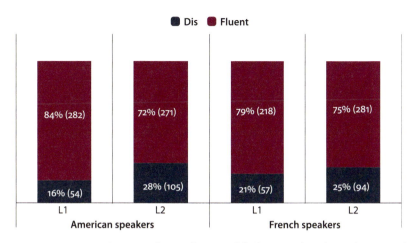

Figure 18. Proportion of gestures during fluent and disfluent cycles of speech in L1 and L2

Table 17. Proportion of gesture types and subtypes un L1 and L2 (American group)

	L1		L2		Z score	P value
	\multicolumn{4}{c}{Referential gestures % (raw)}			
	28%	(95)	21%	(78)	2.33	0.01*
representational	10%	(33)	7%	(26)	1.40	0.1
deictic-anaphoric	18%	(62)	14%	(52)	1.67	0.09
	\multicolumn{4}{c}{Pragmatic gestures % (raw)}			
	72%	(241)	80%	(301)	−2.60	0.009*
discursive	39%	(131)	44%	(167)	−1.46	0.1
interactive	31%	(104)	31%	(116)	0.02	0.9
thinking	2%	(6)	5%	(18)	−2.25	0.02*

Figure 19 shows the proportion of pragmatic and referential gestures in L1 and L2, more specifically in fluent and disfluent cycles of speech for the American and French groups. A chi-square test of independence was performed to examine the relation between gesture type (pragmatic or referential) and speech type (fluent or disfluent). The relation between these variables was not significant neither for the American group in their L1 (χ^2 (1, N=336)=0.5, p=0.4) and their L2 (χ^2 (1, N=205)=0.5, p=0.4) nor the French group in their L1 (χ^2 (1, N=275)=0.3, p=0.5) and their L2 (χ^2 (1, N=376)=0.7, p=0.4). This may suggest that fluencemes have little impact on the speakers' gestural behavior in the data, but this finding may also be due to the limited number of gestures that actually co-occur with them.

Table 18. Proportion of gesture types and subtypes un L1 and L2 (French group)

	L1		L2		Z score	P value
	\multicolumn{4}{c}{Referential gestures % (raw)}			
	28%	(76)	20%	(76)	2.19	0.02*
representational	15%	(40)	9%	(35)	2.05	0.03*
deictic-anaphoric	13%	(36)	11%	(41)	0.84	0.8
	\multicolumn{4}{c}{Pragmatic gestures % (raw)}			
	71%	(194)	74%	(278)	−1.01	0.3
discursive	39%	(108)	41%	(152)	−0.32	0.7
interactive	31%	(86)	34%	(126)	−0.62	0.5
thinking	2%	(5)	6%	(21)	−2.43	0.01*

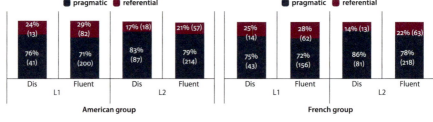

Figure 19. Proportion of pragmatic and referential gestures in fluent and disfluent cycles of speech

Tables 19 and 20 further show the distribution of all gesture subtypes in L1 and L2 and in fluent versus disfluent speech, and just like the distribution of gesture types, none of the values found in the two sample proportions reached statistical significance, except for French speakers who produced slightly more interactive gestures outside fluencemes in their L2 (37% during outside fluencemes as opposed to 23% during fluencemes).

Despite the lack of statistical evidence overall, it is still interesting to note that thinking gestures almost never occurred during fluent speech both in L1 and L2 and in the two groups. Therefore, this finding can be interpreted as a sign that thinking gestures are closely associated to (dis)fluency phenomena, and may thus be an *embodiment* of inter-(dis)fluency behavior. This hypothesis is further discussed in Chapter 6.

Figure 20 reports the proportion of shifts in gaze direction in L1 and in L2 for the two groups,[62] but it should be noted that the findings yielded no statistical

---

62. Raw values can be found in Appendix 2, Table 46.

Table 19. Proportion of gesture subtypes in fluent and disfluent speech (American group)

	L1				L2			
	DIS		FLUENT		Z (p)	DIS		FLUENT		Z (p)
deictic-anaphoric	15%	8	19%	54	−0.75 (0.4)	10%	11	15%	41	−1.17 (0.2)
representational	9%	5	10%	28	−0.15 (0.8)	7%	7	6%	16	0.2 (0.7)
discursive	35%	19	40%	112	−0.62 (0.5)	43%	45	45%	122	−0.37 (0.7)
interactive	30%	16	31%	88	−0.23 (0.8)	25%	26	33%	90	−1.59 (0.1)
thinking	11%	6	0%	0	N/A	15%	16	1%	2	N/A

Table 20. Proportion of gesture subtypes in fluent and disfluent speech (French group)

	L1				L2			
	DIS		FLUENT		Z (P)	DIS		FLUENT		Z (P)
deictic-anaphoric	12%	7	13%	29	−0.20 (0.8)	9%	8	12%	33	−0.87 (0.3)
representational	12%	7	15%	33	−0.54 (0.5)	5%	5	11%	30	−1.54 (0.1)
discursive	42%	24	39%	84	0.49 (0.6)	43%	40	40%	112	0.46 (0.6)
interactive	28%	16	32%	70	−0.58 (0.5)	23%	22	37%	104	−2.41 (0.01*)
thinking	5%	3	1%	2	N/A	20%	19	1%	2	N/A

significance overall (cf Table 48 in Appendix 2), except for the American group who gazed towards the piece of paper more frequently in their L2 (12%) than in their L1 (6%) ($z=4.36$; $p<0.002$). However, when we compare gaze behavior in fluent versus disfluent stretches of speech, a number of significant differences can be found both in L1 and L2 and in the two groups. As Figure 21 shows, there is a higher proportion of gaze withdrawal (*gaze away*) in disfluent than in fluent stretches of speech in L1 (59% vs 34%; $z=7.098$; $p>0.002$), as well as in L2 (50% vs 31%; $z=6.364$; $p>0.0002$). Conversely, there is a higher proportion of mutual gaze (*gaze towards interlocutor*) in fluent than disfluent speech in L1 (54% vs 30%; $z=-6.56$; $p<0.0002$) and in L2 (55% vs 28%; $z=-8.83$; $p<0.0002$).

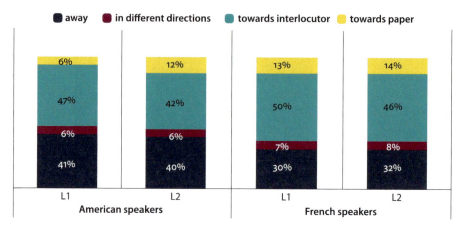

Figure 20. Gaze direction in L1 and L2 (American and French group)

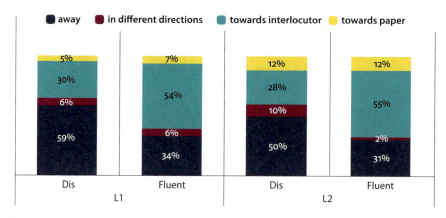

Figure 21. Gaze direction in fluent and disfluent stretches of speech (American group)[63]

Similar results are reported in Figure 22 for the French group, with a higher proportion of gaze withdrawal in disfluent speech both in L1 (39% vs 25%; $z = 4.59$; $p < 0.0002$) and in L2 (47% vs 23%; $z = 7.95$; $p < 0.0002$), and a higher proportion of mutual gaze in fluent speech both in L1 (58% vs 36%; $z = -6.17$; $p < 0.0002$) and L2 (55% versus 28%; $z = -9.24$; $p < 0.0002$).

It is also interesting to note differences between the two groups: French speakers gazed towards the piece of paper 16% of the time in their L1 during fluencemes, as opposed to the Americans who did it only 5% ($z = 4.73$; $p < 0.002$), while Americans spent considerably more time gazing away during fluencemes in their L1 (59%) than the French (39%) ($z = 4.732$; $p < 0.0002$).

---

63. Raw values for this Figures 21 and 22 are found in Appendix 2, Table 46

Chapter 4. Inter-(dis)fluency in native and non-native discourse 123

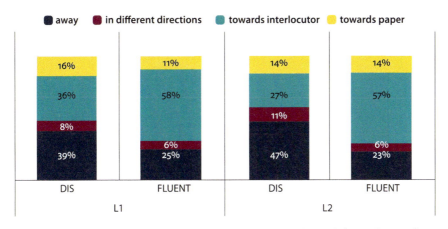

Figure 22. Gaze direction in fluent and disfluent stretches of speech (French group)

To conclude, the aim of this section was to analyze overall patterns of gestural and gaze behavior that are typical of inter-(dis)fluency phenomena in native and non-native productions. The binary opposition between "fluent" and "disfluent" stretches of speech was made explicit here in order to compare the types of gestures that typically co-occur with fluencemes with the ones that do not. However, it has been pointed out several times throughout this book that inter-(dis)fluency phenomena should not be restricted to "disfluent" stretches of speech, but it is interesting to note a number of tendencies in the data, mainly the absence of gestures and mutual gaze during fluencemes, which may indicate a form of disengagement in the gestural and interactional activity. This is one side of DISfluency, characterized by a high rate of verbal fluencemes, complex sequences, and limited gestural activity. The quantitative results observed in this section can be summarized as the following:

Table 21. Summary of the quantitative results

- **Higher rates of fluencemes** in L2 than in L1 both within the French and American groups.
- **Differences in fluenceme distribution between L1 and L2:** more identical repetitions and filled pauses in L2 but more self-interruptions and unfilled pauses in L1 for the American group. For the French group, more self-interruptions and prolongations were found in L1, but more non-lexical sounds in L2.
- **Differences in the form of filled pauses:** more ums in L1 than L2 for the Americans, but more uhs in L1 than in L2 for the French.
- **No significant differences in duration** between L1 and L2 and in the two groups.
- **More complex sequences in L2** than in L1 for the American group. But no significant differences for the French.

Table 21. *(continued)*

- **Higher number of markers combined in L2 for the American group**. But no significant differences for the French.
- **Slight differences in utterance position**: more instances of medial position in L2 for the Americans, and more instances of final position in L2 for the French.
- **More instances of held gestures during fluencemes** in L2 than in L1 for the two groups.
- **Higher rate of gestures in L2** (both during and outside fluencemes) for the two groups.
- **More pragmatic gestures and thinking gestures during fluencemes** than outside fluencemes both in L1 and in L2 for the two groups.
- **More instances of gaze withdrawal during fluencemes** than outside fluencemes both in L1 and in L2 for the two groups.

These findings, which are further discussed in Section IV, give an overall idea of the form, distribution, and co-occurring visible bodily behavior of fluencemes; they do not, however, paint a full picture of the present phenomena, as they do not portray the multimodal deployment of fluencemes in situated tandem activities. This leads us to the following section, which presents the qualitative analyses.

III. Qualitative analyses

In this section, I further explore the interactional ambivalence of fluencemes by illustrating their multimodal quality in situated sequences. I begin with an overview of their distribution with regard to *communication management* in L1 and in L2 by crossing different variables (mainly sequence type and gesture), before presenting micro-analyses of several excerpts taken from the data.

3.1 Communication management: Overview of the data

As mentioned earlier (cf Chapter 1, Section II.2.2.1), Allwood et al., (2015) distinguished between two types of fluencemes (*communication management* in their terms) based on their function in communication. They presented a model with two main systems, one that is concerned with the speaker's management of his or her "linguistic contributions to communicative interaction" (Allwood et al., 2005, p. 2), in other words, speakers' own planning processes (*own communication management*, henceforth *OCM*), and another that pertains to the interactional exchange and the interactants' turn-taking mechanisms and multimodal feedback (*interactive communication management*, henceforth *ICM*). In the present study, I adopted a similar labeling system and annotated fluencemes based on whether they were more intrapersonal, in relation to internal production processes (OCM), or whether they were more interpersonal, and contributed to the sequential development of the interaction through the enactment of speech acts and the co-achievement of intersubjectivity (ICM).

Figure 23 shows the proportion of fluencemes performing ICM and OCM functions in L1 and in L2 and in the two speaker groups. As the numbers show, the proportion of OCM is overwhelmingly greater both in L1 and in L2, and in the two groups. A chi-square test further showed that there was no significant association between language proficiency and functions of fluencemes both for the American group, χ^2 (1, $N=821$) = 0.1, $p=0.7$) and the French one, χ^2 (1, $N=746$) = 0.2, $p=0.6$. This is a very striking result, which, to some extent, gives credit to previous psycholinguistic work on (dis)fluency that focused on their role in the speech production system. Neither speaker group nor language proficiency seem to have an effect on the distribution of these functions, as all fluencemes predominantly performed the OCM function. However, despite the high proportion of fluencemes associated with intrapersonal processes (about 80–82%), the remaining proportion (18%) is nonetheless of great value for the present work, as it illuminates the interactional nature of fluencemes, which have often been too restricted to the overwhelming 80%. This is further explored in the qualitative analyses.

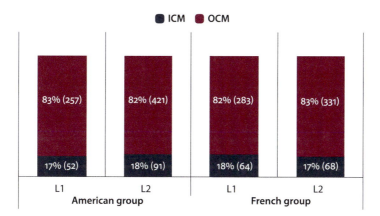

Figure 23. Proportion of OCM and ICM functions in L1 and L2

3.2 Non-native speakers' multimodal communication strategies

Gullberg (2011) distinguished between three major types of difficulties experienced by L2 learners during their non-native productions, mainly lexical, grammatical and interactional related difficulties. In her paper on multimodal communication strategies, she aimed to investigate whether the different types of communicative difficulties would yield different types of multimodal behavior, and explored the role of individual communicative style, by presenting several micro-analyses from her data. Regarding interactional related difficulties, Gullberg showed that L2 learners relied on several multimodal resources to manage problems that resulted from their "non fluent hesitant productions" (Gullberg, 2011, p. 139). She further noted that "every disfluency is a potential locus for loss of face and of floor" (p. 143). However, I do not exactly agree with this view, as I have pointed out before that fluencemes are not necessarily the *result* of interactional difficulties, but that some of them, when coordinated with visible bodily behavior, may in fact be used to *resolve* such difficulties. I thus claim that certain fluencemes can also *act* as communication strategies to a certain extent, and this is illustrated in the following qualitative analyses, each one reflecting a speaker's strategy.

Strategy 1. *Use of an explicit editing phrase and a combination of visual-gestural activities: Projecting the progressivity of the word search*

The first excerpt is taken from the interaction in English between Sally (F11, the French speaker) and Harry (A11, the American speaker). In this particular sequence, Sally is talking about the people who were once part of a reality TV show and then had to go on with their lives after the show ended.

Excerpt 1A. Pair 11
```
  1 *SAL: (0.900) everybody saw um [/] saw you in this tv show so they can't have
→   *SAL: um (1.250) [!] um (2.160) I don't know how the word uh (1.490)
        ****************************************************
```

```
    ((looks away, hands held together, finger snap gesture, smile))
    they can't trust on you.
  2 *HAR: ok.
      ((head nod, gaze towards SAL))
  3 *SAL: on you:ur um (0.510) [/] on <you> +/.
            ********************
((both hands coming together, palms facing upwards; looks away; pouts))
  4 *HAR:              +< uh reliance.
                         ((gazes at SAL))
```

In line 1, Sally (French NNS) produces a fairly long fluenceme sequence comprised of 9 different markers (a filled pause, an unfilled pause, a tongue click, a second unfilled pause, an explicit editing phrase, a second filled pause, and a third unfilled pause, following the *MIX* combination). The length[64] of this sequence (9 markers) is considerably greater than the average of her group (1.9 markers), as well as her own (2.1), which underlines the degree of variation found in fluenceme use. In this particular case, Sally is experiencing lexical difficulties, as she is looking for a specific lexical item and does not have the word for it, and this is overtly expressed in her explicit editing phrase ("I don't know how the word"). Explicit editing phrases (EDT), which can be classified as peripheral markers of fluencemes (cf Chapter 2, Section II.2.2.1), refer to lexical expressions by which the speaker signals some production trouble (Crible, 2017, p. 108). EDTs are rather relatively fixed chunks that are stored in speakers' memories (e.g. formulaic units, see Gürbüz, 2017) and can easily be retrieved without any processing time (Wood, 2001). Even though the speaker failed to produce the correct multi-word expression in her target language, she still used it competently for pragmatic purposes. Indeed, she relied on this EDT to signal production difficulties to her partner, but also perhaps to keep the floor as not to be interrupted (Maclay & Osgood, 1959), and display the progressivity of her word search (Goodwin & Goodwin, 1986; Hayashi, 2003). These cues are in fact understood by her partner, who does not interrupt her right away, but rather provides verbal ("ok") and visual ("head nod") backchannel (l.2) before offering assistance (l.3). Therefore, the production of this ungrammatical verbal expression, does by no means impede the overall interactional flow, as Sally manages to keep her turn while dealing with her lexical difficulties until Harry offers his help.

In addition, the L2 speaker does not only rely on verbal and vocal fluencemes to work on her production, but on several multimodal resources as well. The complexity of her sequence, composed of different clustered fluencemes, is also visible in her gestural activity, as she first holds her arms and hands in the same position during the production of the filled pause, then produces a finger snap gesture with her right hand during her unfilled pause, and then holds both her arms and hands again while looking down, and finally she starts smiling when she produces the EDT. This example shows a synchrony between the complexity of the fluenceme sequence and the complexity of the gestural activity, which further underlines the multimodal dimension of inter-(dis)fluency. This point is further developed in Chapter 6.

The second excerpt is taken from Pair 13 in English between Elena (F13-NNS) and Francis (A13- NS) during which the two speakers are talking about University tuiton fees. Just like Sally, Elena is experiencing a number of lexical and grammatical difficulties, as indicated by the series of fluencemes (in her first turn, in bold) but also by her facial expressions, gaze behavior, gestural and head movement.

---

[64]. Note that the term "length" is borrowed from Crible (2017) to refer to the number of markers combined in a sequence, not actual duration (see Chapter 3, Section II).

Excerpt 1B. Pair 13

→ 1 *ELEN: but I [/] I'm not sure (be)cause here um (0.768) [!] [/] here (0.889) if you:u uh I ain't got the w word here
         ((thinking face a.))   ((looks up; smiles b.))

a. here (.) if you:u uh   b.I ain't got the w word here

       eh hhh. um if the <state> didn't
          ((looks towards Francis))
2   *FRAN: +< mm mm.
                    ((head nod))
→ 3 *ELEN: give you som:me do(llars) don do xxx +//.
              ((thinking face c.))
     *ELEN: ((smiles))
4   *FRAN: I repeat.
              ****

       ((cyclic gesture+ eyes closed d.))
5   *ELEN: if the state doesn't give you money.
              ((looks towards Francis))

c. som:me do don xx   d. I repeat

6   *FRAN: mm mm.
7   *ELEN: you have to pay uh four hundred (0.569) euros for a year.

Here Elena is enacting a lexical search activity by coordinating vocal fluencemes and bodily actions which allow her to project the current progressivity of her search. She first displays a state of uncertainty with a thinking face (picture a.), while suspending the course of her utterance (with an "um", a pause, a tongue click, and a lengthening, turn 1) followed by another EDT "I ain't got the word" (also ungrammatical, just like Sally in the previous example) which makes her word search explicit. She makes her current activity even more visible and almost theatrical by raising her head, looking up, and smiling (picture b.), as if the words were going to fall from the sky. She then initiates a new segment "if the state" (turn 1) and gazes towards her partner to display her tentative lexical retrieval success, but then produces a series of truncated words (turn 2) accompanied by a second thinking face which makes her abandon her current utterance and start a new one ("I repeat") which states her current re-adjustment towards the completion of the segment ("if the state doesn't give you money"). This re-adjustment is also embodied in a cyclic gesture (Ladewig, 2014) in which both hands are rotating as to convey the process of starting over (picture d.). Once again, she makes this process visible to her partner, and the notions of suspending, interrupting and restarting, which are inherent to fluencemes, are embodied in several visible activities. Her tandem partner seems to attend to her actions attentively, as he coordinates his behavior with her by punctuating the interaction with several backchanneling devices and tokens of agreement ("yeah" "mm" and head nods) without interrupting her. Just like Sally, Elena's utterances are highly "disfluent" from a strictly verbal perspective, but it doesn't stop her from pursuing her word search activity without her partner's assistance (as opposed to Sally).

To conclude, these two examples have shown that the production of vocal and verbal fluencemes does not only signal that a speaker is currently experiencing trouble, but it also provides solutions as to how to resolve lexical problems, with the help of co-occurring visual gestural resources. Following Goodwin & Goodwin (1986); Rydell (2019) and Hayashi (2003) I further argue that fluencemes embodying word searching activities are not only manifestations of internal cognitive processes, or "symptoms" of a L2 resource deficit, but relevant displays of an ongoing search, marking a shift in the current speaking activity.

Strategy 2. *Mutual gaze and concurrent gesture: Visibly requesting help from the interlocutor*

Many authors have emphasized the crucial role of gaze in interaction (e.g. Goodwin, 1981; Goodwin & Goodwin, 1986; Gullberg, 2011; Sweetser & Stec, 2016, among others). Gaze enables speakers to embody multiple viewpoints when engaged in storytelling activities, and perform a series of discourse and cognitive functions such as visually "checking" for the interlocutor's approval, or finding access to memory space (Sweetser & Stec, 2016). During word searching sequences, gaze shifts can further signal whether a search is self-directed or other directed (Goodwin & Goodwin, 1986; Hayashi, 2003, Rydell, 2019): speakers may wish to look straight at their partner and perform gestures that are relevant for the solutions of problems (other directed), or they may also withdraw their gaze and display a thinking gesture (self-directed, as illustrated in Excerpts 1a and 1b). In this section, I explore the role of mutual gaze during multimodal communication strategies, and illustrate how speakers visibly request help from their partner in ways that are relevant to the current activities they are engaged in.

The first example is taken from Pair 3 in French, with the American speaker Julia (A03-NNS) and the French speaker Marina (F03-NS). In this excerpt, the pair was asked to talk about the differences between being a traveler and a tourist.

Excerpt 2A. Pair 3
```
1     *JUL: e:et peut-être les voyageurs par contre euh (0.790) [!]
            a:and maybe travelers on the other hand euh (0.790) [!]
2           a:a [/] a l'opportunité de:e rester
            ha:ave [/] have the opportunity to:o stay
                      ((gazes away))
→           un plus lointain [//] peu (0.580) +…
            a little longer [//] a little (0.580) +…
                         ********************
```
((hands held in the same position and slightly move down))
((moves her head and gazes towards Marina))

```
1    *MAR:         plus longtemps.
                   longer
                   ((gazes at Julia))
2    *JUL:                         plus longtemps.
                                   longer
     *MAR:                         ((nods, smiles))
```

In this brief example, Julia is experiencing difficulties with the pronunciation of the adverb "longtemps" (longer), as she mispronounces it (the spelled word "lointain" reflects the initial mispronunciation, but it does not necessarily represent her initial intention). Her mispronunciation is related to difficulties in phonological encoding: she produces a sequence of four words (understood as "un peu plus longtemps") which may be challenging for a non-native speaker because of the three rounded vowels in French (*un* /œ̃/ *peu* /ø/ *plus* /y/.).[65] The comparative in French can also be quite challenging for the American speaker as it requires the

---

65. Thank you Céline Horgues, Sylwia Scheuer, and Christelle Exare for your help on the phonetic analysis.

use of an additional word, as opposed to the "er" suffix in English. Julia quickly realized that she mispronounced the word and she paused for 580 ms (which is a little below her average of 629 ms in her L2), held her arms and hands in the same position, and with her gaze fixed on her interlocutor, she slightly moved her head in the direction of her partner, which could be interpreted as requesting for help. The pause thus marks a transition relevant place, where speaker change is made relevant: Marina understands her partner's request, and takes the floor to provide a phonological repair, but she also skips the quantifier ("un peu"), perhaps to facilitate the phonetic realization of the vowels and focus on the target adjective ("longtemps"). In the subsequent turn, Julia repeats the target word, this time with the right pronunciation, which projects the end of her current utterance. This type of activity is known as *doing pronunciation* (Brouwer, 2004, p. 93), which is a specific type of repair sequence in which a L1 speaker typically corrects a L2 speaker at the phonetic level. As Brouwer further noted, during such repair episodes, the conversation is momentarily "put on hold" (Brouwer, 2009; p. 93) and the participants are then oriented to matters related to language competence. The fluenceme here thus functions as an *initiation technique* (Schegloff et al., 1977, p. 369), signaling trouble with regard to the delivery of the turn, during which the non-native speaker implicitly solicits her partner's correction. Following this brief repair sequence, Julia then goes on saying that travelers, unlike tourists, tend to stay in a foreign country for a longer amount of time (omitted from the transcription). Contrary to what the previous examples have shown, Julia did not verbally convey her production problems (with an EDT) but solely relied on sequential, vocal and visual-gestural strategies to request help. Unlike Sally and Elena, she looked straight at her interlocutor, and it functioned as an indication that her partner's participation was now considered relevant for the current activity.

The second example is taken from Pair 13 in French, where this time Francis (A03) is the non-native speaker and Elena (F03) the native speaker. Here Francis is talking about the kinds of sensitive topics that friends can have during a conversation, and he does not exactly find the words for it.

Excerpt 2B. Pair 13 (FR)

```
1 *FRAN: um mais (1.278) en même temps on peu:ut vraiment
         um but (1.278) at the same time we ca:an really
         si [/] si:i (1.033) dans une groupe euh
         if [/] i:if (1.033) in a group euh
         *******************************
         ((left hand held; looks up e.))
         qui:i [/] qui discutons de:es des choses <politiques>.
         who:o [/] who talk about <so:ome> political stuff
               ************************
```

```
                  ((left hand rotating))
       *ELEN:                                  +< mm mm
                                               ((head nod))
→ 2 *FRAN: ou des choses euh (1.655) <quoi tu [/] tu>.
           or things euh (1.655) < like you [/] you >
           **********************************
       ((left hand held e.))  ((left open palm extended f.))
```

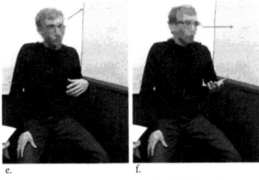

```
  3 *ELEN:        <religieuses politiques> les [/] les choses
                  <religious political > things the [/] the things
                  ****************************************
                  ((left hand rotating + looks at FRAN g.))
                  un peu:u [/] un peu tabou.
                  a little:e [/] a little taboo
```

g. NNS: oui tout ça   NS: religieuses politiques

```
  4 *FRAN:       +< oui tout ça.
                 +< yeah all that.
           ((shoulder shrug and palm up open hands g.))
```

Contrary to Elena in the previous exchange (Excerpt 1b), and just like Julia, Francis does not explicitly signal to his tandem partner that he is looking for a word, but he still displays that his talk is currently being suspended, with the held gesture (picture e.), and the combination of different vocal fluencemes (prolongations "ca:an'", i:if", unfilled and filled pause). After retrieving one noun phrase ("choses politiques" / *political stuff* l. 1) he initiates another one ("des choses" / *or things* l.2) and eventually shifts from his solitary word search project to a joint one by inviting Elena to take part in it. He does so by gazing, and extending his left open palm (which was previously held) towards her (example of a *Palm Up Open Hand Gesture*, cf Müller, 2017; picture f.). This "offering" gesture (Streeck, 2009a) appears to metaphorically hand over Francis' current search to his partner, who joins in and offers a new lexical item, followed by an elaboration further enhancing Francis' initial idea (l.3). A state of mutual understanding is then accomplished when Francis, almost immediately after Elena's prior turn, offers a positive assessment "oui tout ça / yes all that" (l. 4), accompanied by a shoulder shrug, which further displays his affiliation.

These two examples have demonstrated the role of mutual gaze during word searching or repair sequences, which, along with other vocal and gestural cues, signal that a state of co-participation to the joint project may become relevant. This co-participation reflects the interactional dimension of fluencemes, which do not only display internal production processes (self-oriented, OCM) but function as relevant interactional resources (other-oriented, ICM).

Strategy 3. *Gaze towards the piece of paper: Disengaging from the current activity*

The last communication strategy selected for this section illustrates very different modes of behavior, further reflecting the interactional ambivalence of fluencemes. The first example is taken from Pair 09 in which the French participant Emilie (F09-NNS) is interacting in English with her American Partner Arthur (A09-NS). Just like all the other argumentative tasks, the participants were asked to discuss a topic that was written on a piece of paper, and then decide on their level of agreement at the end of the discussion. Here the topic was: "the traveler sees what he sees and the tourist sees what he has come to see." Right from the beginning of the conversation, Emilie had a difficult time grasping the meaning of the topic and expressing herself, which led to interactional-related difficulties. While this context is a little similar to the previous examples, as Emilie is experiencing production difficulties due to her lack of vocabulary in her second language, her behavior is radically different from the previous speakers. The interaction between Emilie and Arthur is organized in terms of a two-pair part exchange involving two adjacency pairs (question-answer) where Arthur, who is actively participating in the interaction, invites his partner to speak by asking her questions (l. 1 and 3), completes her utterances (l.5), and puts an end to the exchange (l.8).

Excerpt 3A. Pair 9
```
1 *ART: (0.410) but um (0.440) what do you think about that distinction in general?
        ((gazes at EMI))
2 *EMI: um (1.870) um +/.
  ((gaze fixed on the paper))
```

```
3 *ART: do you think it makes sense?
4 *EMI: (0.590) &y [//] yes of course because uh the traveler um (0.965) e [//] he
  doesn't &uh (0.520) decide and uh he:e [/] he see what uh (0.930) [/] what uh
  (0.580) +…
  ((gazes at the paper; slight head movement then gazes at ART))
5 *ART: whatever is there.
6 *EMI: yeah.
7 *EMI: (0.490) a:and uh whereas the [/] the [/] the tourist um (0.570) [!] see what's
  he wants to see so.
     ((gazes at the paper))
8 *ART: ok yeah agreed I'd say.
```

Arthur first invites his partner to elaborate on the topic by asking her a question that is quite straightforward (l.1), but Emilie fails to produce a fluent verbal delivery, as the latter is filled with a complex fluenceme sequence, comprised of two filled pauses and one unfilled pause of nearly two seconds (l.2), which is a significant delay (the average duration of her pauses is 450 ms in her L2). As opposed to Sally and Elena in the previous examples who managed to hold the floor while looking for a specific lexical item, Emilie fails to do so, as Arthur interrupts her to rephrase his initial question (l.3). This loss of floor can be explained by the fact that Emilie is totally disengaged from the interaction, as her eyes are fixed on the piece of paper she is holding in her hand. As the quantitative results indicated, French speakers spent half of their time gazing away while producing fluencemes (57%) but also sometimes towards the piece of paper (14%.) Emilie (F09) actually spent 38% of her time gazing towards the piece of paper while producing fluencemes in her L2, which is significantly higher than the average of her group. But it should be noted that she also did it quite frequently in her L1 (32%), which illustrates an idiosyncratic feature. Here Emilie actually repeats the phrase that was initially written on the piece of paper ("see what he wants to see") to finish her argument (l.7). The fluencemes found in this context are thus very different from the ones analyzed previously, as they merely contribute to the flow of the interaction, since Emilie failed to keep the floor and provide a satisfactory answer, which prompted Arthur to end the sequence ("ok agreed I'd say", l. 8).

Chapter 4. Inter-(dis)fluency in native and non-native discourse   135

A similar instance of gazing is found in Pair 18 in French between the American speaker Rosie (A18-NNS) and the French speaker Sophie (F18-NS). In this excerpt, the two speakers are talking about social media (same topic as in Excerpt 1A, "social media makes people more lonely"). After reading the piece of paper aloud to her partner, Sophie first initiated the exchange, and gave her opinion on the matter. The selected excerpt starts from here.

Excerpt 3B. Pair 18

```
 1 *SOP:   (0.500) j(e) pense que:e (0.513) bah ça peut permettre de
          (0.500) I think tha:at (0.513) well that it can enable us to
          rester en contact avec les gens.
          stay in touch with people.
 2 *ROS:   mm mm.
 3 *SOP:   parce-que par exemple sur facebook on peut retrouver des
          because for example on facebook we can find
          personnes qu'on avai:it pas vu depuis longtemps.
          people that we ha:ad not seen in a while
 4 *SOP:   (1.275) et voilà.
          (1.275) and yeah
 5 *ROS:   mm mm.
→ 6 *ROS:  (0.550) j'ai besoin du vocabulaire.
          (0.550) I need vocabulary
         ((reaches toward the piece of paper))
```

```
 7 *SOP:   (laughs).
 8 *ROS:   (0.587) ok.
         ((gazes towards paper))
```

In line 4, Sophie projects the end of her turn with a sequence-final "voilà" (*yeah*), which gives the floor to Rosie. Rosie's turn is delayed by two vocal fluencemes: one during which she leans forward to reach the piece of paper (an unfilled pause of 550 milliseconds), and a second one (an unfilled pause of 587 ms), during which she inspects the piece of paper. These actions thus momentarily disrupt the progressivity of the exchange, as the L2 speaker is not oriented to the current argumentative task anymore, but to her own expressive difficulties. This is overtly expressed in line 6: "j'ai besoin du vocabulaire" (*I need vocabulary*), which further justifies her need to perform these actions, which are now deemed relevant in order to pursue the exchange. The piece of paper thus becomes a relevant *pedagogical* tool, which provides the right expressions and vocabulary in the target language. Rosie also constantly shifted her gaze, alternating between the piece of paper and her interlocutor, and swinging back and forth between her lack of vocabulary and the interactional task at hand. In this case, the L2 speaker's strategy is to delay parts of her delivery and rely on the piece of paper, in order to provide parts of her answer that are written on the piece of paper. These examples show the importance of material objects in multimodal communication (cf Boutet, 2018, Goodwin, 2003, Streeck et al., 2011,) and how they may influence speakers' actions. This is further discussed in Chapter 5 when I report the results from the DisReg corpus.

In brief, word searching or repair episodes present a number of possibilities for the learners to either put the interaction on hold to display embodied thinking and the progressivity of the word search (Strategy 1), request help from their interlocutor (Strategy 2), or retreat into a more solitary activity with the help of an external object (Strategy 3). This diversity of behaviors reflects individual preferences, in line with Gullberg (2011), but it also further demonstrates the multifunctionality of fluencemes, which can either create "fluency" or "disfluency", depending on the point of view taken. While they may disrupt the flow of speech by inserting significant delays in the acoustic channel, these delays can embody an interactional process, thus ensuring continuity between the interactants' co-actions (or on the contrary, they may also momentarily disrupt the continuity of the exchange, cf Excerpts 3a and 3b).

To conclude, detailed qualitative analyses of the data have exemplified how L2 (dis)fluency is not necessarily associated with a "lack of skill" or a "resource deficit", but is largely embedded within a set of interactional practices involving the gesturers' active co-participation in the talk. The degree of (dis)fluency found in those markers is neither fixed nor systematic and is highly determined by their context of use, as well as their accompanying visual-gestural features. Since fluencemes carry little semantic or pragmatic information, their accompanying visible behavior can further determine whether they display instances of *interactive communication management* (ICM) or *own communication management* (OCM), and their status is constantly being re-shaped in the course of the multimodal talk, depending on the gesturers' available resources. The aim of this section was to bridge the gap between quantitative and qualitative findings in order to better illustrate the ambivalent nature of fluencemes which can both be the result of internal speech processes and social interactional practices.

IV. Discussion

The present section addresses the research questions formulated earlier by drawing on a selection of findings obtained from the statistical treatments (Section II.2.1) as well as the qualitative analyses. This section is structured as follows: I first report on the differences between L1 and L2 fluency in the American and French groups (4.1), and discuss the role of fluency in situated tandem discourse and the multimodal strategies yielded by non-native speakers to deal with language difficulties in their L2 (4.2).

4.1 Specificities of L1 and L2 Fluency

One of the main questions this chapter sought to answer was whether L2 fluency differed significantly from L1 fluency, or whether the two were correlated (RQ1). As we have seen, these differences can be measured by looking at temporal variables and fluency rates (e.g. Tavakoli, 2011; Riggenbach, 1991). In addition to temporal variables, I also looked at sequential (i.e. patterns of co-occurrence), positional (utterance position), and visual-gestural features.

4.1.1 *Fluenceme rate, distribution, and patterns of co-occurrence in the American and French groups*

In line with previous studies in SLA (e.g. De Jong, 2016a, Fehringer & Fry, 2007; Gilquin, 2008) results confirm earlier predictions that non-native speakers produce significantly more fluencemes in their L2 than in their L1, and this was true for both the American and French groups. However, fluency is not only assessed by frequency measures, but durational features as well; unlike previous studies (e.g. Cenoz, 1998; Rasier & Hiligsmann, 2007), no significant differences were found in the average duration of the vocal markers (i.e. filled and unfilled pauses and prolongations) in L1 and L2 for the French and American groups. This can be explained by the high degree of variability and dispersion found in the data, reflecting individual differences.

At the sequence level, a number of differences were found. American speakers were more likely to produce complex sequences in their L2 than in their L1, and their sequences contained a higher number of markers in their L2. This finding may indicate one salient feature of L2 fluency, characterized by a higher rate of long and complex sequences. However, this was not true for the French group where no significant differences were found, so this difference may also be language-specific. Differences were also found in the sequence configurations: American speakers showed a tendency to produce sequences which mainly consisted in the *VOC+MS* (vocal marker + morpho-syntactic marker) configuration in their L2, and the *VOC+VOC* configuration in their L1, suggesting preferences for stalling strategies in the L1, as opposed to a mixture of stalling and repair mechanisms in the L2. For the French group, the *VOC+MS* pattern was used more frequently in their L1 than in their L2, showing the opposite tendency. Overall, these results seem to suggest that some specific patterns are more prominent than others, especially *VOC+MS* and *VOC+VOC*,[66] but their use is not systematically determined by levels of proficiency. This does not support my initial hypothesis which claimed that non-native speakers would produce fewer recurrent patterns of combination (cf RQ1), since the *VOC+MS* pattern was used 50% of the time by American speakers in their L2. It is still interesting to note, however, that the speakers used different types of patterns in their L1 and L2. This further emphasizes the idea that fluencemes are made of dynamic and flexible structures with different possible configurations, which are more or less fixed depending on language and other contextual features, following assumptions from Cognitive Grammar and usage-based linguistics (cf Chapter 1, Section III.3.1.2).

As to the utterance position of the fluenceme sequences, not many significant differences were found between L1 and L2 in the two groups, except for the medial and final position. The American group was found to produce more sequences in medial position in their L2 than in their L1, and the French group produced slightly more sequences in final position in their L1 and their L2. However, contrary to previous studies (e.g. Cenoz, 1998; Rasier & Hiligsmann, 2007) the position of the sequences was not annotated with regard to syntactic structure (e.g. intra-clausal versus inter-clausal, or inter-propositional versus intra-propositional) or at the level of the word or morpheme, but more in terms of the overall stream of speech, in line with the notion of multidimensional flow presented in this book (cf Chapter 1, Section IV.4.2).

In addition, several crosslinguistic differences were found between the two groups, perhaps reflecting language-specific or cultural-specific preferences, to name but a few: while the American speakers produced a significant number of unfilled pauses compared to French speakers in their L1, French speakers produced more filled pauses than American speakers in their L2. Another interesting finding was the realization of the filled pause ("(e)uh" versus "(e)um"), which showed opposite tendencies in the two groups. While American speakers used predominantly the um-type filled pause in their L1 as opposed to the uh-type in their L2, French speakers did exactly the opposite, with a strong preference for uh-type filled pauses in their L1 and um-type filled pauses in their L2. This

---

66. These combinations could include a more fined-grained level of abstraction by identifying the specific types of vocal markers that typically occur with specific types of morpho-syntactic markers (e.g. Crible, 2018), but this was not the primary goal of this chapter.

finding validates cross-linguistic preferences, further in line with Clark & Fox Tree's (2002) and Candea et al.'s (2005) argument that filled pauses are language-specific. It is thus important to note that L2 fluency is not only determined by overall differences in language proficiency, as it can also be speaker-, and to a larger extent, language-specific.

4.1.2 *Fluency and language proficiency*

A second closely related question concerns the correlation between fluency and language proficiency (RQ2). While the present study does not aim to target these aspects specifically, it was still deemed relevant to investigate a potential relation between fluency and proficiency, in line with previous work (e.g. De Jong, 2016a, Riggenbach, 1991). Even though the proficiency levels of the participants were not officially assessed but self-evaluated by the students themselves, it is still interesting to study the relationship between *perceived proficiency* and fluency rates.

As findings indicated, no significant correlation was found between the two variables in the two groups. This is consistent with Brand & Götz (2013) who found no trend for a correlation of accuracy (i.e. levels of oral competence in terms of grammatical, lexical, and phonological proficiency) and fluency, but this was perhaps due to the limited size of their sample (only 5 speakers). Similarly, the size of the selected sample is quite small, which makes it difficult to draw general conclusions. However, this finding does show to a certain extent that L2 fluency is not systematically associated with (perceived) proficiency. This further questions the extent to which fluency rates are a valid indicator of L2 proficiency, as previously challenged by a number of authors (see De Jong et al., 2015, Derwing et al., 2010; Zuniga & Simard, 2019).

4.1.3 *Gestural and gaze behavior*

One of the major contributions of the present study is to analyze inter-(dis)fluency in terms of gaze and gestural behavior, in order to go beyond the traditional view of L2 fluency in SLA which has too often been restricted to temporal variables. Following previous work (e.g. Gullberg, 1998; Kita, 1993; Stam, 2006), a higher rate of gestures in L2 than in L1 was expected, and the findings confirmed this prediction, as the two speaker groups produced significantly more gestures in their L2 than in their L1, both in fluent and disfluent cycles of speech (even though gestures did not frequently co-occur during fluencemes). In addition, speakers showed a tendency to hold their gestures during the production of fluencemes, which further confirms the relationship between speech suspension and gesture suspension (e.g. Esposito & Marinaro, 2007; Graziano & Gullberg, 2018). This is further developed in Chapter 6. In addition, both the American and French speakers were found to hold their hands during fluencemes more frequently in their L2 than in their L1, which may reflect a need in the L2 to hold different modalities (vocal and gestural) at the same time in order to put the interaction on hold and buy more time. This observation is also consistent with the prominence of the *VOC+VOC* pattern in the Americans' L1, which further reflects a different type of time-buying strategy at the vocal level.

Additionally, results showed that the two speaker groups produced a higher proportion of referential gestures in their L1 than in their L2 overall, which challenges the idea that speakers produce more referential gestures in their L2 to deal with lexical difficulties (e.g. Stam, 2001). This is further discussed in Section 3.2. Moreover, a large majority of the gestures found during fluencemes were pragmatic, and not referential, contrary to what the Lexical Retrieval Hypothesis (Krauss et al., 2000) suggests (cf Chapter 2, Section 1.1). In addition, it is worth noting that speakers produced a higher proportion of thinking gestures in their L2 than in their L1 (and almost exclusively during fluencemes), which may reflect one prominent feature of L2 (dis)fluency as a display of *doing thinking* (Heller, 2021, cf Chapter 6). Such gestures, along with thinking faces, were also examined in the qualitative analyses, and showed how they were used as an interactional practice to display the progressivity of a word search (Excerpts 1b and 2B). When it comes to gazing behavior, the two groups showed a tendency to withdraw their gaze during fluencemes (i.e. gaze away, or towards the piece of paper), and this was the case both in L1 and in L2, which demonstrates a notable feature of (dis)fluency in general, regardless of language proficiency.

To conclude, many inter-related features need to be taken into account when examining the relation between L1 and L2 fluency, from temporal variables and sequential features to visual-gestural behavior during fluencemes and outside fluencemes. Table 22 summarizes the different variables used to analyze the distribution of fluencemes and fluenceme sequences, as well as gaze and gestural behavior, across the two speaker groups. In sum, many differences can be found between the two speaker groups, as well as instances of individual variability which prevented some variables (i.e. duration, position, type, and length) to reach significance. What these results suggest is that specific aspects of L1 and L2 fluency do differ on some levels (i.e. frequency, form, type, length, configuration, gesture phrase and gesture rate), but not systematically across the two speaker groups, suggesting speaker-and language-specific patterns of behavior, in line with Gullberg (2011) and De Jong (2018). The most salient feature remains frequency, as nearly all speakers from both groups produced significantly more fluencemes in their L2 than their L1, as well as more gestures. This difference in frequency does not mean, however, that L2 fluency is necessarily associated with a lack of proficiency in the L2, but it can be further interpreted as a sign that non-native speakers require more stalling and repair strategies in their L2 to perform a variety of actions such as word search, planning, turn-taking or time-buying.

Chapter 4. Inter-(dis)fluency in native and non-native discourse   141

Table 22. Summary of (dis)fluency variables for the American and French group

		American group	French group	Inter-group differences
Fluenceme level	Rate	Higher rate in L2 than in L1	Higher rate in L2 than in L1	AM speakers produced a higher rate in their L2 than the FR
	Marker Type	More IR and FP in L2, more SI and UP in L1	More SI and PR in their L1, and more NL sounds in their L2	AM speakers produced more UP than FR speakers in L1, but FR speakers produced more FP in their L1 than AM speakers
	Form	More ums in L1 than L2	More uhs in L1 than L2	AM used um more often than the FR in their L1
	Duration	no significant differences	no significant differences	no significant differences
Sequence level	Type	more complex sequences in L2	no significant differences	no significant differences
	Lenght	higher number of markers combined in L2	no significant differences	no significant differences
	Configuration	more stalling strategies in L2 (VOC+VOC) and a combination of stalling and repair in L1 (VOC+MS)	higher proportion of VOC+MS pattern in L1	no significant differences
	Position	more instances of medial position in L2	more instances of final position in L1	no significant differences
Visual-gestural level	Gesture phrase	more holds in L2 than L1	more holds in L2 than L1	no significant differences
	Gesture production	more gestures in L2	more gestures in L2	no significant differences
	Gesture types and subtypes	more pragmatic gestures during fluencemes both L1 and L2, and more thinking gestures in L2	more pragmatic gestures during fluencemes both L1 and L2, and more thinking gestures in L2	no significant differences
	Gaze direction	more instances of gaze withdrawal during fluencemes (both L1 and L2)	more instances of gaze withdrawal during fluencemes (both L1 and L2)	FR speakers gazed towards paper more often than AM in L1, while AM speakers gazed away more frequently than the FR

4.2 How L2 learners deal with language difficulties: Beyond lexical retrieval

4.2.1 *L2 fluency anchored in language use*

Further in line with the framework of *CA-SLA* (Pekarek-Doehler, 2006) and the notion of interactional competence (Galaczi & Taylor, 2018) I claim that L2 competence, and to a larger extent L2 fluency, is not only the result of individual and internal cognitive processes related to encoding difficulties (e.g. Hilton, 2009) but may also constitute a relevant interactional tool for maintaining the fluency of the exchange (Peltonen, 2020). In this view, L2 speakers make use of a variety of features to deal with language difficulties in the course of the interaction. Even though vocal and verbal fluencemes remain the default mode (according to the scope of relevant behaviors (SRB) theory, cf Cienki, 2015a) for dealing with such difficulties (since they occur predominantly without gestures),I have shown specific instances during which speakers mobilized a combination of vocal and visual-gestural features to perform a series of actions, such as requesting help, putting the current speaking activity on hold, displaying the progressivity of the talk, and the like.

4.2.2 *The interplay of vocal, verbal, and visual-gestural resources in the multi-level ambivalence of fluencemes*

Following Graziano & Gullberg (2013, 2018) results showed that speakers produced predominantly more pragmatic gestures during fluencemes than referential ones both in L1 and L2, which makes it difficult to assess theories like the Lexical Retrieval Hypothesis (LRH) which claims that referential gestures facilitate access to lexical memory and compensate for speech failure. In this view, I do not believe that learners make use of referential gestures to compensate for a lack of skill or to activate a spatio-motoric mode of thinking (e.g. Kita, 2000), which would imply that such gestures accompanying fluencemes are exclusively based on internal processes reflecting models of speech production, thus completely disregarding interactional dynamics.[67]

While a lot of emphasis has been laid on the role of gestures as a window onto thought and cognition, facilitating access to mental spaces, working memory, or leading towards a different mode of thinking (e.g. Kita, 2000; McNeill, 1992; Stam, 2018; Sweetser, 2007) the present study focused more specifically on the communicative aspects of gestures, and their emergence in situated interaction (i.e. tandem settings), which can further our understanding of fluencemes and their interactional ambivalence (RQ4).

---

67. Read Kosmala (2020) for detailed qualitative analyses of representational gestures in the same data.

In addition, a majority of the fluenceme sequences performed Own Communication Management (henceforth OCM) both in L1 and L2, with only a small proportion of Interactive Communication Management (henceforth ICM) overall. This result may explain why a great number of studies on (dis)fluency have not explored their interactional quality in detail and rather focused on internal and cognitive processes, as the latter uncover a wider range of fluencemes. However, the fact that the interactional dimension of fluency has often been overlooked in past studies is also largely explained by the differences found in theoretical and methodological frameworks (cf Chapter 1). In line with McCarthy (2009); Peltonen (2020), and Pekarek-Doehler (2006), and further grounded in an multidisciplinary framework (cf Chapter 1, Section IV) the present study aims to bridge the gap between quantitative production-based (mostly psycholinguistic or phonetic) studies conducted on disfluency and usage-based, interactional, multimodal approaches to social interaction, to integrate different levels of analysis. In particular, we have seen that visual-gestural features played a certain role in the type of communication management, with a higher proportion of gestures found during ICM than OCM in L2 for the American group (however, no differences were found for the French group). This further questions the extent to which gaze and gesture may reflect the multi- layered ambivalence of fluencemes (RQ4): while certain highly complex fluencemes mark a significant suspension or interruption in the speech flow because of their length and complexity (speech DISfluency), they may also display relevant interactional work signaling that a search is currently being performed, and that it may require the partner's co-participation (interactional fluency). Such interactional displays are made visible with the help of mutual gaze and co-occuring gestures performing interactive functions (i.e. enact a stance, give the floor, perform a speech act, see Excerpts 2a and 2b). On the other hand, short vocal fluencemes that do not severely interrupt the flow of speech may in fact DISrupt the progressivity of the exchange (e.g. Excerpts 3a and 3b) if speakers are not oriented towards it.

Conclusion to the chapter

While the general aim of this chapter was to address differences between L1 and L2 fluency overall, in line with the SLA literature, the present study has shown several aspects of inter-(dis)fluency that go beyond the notions of L2 competence, proficiency, and accuracy, by integrating different variables (form, position, sequence complexity, visual-gestural behavior) and levels of analysis (speech, interaction, and gesture). This study corroborates previous findings in SLA, mainly that fluencemes are significantly more frequent in L2 than in L1, but we have also seen that they tend to form more complex sequences (for the American group), and that specific fluencemes or patterns are preferred in the L2, depending on the speaker group. Overall, findings have shown individual and language-specific differences, which calls for further investigation in other fields of research, such as phonetics, but which also stresses the impact of individual speaking style, in line with Gullberg (2011) and De Jong (2018). Given the size of the data, however, no general conclusions can be drawn, and the number of tendencies which were reported within fluency behavior may only be specific to my type of data (i.e. semi-guided interactions in tandem settings at a French university).

In addition, unlike previous work on gesture in SLA, the goal of this chapter was not to study the role of gestures in language learning specifically (i.e. Adams, 1998; Gullberg, 1998; Tellier, 2008a) or their role in cognition (i.e. Alibali et al., 2000; Kita, 2003; Stam, 2001), but rather to present ambivalent fluencemes as potential interactional components of L1 and L2 fluency, by examining their co-occurrence with visual and gestural behavior. Even though fluencemes tend not to co-occur extensively with gestures, a majority of gestures accompanying fluencemes perform pragmatic functions, which can be used by speakers to regulate the interaction and provide metacommunicative comments on their performance. While only a small percentage of fluencemes occurred in interactional contexts (18% approx.) it is still essential to provide a closer examination of such fluencemes in situated discourse in order to understand how they may contribute to the interactive flow. Qualitative examples have shown that they can be used as individual communication strategies, or in joint productions to negotiate meaning, and they are deployed differently by speakers, who make use of vocal fluencemes as well as gestures to resolve language difficulties and/or to maintain a speaker-hearer relationship, which is in line with Peltonen (2019) and McCarthy (2009). Once again, this underlines the interactional ambivalence of fluencemes and the fact that their usage is highly contextual and depends on a number of situational features.

However, some limitations in the study should be noted. As stated earlier, (e.g. Chapter 3, Section I.1.4) the size of the sample is relatively small compared to most corpus-based studies on L2 fluency, which makes it difficult to draw general conclusions, so the findings must be interpreted with caution. In addition, the statistical methods were rather "basic" as opposed to previous authors who used mixed-linear regression models (e.g. Graziano & Gullberg, 2018) or multiple correspondence analysis (e.g. Grosman et al., 2018) which make use of fixed and random effects (in the case of the linear mixed model) and further display the relationship between different variables (in the case of the multiple correspondence analysis). For future work, a more thorough statistical methodology should be applied to a larger sample of the data to perform a more robust quantitative analysis. However, it should be noted that the aim of the present study was to combine quantitative and qualitative analyses (cf Stivers, 2015), which has not been systematically done before in (dis)fluency research. This further motivated my choice to work on a small sample (cf Chapter 3, Section I.1.4). In addition, the present study focused more specifically on fluenceme sequences to explore their patterns of co-occurrence and accompanying visual-gestural behavior, but it did not analyze individual fluencemes in detail (except for the duration and form of certain markers). This drawback was already pointed out by Lopez-Ozieblo (2019) in a recent paper which examined different types of fluencemes (i.e. cuts-offs) and their co-occuring gestures. It will be helpful for future work to compare the production of the different fluencemes and their accompanying gestures in order to better capture the differences in L1 and L2 behavior.

CHAPTER 5

Inter-(dis)fluency across communication settings

This chapter presents the findings obtained from the DisReg corpus, covering "ordinary" versus "institutional" aspects of multimodal talk, comparing productions of French students in two different language styles and communication settings (i.e. class presentations versus face-to-face interactions, cf Chapter 3, Section I.1.3). As we have seen (cf Chapter 2, Section II), these differences cover many dimensions, ranging from the type of delivery, the degree of preparation, to other social factors (i.e. register and type of addressee). The main research question addressed in this chapter is whether all these inter-related factors do have an impact on the distribution of fluencemes and gestures, and, if it is the case, how it is manifested in both the vocal/verbal and visual-gestural channel.

This chapter is structured as follows: I first present research questions and hypotheses, some of which stem from the ones formulated in Chapters 1 and 3. In Sections II and III I present the quantitative and qualitative findings extracted from the annotations of the data, which, similarly tot the study of SITAF, integrates different levels of analysis (speech, visuo-gestural, and interactional) and mixes statistical and conversation-analytical methods. These findings are then discussed in Section III.

I. Research questions and hypotheses

This chapter aims to address other features, such as setting, register, or style, and their potential effect on fluency and gesture, following the literature review presented in Chapter 2 (Section II). My primary assumption is that all these features are interrelated and go beyond differences in mode or delivery (e.g. dialogue vs monologue, prepared vs spontaneous speech). My research questions are addressed below, followed by my hypotheses:

RQ1: Do style and setting play a role on (dis)fluency and gesture production?
– H1: In line with previous work on (dis)fluency (cf Chapter 2, Section II) I hypothesize that fluencemes are dynamic systems which are highly sensitive to situational factors, and are thus inevitably affected by style and setting. While they may also be affected by other variables (i.e. topic

difficulty or anxiety), these factors cannot be directly observed in the corpus since I did not manipulate (dis)fluency with task difficulty (as opposed to previous experimental studies, e.g. Hartsuiker & Notebaert, 2010), so the main focus will be on the effect of style and setting, as well as individual differences across speakers.
- **H2**: I expect speakers to constantly adjust their body and talk for their audience, and rely on a multiplicity of semiotic resources and diverse media to build meaning (stream of speech, body, material objects, etc.,) which will inarguably have an impact on their visual-gestural behavior.

RQ2: If (dis)fluency and gestures are influenced by these factors, how are these differences characterized?
- **H3**: Given the lack of interactivity and the temporal constraints imposed on oral presentations, more fluencemes are expected in institutional settings than in conversational ones. I do not believe that the distinction between "read" versus "spontaneous" speech will affect (dis)fluencies positively, i.e. read speech associated with fewer fluencemes (e.g. Goldman et al., 2010). Even though speakers were indeed reading their notes and their speech was prepared beforehand, they were not asked to simply "read aloud", but to give an actual performance, which still requires the student to be "spontaneous" at times, and deal with the planning of their discourse (Tottie, 2016).
- **H4**: I further hypothesize that the fluencemes produced during class presentations will be closely associated with planning and repair processes, with more instances of pauses (of longer duration). Since the presenters pay great attention to their own production, I also expect them to produce more morphological repairs (i.e., if they misread a word, they may wish to correct it).
- **H5**: I also predict that the mean length of utterance (MLU) would be longer in class presentations than in conversations, and I expect it to correlate with higher fluenceme rates (in line with Shriberg, 1994 and Oviatt, 1995).
- **H6**: Since gestures are one salient characteristic of social interaction, I expect fewer gestures in class presentations than conversations overall (following Bavelas et al., 2008), as well as differences in distribution, with more interactive gestures in conversation and more discursive gestures in class.

- H7: Fewer instances of mutual gaze are also expected in class presentations. I further predict that the students will predominantly gaze towards their notes written on a piece of paper, or laptop, which will be used as resources to maintain the continuity of their presentation (cf H9).

RQ3: Can we identify specific multimodal social practices that reflect these potential differences in style and setting? If yes, how would it influence the use of fluencemes?
- H8: In conversations, interactants rely on joint productions. Fluencemes will therefore occur more frequently in contexts of turn-taking where they embody visible displays of active participation in the talk, and occur in specific interpersonal contexts where speakers rely on shared experience, such as storytelling. Several of these fluencemes will reflect instances of Interactive Communication Management (ICM), hence reflecting the more communicative, fluent, side of inter-(dis)fluency.
- H9: In class presentations on the other hand, fluencemes will be used as a resource to deal with trouble in the talk, as students must find ways to deal with the temporality of their presentation within their material and spatial environment (their notes, their book, and the audience), as well as how to switch from different modes (reading and talking). Therefore, most of these fluencemes will reflect instances of Own Communication Management (OCM) reflecting the more production-oriented, DISfluent, side of inter-(dis)fluency.

II. Quantitative findings

The present analyses compare fluenceme rates, gesture distribution, and gaze behavior across two language styles and communication settings (formal class presentations in front of a classroom versus face-to-face dyadic casual conversations between friends). Just like Chapter 4, values are provided in raw/absolute and relative frequency (e.g. proportion or ratio), and the basis of normalization for the rate of fluencemes and gestures is *per hundred words* (henceforth phw).

2.1 Marker level: Rate, form, and duration of individual fluencemes

A total of 2870 fluencemes were annotated in the data, with 1472 tokens during class presentations, versus 1398 during face-to-face conversations. Figure 24[68] reports the rate of fluencemes per hundred words and per speaker in the two settings, and a test of log-likelihood indicated that these differences were significant statistically: the French students produced significantly more fluencemes overall during class presentations (28.4 phw) than during conversations (20.4 phw) ($LL = 325.38$, $p < 0.0001$).

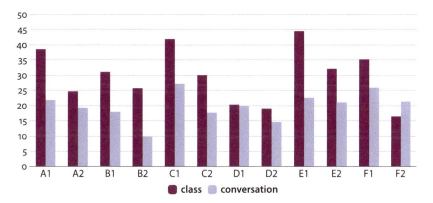

Figure 24. Rate of individual fluencemes per hundred words

Some individual differences can be noted. For instance, F2 is the only speaker who actually produced fewer fluencemes during the class presentation (16.5) than the conversation (21.4), and D1 produced about the same amount in the two situations (20.2 and 19.9). Others, like B2, produced considerably more fluencemes during the presentation (25.6) than when she was engaged in the interaction (9.7). In fact, she produced relatively few fluencemes during the conversation in comparison to the average in her group (20.4).

Table 23 identifies all the fluencemes that were annotated in the data (excluding additions which were extremely rare overall, $N = 5$). Results further show that the proportion of identical repetitions,[69] self-interruptions, and prolongations was significantly higher in conversations than class presentations, but the propor-

---

[68]. Raw frequencies are reported in Appendix 3, Table 57.
[69]. Note that the proportion of identical repetitions (based on the total number of fluencemes) is higher in conversations than in presentations, but they showed no differences in overall rate per hundred words (about 2.4 in both situations, cf Table 51 in Appendix 3). This shows that both situations may require about the same amount of fluencemes globally, but more fine-grained differences can be found within the structure of (dis)fluency.

tion of filled pauses and non-lexical sounds was higher during class presentations. Additionally, morphological repairs were slightly more frequent in class (0.9 per hundred words) than in conversation (0.4 per hundred words, $LL=9.39$, $p=0.01$, cf Table 52 in Appendix 3), as expected (cf H4) and unfilled pauses were found to have a higher rate per hundred words in class (6.7) than in conversation (4.7; $LL=21.15$, $p=0.001$) despite no differences in proportion. Overall, these differences in distribution confirm most of my hypotheses, and may reveal characteristics of institutional and conversational talk with regard to (dis)fluency; I will return to this point in Section IV.

Table 23. Proportion of fluencemes in class presentations and conversations[70]

	Class (raw)		Conversation (raw)		Z score	P value
Morpho-syntactic markers						
lexical repair	1.3%	(19)	1.1%	(16)	0.346	0.7
morphological repair	3.1%	(45)	2.1%	(29)	1.645	0.1
syntactic repair	3.4%	(44)	4%	(56)	−1.503	0.1
identical repetition	8.2%	(121)	11.6%	(161)	−2.997	0.002*
self-interruption	0.5%	(7)	3.2%	(45)	−5.521	< 0.0002*
truncated word	3.8%	(56)	4.5%	(63)	−0.963	0.3
Vocal markers						
filled pause	26.3%	(387)	20.2%	(281)	3.871	< 0.0002*
prolongation	11%	(162)	20.2%	(280)	−6.736	< 0.0002*
unfilled pause	23.4%	(345)	23%	(319)	0.341	0.7
Peripheral markers						
NL sound	18.9%	(278)	9.6%	(134)	7.103	< 0.0002*
explicit editing phrase	0.5%	(8)	0.8%	(11)	−1.22	0.2

Turning now to the duration of the vocal markers, the Shapiro-Wilk test revealed that neither filled pauses, unfilled pauses, nor prolongations had a normal distribution ($W=0.86$; $W=0.59$; $W=0.76$), so the duration values (aggregated per speaker) were submitted to a Wilcoxon test for comparison of means. Results show that, despite numerical evidence, no significant differences were found between the average duration of filled pauses during class presentations ($M=412$ ms, $SD=$

---

70. Just like Chapter 4, the rate of markers per hundred words can also be found in Appendix 3, Table 51. This table focuses on the proportion of fluencemes to highlight the different ways they are distributed compared to one another.

240 ms) and conversations ($M=340$ ms, $SD=199$ ms; $p=0.06$). Similarly, no significant differences were found for prolongations ($M=351$ ms, $SD=142$ ms in class; $M=350$ ms, $SD=155$ ms in conversation; $p=0.4$). Unfilled pauses, however, were found to be of longer duration in classroom settings ($M=695$ ms, $SD=543$ ms) than conversational ones ($M=594$ ms, $SD=323$ ms; $p=0.01$). Despite no significant differences in proportion (they represent about 23% of the total fluencemes both in class and in conversations), unfilled pauses show significant differences in duration and frequency. This may reflect one specific temporal feature of class presentations during which students rely on time-buying strategies to deal with their production. Just like the vocal fluencemes in SITAF (cf Chapter 3), the data shows a wide range of variation in the duration values,[71] as illustrated in the boxplots from Figure 25.

Filled pauses' duration values ranged from 60 ms to 1455 ms during the presentations, and 72 ms to 2085 ms during the conversations, with two outliers (i.e. data points) situated at a great distance from the median.[72] For the unfilled pauses, the values ranged from 255 ms (lowest outlier) to 4965 ms (highest outlier) during presentations, whereas during conversations the largest outlier is situated at 2220, which is almost 2000 ms below. Lastly, for the prolongations, a wider distribution is found during conversations, with values ranging from 105 ms to 2016 ms, as opposed to presentations which have a lower range (156 ms–1196 ms). In sum, filled pauses and prolongations show a much wider distribution during presentations, which may explain the lack of statistical significance between the two means, but unfilled pauses show almost the opposite tendency during presentations, with extremely high maximum values (up to 5 seconds, which is very far from the mean and the median). As we shall see, these very long silences, may reflect a *relevant absence of talk* (Hoey, 2015), during which students may go through their notes in a way that is relevant to pursue the next steps of their presentation. This is further elaborated in Section III.

Turning now to the distribution of filled pause types, Figure 26 reports the proportion of "euh" and "eum" across the two situations. Overall, the *euh* variant was the most widely used in both situations, but it was more frequent in conversation ($z=-5.144$, $p<0.0002$), as opposed to "eum" which was over twice as frequent in class ($z=5.144$, $p<0.0002$).

In the previous Chapter, I observed crosslinguistic differences in form distribution, which supported the view that filled pauses were essentially language-specific, and this finding provides additional evidence that their form is also sensitive to the type of situation.

---

[71]. The exact values are found in Tables 53, 54, and 55 in Appendix 3.
[72]. A second Wilcoxon test was conducted after removing these two extreme values, but the differences between the two means still did not reach significance ($p=0.06$).

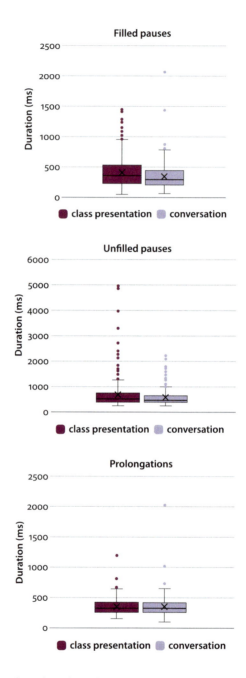

Figure 25. Duration of vocal markers during class presentations and conversations

Chapter 5. Inter-(dis)fluency across communication settings 153

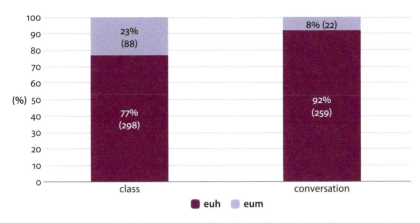

Figure 26. Proportion of filled pause types ("euh"/"eum") in class and conversation

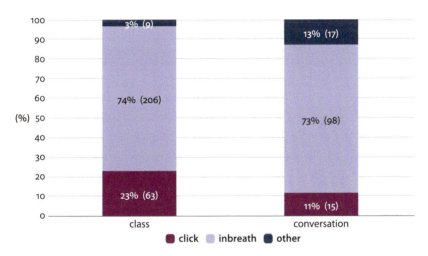

Figure 27. Proportion of NL sounds in class and conversation

Figure 27 illustrates the proportion of the different non-lexical sounds per type (audible inbreaths, tongue clicks, and other). There is a greater proportion of tongue clicks in class (23%) than in conversation (11%), and this was found to be statistically significant ($z=2.783$; $p=0.005$). In addition, the proportion of non-lexical sounds, i.e. laughter, sigh, creaks (see Table 56 in Appendix 3) was greater in conversation than in class ($z=-3.695$; $p=0.002$). The proportion of audible inbreaths, however, did not differ significantly across the two situations ($z=0.048$, $p=0.9$). These differences in distribution may further reflect specificities of oral presentations versus face-to-face interactions: while inbreaths are common across the two situations, the proportion of clicks was found to be higher in class, while other types of non-lexical sounds, which are perhaps more typical of social interactions, were more frequent in conversation.

Table 24 reports the mean length of utterance (MLU) per speaker in the two settings. The data showed a normal distribution ($W=0.96$), so a two-paired t-test was conducted to compare the differences between the two samples. Results show that speakers produced significantly longer utterances during their presentations than during the conversations ($t(11)=5.308$, $p=0.0002$), which can be explained by the lack of interactivity in presentations which leads to fewer interruptions, and may hence result in longer utterances. This may also explain the high rate of fluencemes found in presentations, which could reflect the effect of utterance complexity on (dis)fluency (in line with McLaughlin & Cullinan, 1989). However, a Pearson Correlation Coefficient was computed to test the potential positive relationship between fluenceme rate and utterance length, but it did not reach significance ($r=0.37$, $p=0.07$).

Table 24. Mean length of utterance per speaker in class and conversation

Speaker	Class presentations		Conversations	
	MLU	SD	MLU	SD
A1	12.6	1.5	10.2	7.8
A2	15.9	6.8	8.3	5.9
B1	11.9	7.1	10	8.5
B2	13.8	5.8	12.3	7.9
C1	15.5	9.3	8.2	6.8
C2	16.8	9.7	10.6	8.3
D1	19.5	8.3	8.9	11
D2	14.7	7.4	6.5	5.7
E1	13.3	6.2	9.4	9.3
E2	12.3	6.5	13.2	8.1
F1	20	11.1	10.8	8.9
F2	13.1	6.2	7.3	7.9
Total	14.7	7.4	9.6	8

This shows that despite a higher rate of fluencemes and a longer length of utterances in class, these two variables are not necessarily related in the data. Given the significant differences found in the duration of unfilled pauses (cf Figure 25), an additional test was conducted to measure the relationship between the mean duration of unfilled pauses and the mean length of utterance, and this time, a moderate positive correlation ($r=0.52$, $p=0.0008$) was found between utterance length and unfilled pause duration, as illustrated in the scatter plot (Figure 28).

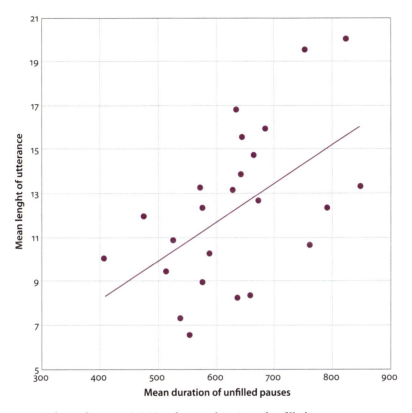

Figure 28. Relation between MLU and mean duration of unfilled pauses

Although it does not show a perfect positive correlation, the data still indicates a tendency for unfilled pauses to last longer when speakers produce longer utterances. This further reflects specific temporal characteristics of class conversations, characterized by lengthy utterances and long pauses, among other processes described in the following sections.

2.2 Sequence level: Type, length, position, and patterns of co-occurrence

A total of 1576 sequences was identified, with 759 in class presentations, and 817 in conversations. Figure 29 illustrates the proportion of simple versus complex sequences in the two settings.

156   Beyond Disfluency

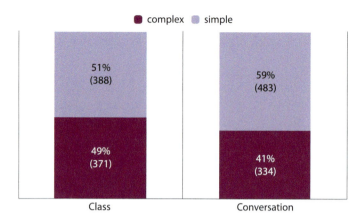

Figure 29. Proportion of simple and complex sequences in class and conversation

A slightly higher proportion of complex sequences is found in class (49%) than in conversation (41%; $z=3.91$, $p=0.001$). This indicates that, in addition to longer utterances and pauses, class conversations are also characterized by more complex sequences, in line with Moniz (2014), and this variable is shown to have an effect on setting; $\chi^2(1, N=1576)=10.1$, $p=0.001$. However, no significant differences are found in the average number of markers found within these sequences, as illustrated in the boxplot[73] in Figure 30. As the Shapiro-Wilk test revealed, the values were not normally distributed ($W=0.67$) so a Wilcoxon test was performed to measure differences between the two samples. On average, speakers combined 2.9 markers ($SD=1.3$) during their class presentations, ranging from 2 to 11, and during the conversations they combined 2.7 markers on average ($SD=1.1$), ranging from 2 to 9, which is not a significant difference ($p=0.6$).

However, a few individual differences can be found: for instance, A1 produced fewer clustered markers during his presentation (2.8) than when engaged in the interaction (3.7), while F1 did the opposite, and produced longer sequences during her presentation (3.3) than the conversation (2.7).

Table 25 reports the proportion of the different sequence configurations across the two settings. Two main patterns emerge, and reveal significant differences in the two situations, mainly *VOC+MS* and *VOC+NL*. Once more, class presentations and face-to-face conversations exhibit differences within the structure of (dis)fluency, with half of the fluenceme sequences composed of vocal and morphosyntactic markers in conversation, as opposed to 30% in class.

This pattern seems to be fairly recurrent, and may reflect a tendency in French conversation to combine stalling and repair strategies in order to (co)-construct

---

73. The exact values are found in Table 57, Appendix 3.

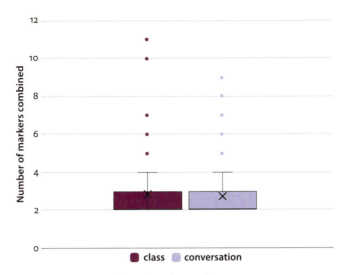

Figure 30. Range of markers combined in class and conversation

Table 25. Proportion of sequence configurations in class and conversation

Seq. conf.	Class (raw)		Conversation (raw)		Z score	P value
MIX	2%	7	3%	10	−0.957	0.3
MS+MS	6%	23	7%	22	−0.21	0.8
MS+NL	1%	5	1%	4		N/A
NL+NL	1%	4	0%	0		N/A
VOC+MS	30%	113	49%	164	−5.061	<0.0002*
VOC+MS+NL	8%	28	6%	21	0.657	0.5
VOC+NL	32%	118	13%	43	5.979	<0.0002*
VOC+VOC	20%	73	21%	70	−0.423	0.6

discourse. In fact, it is interesting to note that this pattern was also used about 50% of the time by the French speakers in their L1 in the SITAF corpus (See Chapter 4)

During class presentations, however, speakers equally made use of two patterns, mainly *VOC+MS* and *VOC+NL*, and the latter has a much higher proportion in class (32%) than in conversation (13%). This is a striking result, which further accounts for the prevalence of vocalizations, such as clicks and inbreaths, in class presentations. The latter, along with other vocal markers, such as (un)filled pauses and prolongations, seem to play a major role in the fluency of presentations; they may be used to mark discourse structure, index a new sequence of talk, or project an upcoming delay.

Lastly, Table 26 shows the different utterance positions of fluenceme sequences across the two situations. Fluencemes occurred slightly more frequently in initial position in class (43%) than in conversation (37%), but they were more frequent in final position in conversation. This further reflects the degree of interactivity and turn-taking mechanisms found in face-to-face interactions, where speakers are more likely to produce utterance-final fluencemes to cede the floor. During presentations, on the other hand, speakers may prefer to produce utterance-initial fluencemes for planning purposes at the macro level.

Table 26. Utterance position of fluenceme sequences in class and conversation

Seq. position	Class (raw)		Conversation (raw)		Z score	P value
final	3%	22	11%	91	−6.335	< 0.002*
interrupted	0%	0	2%	19		N/A
initial	43%	326	37%	302	2.246	0.01*
medial	54%	410	48%	396	2.202	0.02*
standalone	0%	1	1%	9		N/A

So far, I have noted a number of significant differences across the two situations, mainly a higher rate of fluencemes, longer pauses, a slightly higher proportion of complex sequences, as well as specific combinatory and positional patterns. I will summarize these findings at the end of this section, moving now to the visuo-gestural level of analysis.

2.3 Visuo-gestural level: Gesture production and gaze behavior

Table 27 reports the rate of fluencemes during phases of gestural action (Kendon, 2004) in class and conversation. Speakers overwhelmingly kept their hand in rest position when they produced fluencemes in both situations (about 67% of the time), which is consistent with the findings from the SITAF corpus (cf Chapter 4). This is further confirmed by the proportion of gestures found during utterances produced with fluencemes and outside fluencemes, which shows that a majority of gestures were produced without fluencemes both in class and in conversation, as illustrated in Figure 31.

However, unlike the previous study on native and non-native productions, no significant differences are found in the distribution of gestures and gesture phases between the two settings, whether they co-occurred with fluencemes or not. This may reveal that while language proficiency may have an effect on the type of gestural behavior accompanying fluencemes, setting and style seem to have very lit-

Table 27. Distribution of fluenceme sequences during gesture phases in class and conversation

	Class (raw)		Conversation (raw)		Z score	P value
stroke	14%	107	15%	120	−0.545	0.5
hold	12%	88	9%	71	1.913	0.05
preparation	8%	58	6%	46	1.607	0.1
rest position	63%	478	67%	551	−1.86	0.06
retraction	4%	29	3%	27	0.553	0.5

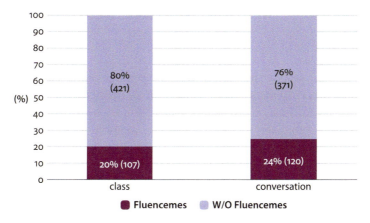

Figure 31. Proportion of gestures that occurred in utterances with or without fluencemes in class and conversation

tle. However, this table only gives information about the types of gesture phases that typically co-occur with fluencemes, which only offers a partial view of the gestural practices characterizing class presentations and face-to-face interactions. This needs to be completed with information regarding the distribution of all gestures, regardless of fluency, which is provided in Figure 32.

Students produced 10.2 gestures phw on average during their class presentations ($N=528$) and 7.6 phw during the conversations ($N=491$), which is a significant difference ($LL=20.46$, $p<0.0001$). Contrary to my expectations (H5, cf Section I) students produced significantly more gestures when they performed a monologic task than a dialogic one, which further refutes Bavelas et al., (2008)'s findings that speakers produce more gestures in dialogue than in monologue.

This further demonstrates that mode of speech alone is not sufficient to characterize differences between formal class presentations and casual interactions. Unlike Bavelas et al.'s (2008) study, the students from the DisReg corpus did have

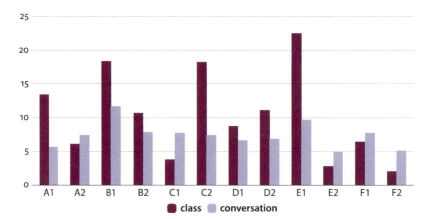

Figure 32. Rate of gesture strokes (phw) in class and conversation

an audience, and despite the lack of interactivity between the speaker and the group of hearers, it appears that a majority of students still produced gestures like they would do in a conversation, which is more in line with Sweetser & Sizemore (2008). However, this needs to be confirmed by looking at the specific types of gestures that were most frequently deployed in the two situations, which is provided in Table 28 further below. In addition, as Figure 32 shows, a number of individual differences are found, as students display very different gesturing behaviors: while some (i.e. A1, B1, C2, and E1) mobilized a significant amount of gestures to deliver their presentations, others (i.e. F2, E2 and C2), showed the opposite tendency. This further demonstrates that speakers have their own stylistic idiosyncrasies, which reflects their own individual language style when it comes to fluency and gesturing behavior, regardless of setting or register.

Table 28 provides more information about the distribution of gesture types and subtypes in class and conversation. Overall, students produced significantly more pragmatic gestures in class than in conversation, especially discursive ones (i.e., gestures used for presentation and emphasis) which represent 83% of all their gestures. Conversely, they mobilized a higher proportion of referential gestures in conversation than in class, and especially representational ones (17% in conversation versus 4% in class).

Additionally, students produced considerably more interactive gestures when they were engaged in the conversational task, which is not surprising, given the lack of interactivity in class presentations, which offers little room for communicative gestures. Interestingly, students produced an equal amount of thinking gestures in the two situations, which represent a very small proportion (3%) of all the gestures overall. Similarly, in the SITAF corpus, thinking gestures amounted to about 3–4% of all the gestures in L1 in the two speaker groups, but significant

Table 28. Proportion of gesture types and subtypes in class and conversation

	Class		Conversation		Z score	P value
	Referential gestures % (raw)					
	17%	(89)	36%	(175)	−6.822	< 0.002*
representational	4%	(21)	17%	(85)	−0.1333	< 0.002*
deictic-anaphoric	13%	(68)	18%	(90)	−2.389	0.01*
	Pragmatic gestures % (raw)					
	83%	(439)	64%	(316)	6.9	< 0.002*
discursive	69%	(363)	22%	(108)	14.992	< 0.002*
interactive	11%	(60)	39%	(191)	−10.178	< 0.002*
thinking	3%	(16)	3%	(17)	0.384	0.7

differences were found in their distribution in L1 and L2. It would appear that in the case of DisReg, setting, unlike language proficiency, did not have a strong effect on these gestures.

Table 29 gives more information about the distribution of gesture subtypes[74] based on whether they occurred with or without fluencemes, across the two settings.

Table 29. Proportion of gesture subtypes with or without fluencemes in class and conversation

	Class					Conversation				
	Fluencemes		W/O		Z (p)	Fluencemes		W/O		Z (p)
deictic-anaphoric	8%	9	14%	59	−1.51 (0.1)	12%	14	20%	76	−2.17 (0.03*)
representational	5%	5	4%	16	0.41 (0.6)	28%	33	14%	52	3.39 (0.0007*)
discursive	69%	73	69%	299	0.04 (0.9)	20%	24	23%	84	−0.60 (0.5)
interactive	4%	4	13%	56	N/A	27%	32	43%	159	−3.16 (0.001*)
thinking gesture	14%	15	0%	1	N/A	14%	17	0%	0	N/A

---

74. Information regarding the distribution of the two main gesture types (referential and pragmatic) can be found in Figure 41, Appendix 3.

Not many differences are found in the distribution of gestures during fluencemes and outside fluencemes in class presentations, except for thinking gestures that virtually never occurred outside of fluencemes. In conversations, however, we find a number of differences, with a higher proportion of deictic-anaphoric gestures without fluencemes (20%) than with them (12%), but more representational gestures during fluencemes (28%) than without them (14%). Lastly, a higher proportion of interactive gestures are found outside fluencemes. Overall, these findings reveal a significant association between gesture type and setting; χ^2 (1, $N=1019) = 247.1$, $p < 0.00001$).

In addition, if we further compare the two settings, results show that students produced more interactive gestures during fluencemes in conversation than in class, as well as more representational gestures ($z = -4.57$, $p < 0.0002$), but they produced more discursive gestures during fluencemes in class ($z = 7.407$, $p < 0.0002$). This is the same pattern of distribution described earlier (cf Table 28), which reviewed the proportion of gestures found in presentations and conversations. This further confirms that, regardless of (dis)fluency, a certain category/type of gestures is preferred in a specific setting, reflecting a number of situational factors, such as audience design (interactants are more likely to deploy interactive gestures in a conversation because of their familiar relationship), or style (students need to deliver a clear presentation and they may do so with the help of discursive gestures).

Figure 33 reports the proportion of different gaze directions in class and conversation, excluding "in different directions" and "towards camera"[75] which were too rare overall (the exact values are found in Table 59, Appendix 3). Students spent nearly 70% of their time gazing towards their notes (or laptop, book etc.,) during the class presentations, and only looked in direction of their audience 27% of the time. Conversely, during the interactions, speakers gazed considerably more frequently towards their interlocutor (58%, $z = 43.798$, $p < 0.0002$). It is also interesting to note that they gazed more frequently away during the interactions (27%) than the presentations (4%, $z = -24.98$, $p < 0.0002$). This is a surprising result, as it is very common to withdraw one's gaze when engaged in an interactional practice, as to display a state of disengagement, a word search, or the end of a sequence, among other actions (e.g. Goodwin & Goodwin, 1986; Kendon, 1967; Rossano, 2013; Streeck, 2014).

---

75. It is interesting to note that 25 instances of gazing towards the camera were found during the class presentations, while it happened only once during the conversations (see Table 59 in Appendix 3). The students were asked explicitly not to look in direction of the investigator (who was holding the camera) to avoid being distracted, but it appeared that some students could not help doing so while they were delivering their presentation; perhaps it was a way for them to include the investigator in the audience.

Chapter 5. Inter-(dis)fluency across communication settings 163

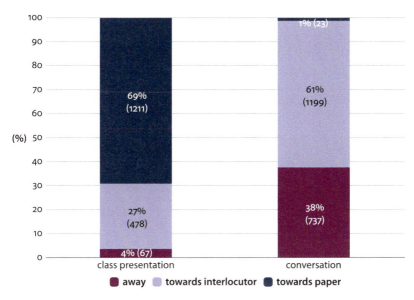

Figure 33. Proportion of gaze direction in class and conversation

This finding may reveal that looking away is a pattern of gazing more commonly found in face-to-face conversations rather than formal class presentations. Perhaps presenters did not want to be seen gazing away by their audience, which could potentially reflect a loss of face or control over their presentation; or perhaps they did not find it necessary to gaze away, since they were extensively relying on their notes.

Overall, there seems to be a mismatch between the students' gesturing and gazing behavior. While they gestured quite frequently during their presentations, and even more frequently than they did during the conversations, they constantly gazed towards their notes, suggesting that they were barely orienting to their audience and were much more focused on performing the task at hand. The latter seems to have a significant effect on gazing behavior, and this was confirmed by a chi-square test of independence which showed a significant relationship between gaze direction and setting; χ^2 (1, $N=3715$) = 206.9, $p < 0.00001$.

Figure 34 illustrates the proportion of gaze direction within and outside fluencemes. In class presentations, we find a higher proportion of gazing towards the piece of paper during fluencemes ($z = 5.602$, $p < 0.0002$), but a higher proportion of gazing towards the interlocutor without them ($z = -6.542$, $p < 0.0002$). Overall, these findings account for a strong association between fluency and gaze direction (χ^2 (1, $N=1756$, $p < 0.0001$). Similarly, in conversations, a slightly higher proportion of gazing towards the interlocutor is found without fluencemes ($z = -6.26$; $p < 0.0002$) but the proportion of gaze withdrawals is greater during fluencemes ($z = 6.407$, $p < 0.0002$).

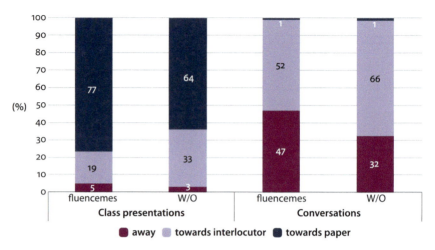

Figure 34. Proportion of gaze direction with and without fluencemes in class and conversation

Overall, these findings show that speakers were more likely *not* to establish eye contact when they produced fluencemes in both situations, which is consistent with the findings from the SITAF corpus where the two language groups were found to withdraw their gaze more frequently during fluencemes both in their L1 and L2 (see Chapter 4). This further emphasizes the fact that gazing away is a very common practice of (dis)fluency, as it enables speakers to momentarily retreat from the current activity to attend to other relevant ones, such as retrieving an item from memory, looking for a specific word, checking for a sentence in a book, etc. Additionally, speakers gazed towards their interlocutor significantly more frequently during fluencemes in conversation than in class ($z = -12.952$, $p < 0.0002$). This further shows that, even though gazing away is a common activity during fluencemes, it varies significantly depending on the situation. Once more, this accounts for the dynamic and fluid nature of fluencemes that are constantly being (re)shaped by local and global situational features.

To conclude, this section has outlined several differences regarding (dis)fluency and visible bodily behavior in two distinct communication settings and language styles, i.e. formal class presentations and casual interactions. As we have seen, these two situations cannot be solely distinguished on the basis of type of delivery (read versus spontaneous) or mode of speech (dialogue versus monologue) since the findings have shown a greater rate of fluencemes and gestures in class presentations, which reveals that the latter is not necessarily characterized by carefully read speech and a total lack of interactivity, as is often expected of "monologues".

In sum, many significant differences were found in the two situations, which are briefly summarized in Table 30. These findings, which are discussed in Section IV, give an overall idea of the rate, form, and distribution of fluencemes, as well as the frequency and distribution of gestures and gazing behavior. In addition, many individual differences were found across the two settings, further reflecting individual speaking styles and idiosyncrasies. These differences are further highlighted in the following section.

Table 30. Summary of the quantitative findings

	Class presentations	Conversations
VOCAL-VERBAL FEATURES (FLUENCEMES)		
Fluenceme rate	Higher rate in class presentations than conversations	
Distribution	more NL sounds, filled pauses and longer unfilled pauses (correlated with utterance lenght)	more repetitions, interruptions and prolongations
Filled pause type	more eum-type filled pauses	more euh-type filled pauses
Combination type	more complex sequences	more simple sequences
Utterance position	more instances of utterance-initial fluencemes	more utterance-final fluencemes
VISUAL-GESTURAL FEATURES (WITHIN AND OUTSIDE FLUENCEMES)		
Gesture rate	Higher rate in class presentations than conversations	
Gesture distribution	more pragmatic gestures overall, and more discursive gestures (with and without fluencemes)	more referential gestures overall, and more interactional gestures (with and without fluencemes)
	no significant differences for thinking gestures but occurred almost exclusively during fluencemes	
Gaze behavior	more instances of gazing towards piece of paper (with and without fluencemes)	more instances of gazing away and towards the interlocutor (with and without fluencemes

III. Qualitative analyses

In this section, I further explore the differences between formal class presentations and casual face-to-face conversations in relation to inter-(dis)fluency by presenting a number of micro-analyses from the data. Just like Chapter 4, I begin with an overview of their distribution with regard to *communication management* in the two situations, and further explore the functional and interactional ambivalence of fluencemes across the two situations. I then present several analyses from selected excerpts of the data to further illustrate the multimodality and multifunctionality of inter-(dis)fluency with regard to audience design, common ground and participation framework. Just like Chapter 4, the participants were assigned pseudonyms specifically in this section to render the exchanges more authentic.

3.1 Overview of Communication Management in the two situations

Figure 35 reports the proportion of fluencemes with ICM and OCM functions in class and conversation. Only 1% of the fluencemes performed the ICM function during the class presentations, as opposed to 27% in the conversations. This result is very striking, although not surprising, given the interactional constraints imposed on the presentations. Unlike the previous study on the SITAF corpus which showed no significant differences between L1 and L2, here the data suggests a strong effect of setting on the functions of fluencemes $\chi^2(N(1) = 1756, p < 00001)$, thus giving more support to their ambivalent nature. This is illustrated in the next subsection which focuses on tongue clicks.

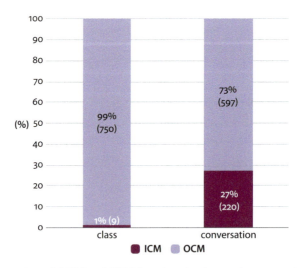

Figure 35. Proportion of OCM and ICM functions in class and conversation

3.2 The case of tongue clicks: Blending vocal and kinetic behaviors

Tongue clicks (*tsk, ttut*) can be described phonetically as "a click articulated with the tongue tip, with central release which is generally slow and affricated" (Ogden, 2013, p. 302). Additionally, clicks are often associated with a number of visible and kinetic behaviors, such as eyebrow flashes, or swallowing (Ogden, 2020, 2018) and manual gestures (Pinto & Vigil, 2019), which further accounts for their multimodality. However, while a lot of work has been done on tongue clicks in Conversation Analysis and phonetics, their analysis is virtually absent from (dis)fluency research, as they have not traditionally been labeled as fluencemes. Yet, quantitative results have shown that tongue clicks, among other vocalizations and breathing phenomena, often cluster with other fluencemes, so they should not be overlooked. In the next examples, I further explore their functional ambivalence, and the different ways they may contribute to the fluency of multimodal discourse.

Excerpt 1.1 CLASS

This excerpt is taken from Jenny's (D2) presentation in class about a French novel which tells the story of a man, named Barnaba, who has become fond of paintings after becoming blind. Here she is analyzing the ways one particular painting becomes a key figure in the life of Barnaba.

```
  1   c:c'est une figure presque obsessionelle à laquelle i [//] il
      i:it's almost a quasi obsessional figure to which e [//] he
      revient toujours.
      always come back to
→ 2   (0.649) [!] hhh. c'est donc un point de départ dans le musée
      ~~ ~ ~~~~ ~ ~~~~
      (0.649) [!] hhh. it is thus a starting point in the museum
   ((parted lips, eyebrow flash, swallowing activity, open mouth, right hand
   preparation))
```

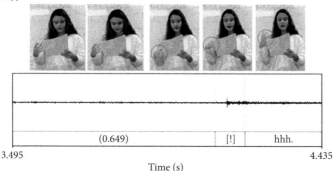

The tongue click occurs in line 2, clustered with an unfilled pause of 649 ms and an audible inbreath. This complex fluenceme sequence, following the *VOC+NL* pattern, is produced in initial position, and projects a new sequence of talk which marks the conclusion of her current argument (the fact that this painting is a recurrent theme in the character's life). This new stretch of talk is also made visible in her visual-gestural behavior, as we can see her opening her mouth and moving her right hand in preparation during the audible inbreath, following the tongue click. The latter is clearly visible in the waveform, as clicks tend to be relatively "loud transient sounds" (Ogden, 2013, p.307).[76] It is also surrounded by silence and an inhalation, during which the speaker deploys several physical actions; we can see her swallowing, flashing her eyebrows, and slightly frowning prior to the production of the click. As Ogden (2013) explained, clicks can be regarded as the culmination of a swallow, which, along with breathing, are basic activities that are closely associated to their production in English conversation. A very similar pattern of distribution was also found here, during a French oral presentation, which calls for more crosslinguistic comparisons.

In the following excerpt, with the same speakers (Jenny and Alex, pair D) engaged in the interactional task, we find another instance of a tongue click, but this time initiated at the beginning of a turn, in response to a prior one.

Excerpt 2.1 Conversation

In this excerpt, the two friends are talking about a TV show that Jenny highly recommends to Alex, although she has not watched it yet. They are also talking about two actors, Yvan Attal (not included in the transcription) and Neil Schneider, who both play in the show.

```
     6  *ALX:     parce-qu'il joue dedans aussi lui?
                  because he also plays in the show?
     7  *JEN:     (0.531) hhh. euh ouais.
                  (0.531) hhh. euh yeah.
     8  *ALX:     (0.631) mais il a un rôle euh (0.924) +…
                  (0.631) but he has a role euh (0.924) +…
  → 9  *JEN:     [!] je sais pas je l'ai pas vu encore.
                  [!] I don't know I haven't seen it yet
        ((gazes away, smacks her lips))((gazes towards ALX; raised eyebrows))
```

---

76. As pointed out several times in this book, the present study does not aim to extensively explore the phonetic aspects of tongue clicks and other fluencemes, but rather focuses on local durational, phonetic, or intonational patterns and the way they synchronize with other types of bodily behavior.

Chapter 5. Inter-(dis)fluency across communication settings 169

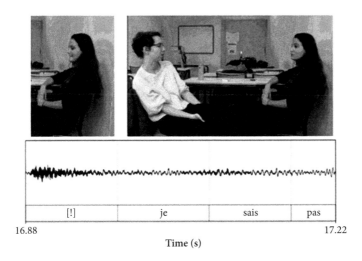

The tongue click occurs in line 9 in turn-initial position, following Alex's invitation to take the turn and elaborate on the show. Here the click prefaces Jenny's lack of knowledge in the form of a non-response "je sais pas" (*I don't know*), suggesting a dispreferred next action. This is further displayed in her visible behavior, as she is seen raising her eyebrows, and slightly pouting, shortly after producing the non-response. In this case, the click displayed epistemic stance, but also indexed the next turn-at-talk, following a transition relevant place in the prior turn. Once again, this further shows that the same forms can follow different patterns of distribution, and occur at different positions within the turns-at-talk, hence displaying radically different functions. In the two previous excerpts from the class presentations, the clicks were mostly used to index a new sequence of talk while the presenters were going through their notes and presenting their next argument; in this excerpt, however, the click was used as a response to a prior turn, hence more oriented towards the ongoing exchange. While the different types of practices underlying the uses of clicks in conversation have already been documented several times before (e.g. Ogden, 2013, 2018; Wright, 2005; 2011), they have almost never been analyzed within the scope of (dis)fluency. Just like other fluencemes, clicks have the potential to serve both production-oriented (OCM) and more interaction-oriented (ICM) functions, depending on the setting and style used. The interactional contribution of fluencemes is further described in the following section.

3.3 Embodied displays of intersubjectivity in storytelling: The interactive dimension of fluencemes

In the conversation-sessions, the students were given a sheet of paper with a list of topics written on it beforehand, to help them start the conversation. One the topics included "amusing anecdote at university", and while this topic of conversation was not covered by all the students, two pairs (Pairs B and D) found it relevant to bring it up in the course of their interaction. The following excerpts are thus taken from the recordings of these pairs. The two extracts are rather long, so several lines are omitted from the transcription.

Excerpt 2.2 The funny-looking shoes

In this extract, Paul (B1) is retelling an amusing encounter he had with a staff member of the university at the beginning of his undergraduate program, who was wearing five FiveFinger shoes at his office. These shoes, which are typically found in outdoor activities, look very unusual and rather ludicrous, as they are designed in a way that shows all individual toes. In this excerpt, Paul takes on different viewpoints through his gaze behavior and body movement to make the scene quite dramatic and very humorous. He begins by setting the scene where the event took place by describing where he was sitting and how he came to see these funny looking shoes and then acts out the entire encounter as if it was a play, by re-enacting, and re-voicing (Goffman, 1981) the dialogue between himself and the "protagonist" of his story. While there are many fluencemes and gestures in this excerpt, I will focus on four particular moments in the interaction (marked by the arrows in the transcription) that are of interest for the present section.

```
→ 1 *PAUL: euh c'était un secrétaire alors c'était l'année où euh +//.
           euh he was a secretary so it was the year when euh +//.
                              ((gazes away))
  2 *PAUL: le saviez vous (0.286)?
           did you know (0.286) ?
                   *******
           ((gazes towards Paula, with index finger from his right hand oriented
   towards Paula))
```

Chapter 5. Inter-(dis)fluency across communication settings   171

```
  3 *PAULA:      (laughs)
  4 *PAUL: l'année dernière ils ont viré tous les (laughs) [/] tous les secrétaires
         last year they laid off all the (laughs) [/] all the secretaries
((lines omitted from the transcription))
  5 *PAUL: donc du coup ce mec qui malheureusement a été viré après
         so this guy who unfortunately got fired later
parce-qu'il était génial s'appelait XX.
because he was great was called XX.
→ 6 *PAUL: [!] (0.400) salut.
         [!] (0.400) hey
                ***********
```

((looks down, index finger from his right hand pointed upwards))

```
  7 *PAULA:      ((laughs))
→ 8 *PAUL: euh il euh [/] il se baladait avec des eum [/] des euh je
  euh he euh [/] he was walking around with some eum [/] some euh I
sais pas si tu vois les [/] le:es [//] des gants de pieds.
I don't know if you know the [/] the:e [///] five finger shoes.
                        *******************************
```

((left POH facing down, extended opposite him, gazes towards his hand))

```
  9 *PAUL:          +< c'est des chaussures avec le:es euh voilà
                   +< they're shoes with the:e eum you know
                              **************
```

((extends index finger to draw a series of circles in the air while moving to the
left; smiles & gazes at Laura))

```
                    avec les orteils.
                    with the toes
10 *PAULA:      +< ah oui je vois très bien c'est celles avec les orteils.
                +< ah yeah I see perfectly it's the ones with the toes
```

Before describing the "protagonist" of his story (the staff member) in detail, Paul first digresses from his initial story to offer a contextual frame, i.e. the background of the event. We can thus observe an interruption within his discourse (l.2) at different levels, i.e., at the *narrative* level, as he abruptly changes the course of his story; at the *syntactic* level, as he interrupts the delivery of his verbal utterance (l. 3) with a complex fluenceme sequence made of a filled pause and a self-interruption; and at the *interactional* level, as he re-shapes the trajectory of his current action by addressing his interlocutor and an imaginary audience ("le saviez-vous"?, l. 2). This "catchline", *le saviez-vous* (*Did you know*?) further contributes to the humorous and dramatic dimension of his story. It is a fixed expression which is often found in Trivia articles[77] advertising jingles, or showcases, and introduces well-known world facts, "mind-blowing" or "fun" facts to a large audience. By uttering this very specific expression, Paul takes on an entirely different discourse identity, by playing the role of a television host at a talk show, addressing an imaginary audience (which includes Paula). This interactional strategy is further reflected in his visual-gestural behavior, as he initiates an interactive gesture immediately after interrupting his verbal utterance, with his index finger slightly oriented towards Paula. This gesture, even though it shares close formational characteristics with deictic gestures (because of the pointing) is considered *interactive* in this case, and belongs to the subcategory of "delivery" gestures, according to Bavelas et al. (1995), i.e. gestures used to "hand over information relevant to his or her main point" (Bavelas et al., 1995, p. 397). The stroke and retraction of the gesture synchronizes with a pause of 286 milliseconds produced in utterance-final position. In sum, the interruption (l.3) or the pause (l.4) are, once more, merely

---

77. Note a similar expression in English, with for example the headline of this article (https://www.rd.com/list/did-you-know-facts-most-people-dont-know/) *Did-you-know Facts That Are Almost Hard to Believe* (last retrieved on August 26th 2021).

Chapter 5. Inter-(dis)fluency across communication settings   173

a sign of "disfluency" per se, but constitute relevant interactional actions which contribute to the humorous dimension of his narrative.

In line 6, another instance of interactional fluency is found, marked by the pause and the tongue click. After describing how a lot of staff members were fired (according to Paul) that year (omitted from the transcription), Paul re-introduces the protagonist (who was also reportedly laid off from the university)[78] who plays a major part in his narrative. Once again, Paul is not only retelling an anecdote, he is dramatizing it, by addressing the protagonist directly ("salut" / *hey*) with a solemn tone, as if he was paying a tribute. He produces a second pragmatic gesture with the same hand configuration as before (index finger extended), but this time he is looking down, and raising his hand and finger upward. This gesture has already been documented as part of a repertoire of German recurrent gestures (see Bressem & Müller, 2014, p. 1583) and is said to draw attention of other participants to particular important topics. Once again, this gesture is manifested during a fluenceme sequence, which further reflects the multimodal and pragmatic dimension of inter-(dis)fluency. In addition, the fluenceme sequence marks a shift in the current status of the co-participant, who does not appear to be Paula anymore, but the staff member from the story, hence reflecting a complex participation framework involving multiple participants (Goodwin & Goodwin, 2004).

Now that Paul has rightly introduced the main character of his story, he shifts back to his status of conversational co-participant in order to build meaning around the funny looking shoes, by extending his left palm open hand downwards, and rapidly wiggling his fingers, as to reproduce the wiggling movement of toes (l. 09). This gestural activity is synchronized with another complex fluenceme sequence, made of multiple fluencemes (i.e. a filled pause, an explicit editing phrase, a repetition, a syllable prolongation, and a syntactic repair). Once more, Paul mobilizes a combination of vocal and visual-gestural actions to establish meaning. By doing so, he manages to make visibly available to his partner the iconic and comical aspect of these atypical shoes, and further relies on common ground (Clark, 1996). These shoes are not very common, so Paul needs to make sure that Paula clearly understands what he is referring to; after placing the referent in the gestural space, Paul further elaborates on the iconic properties of the shoes by drawing a series of circles in the air with his index finger (l. 09), while moving to the left. Paula then takes a look at his gesture, and confirms her understanding.

In sum, this excerpt has demonstrated how Paul positioned himself as an entertaining storyteller, who used a multiplicity of resources other than talk alone,

---

78. It should be noted that this information is purely based on his interpretation of what his teacher allegedly reported, not on actual fact.

which were central to his ability to construct a humorous story and engage with his conversational partner. Once more, this further reflects the close relationship between fluency and gesture, as well as the embodied nature of inter-(dis)fluency and the different pragmatic roles fluencemes may play in interaction.

Excerpt 2.3 Louis garrel
In the following extract, it is Jenny who initiates the retelling of an amusing narrative, but unlike Excerpt 2.1, it is not the story itself that will be of interest to us, but the story *initiation* (Lerner, 1992) i.e., the story preface (Sacks, 1992) leading up to the telling of the actual event. In the previous example, Paul provided some context about the university before retelling the funny anecdote (story preface), and overall, the progressivity of his story was maintained throughout the course of the retelling, without being interrupted by Paula, who closely attended to his talk, displaying tokens of understanding and appreciation. In the following example, however, I will demonstrate how the progressivity of the storytelling becomes immediately disrupted following the story initiation, because of problems in shared understandings.

```
1 *JEN:    hhh. ma:ais euh la dernière fois j'étais au café (il) y'a
           hhh. bu:ut euh last time I was at a cafe and there was
           une pote (laughs) qui me raconte qu'elle avait une pote (laughs)
           a friend (laughs) who was telling me that she he had a friend (laughs)
           complètement bourrée qui était dans un bar.
           completely drunk at a bar
2 *JEN:    et elle était en fait euh assise en face de louis garrel.
           and she was actually uh sitting opposite Louis Garrel
                  ~ ~~ *********************
                               _____
           ((extends her left arm and hand towards ALX))
           ((ALX gives an astonishing look))
```

```
3 *JEN:    hhh. (0.425) parce-qu'il était avec euh des potes e:et
           hhh. (0425) because she was euh with friends a :and
           voilà donc bref xx xx.
           so anyway xx xx.
4   *ALX:  +< comme nous et le type de les choristes.
           +< like us and the guy from The Chorus
                    ************
```

```
((ALX extends her POH towards JEN; JEN's hands return to rest position))
→          (2.220)
   ((JEN first looks left, then leans her head forward))
```

```
5   *ALX: mais t'étais pas là ?
          but weren't you there ?
6   *JEN: (0.470) on le connait lui ? (laughs)
          (0.470) do we know him ? (laughs)
7   *ALX: le type de les choristes Jean Baptiste Maunier au XX.
          the guy from The Chorus Jean Baptiste Maunier at XX.
8 *JEN:   oui [/] oui [/] oui.
          Yeah yeah yeah
9 *JEN:   ah il était au XX?
          ah he was at the XX?
   ((mouth open, raised eyebrows, expression of surprise))
```

Jenny first projects the beginning of her storytelling with turn-initial fluencemes (an inbreath and a prolongation, l.1) and further provides some background about the humorous event. It is important to note that the story is in fact not her own personal narrative (unlike Paul), but a friend of a friend's, so she has not experienced it herself. Just like Paul, Jenny first describes the location and setting where the event took place (at a bar, where the girl in the story was sitting opposite Louis Garrel). However, the progressivity of her story initiation is immediately troubled by Alex's facial reaction (l. 2) who gives an astonishing look after hearing Louis Garrel's name. Louis Garrel is a famous French actor, who is not the kind of person one would casually meet at a bar, which explains Alex's reaction. Alex's visible response to the mention of Louis Garrel momentarily disrupts the progressivity of Jenny's narrative, who delays her upcoming turn (l.3) with a fluenceme sequence made of an inbreath and unfilled pause. She then quickly elaborates on the reason why he may be there, but brushes it aside with a sequence-closing expression "bon bref voilà / *anyway* ", as this part of the story, it would seem, is not deemed relevant to her story-in-progress. However, the mention of a French celebrity becomes a relevant topic of conversation for Alex, who retells their supposedly shared experience, in line 4 "comme nous et le mec de les choristes / *like us and the guy from the Chorus*" by extending her left palm up open hand towards Jenny. A long silence of two seconds follows, during which Alex first looks to her left, then leans forward, as to display trouble in understanding. A series of question-answer sequences are then co-produced within the exchange (from lines 5 to 17) to help them clarify the misunderstanding: Alex is talking about a place (transcribed as *XX*) that both her and Jenny went to in their past common experience, and she seems convinced that Jenny was there when she saw another famous French actor, Jean Baptiste Maunier; while Alex understands who she is referring to (marked by her repetition of the agreement marker "oui" (yes), l. 8), she in fact did not share this experience with Alex. In sum, this excerpt has shown the different ways through which Alex and Jenny have been trying to map their common experience, based on their knowledge of French celebrities and the places they went together in Paris. This provided opportunities for them to address trouble in understanding, request for clarification, and display mutual orientation and intersubjectivity. Both speakers performed these relevant activities by deploying a number of resources among their relevant scope of behavior, mainly, talk, fluencemes, facial expressions, and gestures, which enabled them to co-construct the continuation of the dialogue.

To conclude, these analyses have illustrated the emergence of fluencemes in larger interactional contexts, where they functioned as byproducts of systematic interactional practices, i.e. humorous personal narratives (Excerpt 2.2) and displays of shared (mis)understandings to co-construct meaning (Excerpt 2.3). In the first excerpt, Paul skillfully made use of fluencemes and gestures to pursue the delivery of his humorous narrative quite continuously, and establish a referent by combining vocal and gestural strategies. In the second one, however, fluencemes mainly emerged in contexts of trouble in shared understanding, hence disrupting the progressivity, and to a larger extent, *fluency*, of the storytelling sequence. However, several fluencemes were also used to preface and resume Jenny's storytelling activity, which further illustrates their potential to mark the continuity as well as the DIScontinuity of discourse.

3.4 The interplay of vocal and material resources in the course of class presentations

I shall now conclude this section with two short examples from the class presentations which reflect the ways the students dealt with the different material resources they had within reach, to pursue the delivery of their oral assignment. The excerpts are taken from Paul (B1) and Linda (F1).

Excerpt 1.2 Paul's presentation

In this excerpt, Paul is analyzing the rhyming and rhythmic patterns of a poem, by describing specific instances of assonance (the resemblance in sounds of words or syllables between their vowels or consonants).

Chapter 5. Inter-(dis)fluency across communication settings

```
1 (0.510) eum (0.617) et là ce qui est assez intéressant à noter c'est
  (0.510) eum (0.617) and here what's interesting to note is that
      ((gazes towards notes; brings his hands to his cheeks))
  les euh [/] les assonances en début de mot
  the euh [/] the assonances at the beginning of the words
      ((gazes towards audience))
→ 2 euh qui se reprennent vraiment d'un vers sur l'autre.
  euh which really go one verse over another
      ((gazes towards notes and slightly pushes his book aside))
```

```
2 (0.445) euh entre enflammer et entreprise
  (0.445) euh between inflame and enterprise
       ~~~~~~~~~~~~~********~~~******
((gazes towards audience))
```

```
3 (0.589) débriser dessein
  (0.589) break design
             ****  *****
((lines omitted from the transcription))
4 et mettre en pièce et finesse
  and ripp off and delicacy
          ****          ****
→ 6 qui là sont euh [/] euh sont euh liées avec la:a [/] la rime.
   which here are euh [/] euh are euh linked with the:e [/] the rime.
                               ***-.-.-.-.-.-.-.-.-.-
((gazes towards paper, RH returns to rest position + writes something))
```

Paul is re-arranging the different objects placed opposite him by grabbing his pen with his dominant hand (right hand), and slightly pushing his book to his left side, with his left hand (l.2). Then, he produces a pause of 445 milliseconds clustered with a filled pause ("euh") of 255 ms; and while his left hand is resting on the book, he moves his dominant hand in preparation while holding the pen and raising it in the air. Paul then deploys a sequence of gestures (from lines 4 to 6), characterized by a series of beat movements and flicks of the wrist, still carried out with his dominant hand holding the pen in the air, as he moves across the table in different positions. Each time, the stroke of the gesture is synchronized with specific key words from the poem ("enflammer" "entreprise", "débriser", "dessein" "mettre en pièce", and "finesse"), as he places them in his discourse space, i.e. the desk, marking different components of his verbal discourse. This series of manual operations on relevant objects i.e., the sheet of paper and the book are part of Paul's embodied environment (the classroom). He presents a number of examples from the book illustrating instances of assonance in the poem through speech and gesture, by deploying a series of manual actions directly on his book and notes. The latter, which can be considered as deictic-anaphoric gestures in this context,[79] further offer discourse cohesion, as the same gestural patterns (beat movements and flicks of the wrist) were initiated in the same specific spatial area (the desk) and were repeatedly associated with specific referential expressions found in the text (Levy & McNeill, 1992). Paul also draws a parallel between the paired lexical terms, by making use of space; for instance, "enflammer" is produced on the left side of his notes, while "entreprise" is produced on the right side, with the pen raised in the air. In addition, he is also seen writing something on his notes (l.6), during which he momentarily suspends the course of his multimodal discourse activity, marked by a complex fluenceme sequence following the *VOC+MS* pattern, and a retraction of his manual gesture.

In sum, this excerpt has shown the different vocal and manual actions Paul had to mobilize in order to deal with the task at hand, alternating between (1) presenting his assignment through talk and gesture, (2) engaging with the audience, (3) reading his notes, and (4) writing on his sheets of paper. Paul managed to handle all these activities simultaneously without much disrupting the course of his presentation, but this cannot always be achieved so easily, as presentations have to be carried out quite continuously in an organized manner. This leads us to the following example, taken from Linda's (F1) presentation.

---

79. Note that these gestures were coded as *deictic-anaphoric* in the quantitative analysis (cf Section II2.1.3) because of their use of space to place referents in discourse (cf Chapter 2, Section II2.2.3), but they could also be regarded as *discursive* gestures to a certain extent, since they were also used to mark emphasis. Thus, both functions may overlap here, which justifies the use of intercoder reliability on 15% of the data (cf Chapter 2, Section II.2.2.3).

Chapter 5. Inter-(dis)fluency across communication settings 179

Excerpt 1.3 Linda's presentation
```
1 hh. alors (0.728) mmm pardon (1.132) je cherche la page (smiles)
  hh. so (0.728) mm sorry (1.1.32) I'm looking for the page (smiles)
  (7.512)
((looks through her notes; uses her pen to look for the right page))
```

```
2 hhs donc euh l'auteur nous partage (0.404) tout le long de:e [/] de
  hh. so euh the author is sharing (0.404.) throughout the:e [/] the
cette première partie hhh. eum les [/] ses souvenirs de premier émois.
first part hhh. eum the [/] the memories of his first emotions
        ((gazes towards her notes))
3 (0.304) ses randonnées en montagne e:et ses pêches à la mer.
(0.304) his hiking trips in the moutain a:and his fishing at sea.
                 (1)*******************(2)****
((1. holds out her hand, palm facing up with slightly bended fingers; 2. extends her
palm and fingers with a slight wrist motion))
```

As this brief example shows, Linda's use of her space is not as carefully organized as Paul's, given the multiplicity of objects found on her table, with about 8 different sheets of paper, her laptop, and her book. In fact, she seems to be experiencing difficulties managing these various media simultaneously, as marked by the significantly long silence found in her discourse, lasting up to seven seconds. The author Rendle-Short (2005), in her study on academic lectures, identified periods of "non-talk" i.e, when presenters stop talking and do not engage with their audience, as they attend to other *presentation-relevant* activities, such as looking through one's notes or interacting with the computer. She argued that periods of long talk were not necessarily viewed as problematic, as they marked a period during which presenters transitioned from "topic-talk" to non-talk, and from engagement to disengagement with the audience, and this shift can be achieved through visible bodily behavior. In Linda's case, we can see her gazing towards her different sheets of paper while trying to find the right one, and she also uses her pen at some point to help her. She is thus fully oriented to this activity, and this is signaled by her bodily behavior. Note that this period of nontalk is preceded by a complex fluenceme sequence made of two explicit editing phrases ("pardon / sorry" and "je cherche la page / I'm looking for the page"), a non-lexical sound ("mm"), and two unfilled pauses (of 728 and 1132 milliseconds) during which she is smiling, perhaps to save face. Here the fluenceme sequence functions both as a time-buying and a signaling tool, projecting to the audience that more time is required for Linda, who cannot find the right page from her notes. Therefore, this cessation of talk may be treated as relevant here, as it signals to the audience that the talk is momentarily being put on hold in order for Linda to pursue the delivery of her presentation, which gives her more time to accomplish her actions. After some time, she eventually manages to resume the delivery of her presentation, but she still seems absorbed in her notes, as she still does not gaze towards her audience, despite carrying out a gestural activity (l. 3). In fact, she spent 90% of her time gazing towards her notes during her presentation overall (cf Appendix 3, Table 60), which is considerably higher than the average of her group (about 70%). This shows that, even in periods of "fluent" talk, which tend to be characterized by mutual gaze, she very rarely engaged with her audience, as she was too focused on her own performance.

To conclude, these two examples from the presentation-sessions have shown that the emergence of fluencemes is intricately embedded within the continuous activity of giving an oral assignment, during which speakers must find ways to deal with the content and temporality of their presentation flow, as well as their spatial and material environment. In the first excerpt, Paul successfully shifted between different presentation-relevant activities through talk, gaze, and gesture, by making use of his gesture space to place referents within his discourse in a way that was visible for his audience; in the second excerpt, however, Linda experienced difficulties managing multiple media simultaneously, and had to delay quite significantly the course of her presentation in order to attend to other actions and focus on her own performance. Once more, we can find different degrees of fluency and disfluency at several levels of analysis, mainly speech, content, gesture, and interaction. Despite being a "monologic" task, where audience participation is not expected, the presenters are still delivering a presentation *to* them, and must therefore display mutual orientation and engagement, while still being able to talk quite continuously without too many interruptions. This may present a number of challenges for the students, which could potentially explain the high rate of fluencemes found in their presentations. This is further discussed in the next section.

IV. Discussion

The present section addresses the research questions formulated earlier, by drawing on a selection of findings obtained from our statistical treatments and the qualitative analyses. The section is structured as follows: I first report on differences in distribution between class presentations and conversations, and discuss the effect of style and setting on fluency and gesture; then stress the importance of *audience design* across the two situations, and provide a brief conclusion summarizing the results.

4.1 Effect of style and setting on fluency and gesture

One of the main questions this chapter sought to answer was whether style and setting had an effect on (dis)fluency and gesture production (RQ1), and whether significant differences would be found across the two situations (RQ2). As we have seen, differences in (dis)fluency or gesture behavior cannot solely be measured by isolating one factor, such as task complexity, mode of delivery, or degree of preparation, which has often been done in the literature (except for Bortfeld et al., 2001, among others, cf Chapter 2).

4.1.1 *Beyond the degree of preparation or mode of delivery*

A number of studies in the field of psycholinguistics and (dis)fluency research have insisted on the *spontaneous* nature of fluencemes, and the fact that they are systematically produced in spontaneous productions, as opposed to carefully read speech (e.g. Goldman-Eisler, 1958; Silverman et al., 1992; Shriberg, 1994). However, most of these studies carried out elicitation experiments to obtain such findings, which offers little ecological validity, and hence does not truly reflect the use of fluencemes in situated discourse (see Chapter 2). It would appear that in the case of DisReg, the role of preparation did not affect fluencemes positively, since students produced significantly more fluencemes in class presentations ("prepared" speech) than conversations ("spontaneous" speech). Even though the participants were extensively reading their notes, and had prepared their assignment at home, it did not stop them from producing a high number of fluencemes (with the exception of one participant, F2). A multiplicity of other factors thus needs to be taken into account to interpret such differences in fluency behavior.

Another body of research in corpus-based linguistics and Second Language Acquisition have compared (dis)fluency rates in monologic versus dialogic situations, sampling from different types of speakers and data types, resulting in contradictory results. For instance, Schatcher et al., (1991) found higher rates of fluencemes in interviews than in lectures, and Duez (1982) found that pauses were more frequent in political and casual interviews than political speeches. By contrast, Tottie (2016) found more pauses during narrative turns than in conversations between relatives and friends, and Michel et al., (2007) found fewer filled pauses in dyadic phone conversations than in messages left on a recording machine. As we have seen, other variables, such as topic familiarity and utterance complexity, may also come into play. For example, Bortfeld et al., (2001) showed that (dis)fluency rates were associated with heavier planning demands, in line with Beattie (1979), Oviatt (1995), and Shriberg (1994) who found more (dis)fluencies in longer utterances. Bortfeld et al., (2001) and Merlo & Mansur (2004) also found an increase in (dis)fluency rates when speakers discussed unfamiliar and abstract topics.

I also addressed a gap in the literature regarding the study of gesture with respect to setting (cf Chapter 2, Section II.2.3), which has received little attention, except for Bavelas et al.'s (2008) study that compared the rates of gestures in dialogues and monologues. In sum, I believe that mode of delivery or task complexity alone are not sufficient to interpret differences in fluency and gesturing behavior across situations. This corpus study has revealed quantitative and qualitative differences in fluenceme use, thanks to the multiple formal and functional variables included in the analysis which has shed some light on the interplay of factors impacting inter-(dis)fluency.

4.1.2 *Fluenceme rate, distribution, and patterns of co-occurrence across the two situations*

Overall, significant differences were found in the distribution of fluencemes in the two situations. A higher rate of fluencemes was found in class presentations, with significantly longer unfilled pauses, and a higher proportion of non-lexical sounds, as well as filled pauses. The latter were also more often realized with the nasal variant (*eum*) in class presentations than conversations, suggesting a longer delay (Clark & Fox Tree, 2002). In addition, a slightly higher proportion of complex fluencemes was found in class, but without differences in length. So far, these findings suggest that class presentations require more time for planning and monitoring, which is consistent with Tottie (2016) who found that filled pauses were closely associated with planning demands, as they tended to occur more frequently in utterance-initial position in long narratives or thoughtful presentations of evidence, which require more planning than casual conversations. This is also confirmed by the positive correlation found between unfilled pause duration and utterance length, with longer pauses associated with longer utterances. The latter were significantly longer in class presentations than conversations. A tendency for fluenceme sequences to occur in utterance-initial position was also found in presentations, which could reflect a possible rhythmic and stylistic style, in line with Duez (1982). Indeed, class presentations require students to produce clear intelligible utterances and pay close attention to their speech, in order to present structured arguments with a careful choice of words. However, I also mentioned the role of anxiety and self-consciousness in formal situations with higher stakes (graded assignments in the case of DisReg), which resonates with several previous studies (Broen & Siegel, 1972; Christenfeld & Creager, 1996; Tottie, 2014). Although it is not possible to find a direct connection between anxiety and (dis)fluency production, the effect of stress, or at least self-consciousness could be a possibility, given the amount of time students spent gazing towards their notes and not engaging with their audience, suggesting that they were paying more attention to their own production than to their group of interlocutors.

In addition, let us not overlook the weight of individual differences in the data, as many were found across the two situations. For instance, F2 is the only speaker who actually produced fewer fluencemes during his presentation (16.5 phw) than in the conversation (21.4 phw), and D1 produced about equally the same amount in the two situations (20.2 and 19.9). Others, like B2, produced considerably more fluencemes during the presentation (25.6) than when she was engaged in the interaction (9.7). In fact, she produced relatively few fluencemes during the conversation in comparison to the average of her group (20.4). Similarly, a group of speakers produced on average filled pauses of longer duration during their presentation than in the conversation (e.g. A1, D1, E1, E2, see Table 69, Appendix 4), while others showed the opposite tendency (e.g. D2 and F2). These findings are consistent with the study of the SITAF corpus, where many individual differences were found across speakers within the two language groups, which further confirms that fluency is in part dependent on personal speaking style, regardless of setting or proficiency, in line with De Jong (2016a). These individual differences were also illustrated in the gesturing behavior of speakers, which leads us to the next section.

4.1.3 *Gestural distribution and gaze behavior*

Contrary to what was expected (cf H5), a higher rate of gestures was found in class presentations than in the conversations, which is not consistent with Bavelas et al's., (2008) findings that gestures were more frequent in dialogues than monologues. But once more, these differences can be explained by the type of experimental procedure used in their study, which relied on a picture elicitation experiment to create the monologue and dialogue conditions. This is very different from this study, which is based on semi-naturalistic settings (cf Chapter 3, I.1.1), so specific attention needs to be paid to the ecology of these gestures. In addition, the supposedly "monologue" situation is also quite dialogic in a sense, since the students were presenting their assignment to the group of students facing them. As the quantitative findings revealed, a majority of the gestures produced during the presentations served discursive functions, i.e. they were used to mark emphasis, present an idea, or structure aspects of multimodal discourse, and the latter were used significantly more during class presentations than conversations. Conversations, on the other hand, comprised a higher proportion of interactional and representational gestures. This was also found in Bavelas et al's (2008) study, who reported a similar result. In the conversations, representational gestures were also found to occur more frequently during fluencemes (28% of all gestures during fluencemes) than without them (14% of all gestures outside fluencemes), while interactive gestures occurred more frequently outside fluencemes (43%) than during them (27%). Thinking gestures, on the other hand, almost occurred only exclusively during fluencemes in the two situations, which is consistent with findings from the SITAF corpus (Chapter 4).

As the qualitative analyses further demonstrated, speakers often made use of interactional gestures to perform a series of actions, such as establishing common ground, displaying a stance, or addressing their interlocutor in the course of their interactive practices. During their oral presentations, however, students almost never addressed their audience, except for a few exceptions, but mostly made use of gestures to segment discourse and mark information structure. In particular, I described one example (Excerpt 1.3) in which the presenter made use of his gesture space to emphasize a selection of words, and each change of gesture coincided with a key word. Once again, this further reflects the effect of situation on the functions of the gestures. In addition, a considerable proportion of gazing towards the piece of paper was found in the presentation-sessions, amounting to 70% on average, as opposed to only 27% of gazing towards the interlocutor, which is a significant difference with the conversations. This finding seems somewhat at odds with the considerable number of gestures found in class presentations (10.2 phw as opposed to 7.6 in the conversations), which means that, even though the students were engaged in a relatively dense gestural activity, they did not truly engage with their audience, as they were too engrossed in their notes. In addition, findings showed that speakers were more likely *not* to establish eye contact when they produced fluencemes in both situations, which is consistent with findings from the SITAF corpus where the two language groups were found to withdraw their gaze more frequently during fluencemes both in their L1 and L2 (see Chapter 4). This further emphasizes the fact that gazing away is a very common practice of (dis)fluency, regardless of language or setting, as it enables speakers to momentarily retreat from the current activity to attend to other relevant ones, such as retrieving an item from memory, looking for a specific word, checking for a sentence in a book, etc. However, I also showed several instances of mutual gaze coordinated with fluencemes in the conversations (see Section II) during which speakers were engaged in interactive practices, which further reveals the potential for fluencemes to embody interactive processes as well, and not only intrapersonal ones. In sum, fluencemes enable speakers to transition between periods of planning and monitoring with periods of engaging and conversing with co-participants, and this transition can further be manifested in accompanying visual-gestural behavior; in the case of class presentations however, it would appear that students were primarily focused on their own performance, and this was further confirmed by the overwhelming proportion of fluencemes performing *own communication management* (99%).

4.2 The importance of audience design

This section discusses the importance of *audience design* (Bell, 2006) with respect to language style and setting, within the frameworks of Conversation Analysis. Unlike previous studies from Bavelas et al., (2008) or Michel et al., (2007) the "monologic" productions from the DisReg corpus were elicited in front of an actual *real* audience (not an experimenter alone), and this has a number of consequences on the participants' behavior.

4.2.1 *Discourse identities within complex participation frameworks*

On the one hand, class presentations involve one presenter (or two) and an audience of passive hearers, whose relationship is highly asymmetric, but also fixed and predetermined. Indeed, throughout their presentation, students are acting as *presenters*, and their status is not expected to change until the end of their talk. The audience, too, is bound to remain "passive"[80] at all times, and is not invited to speak, except eventually at the end of the student's presentation.[81] In conversations, on the other hand, the participants' status and discourse identities are continuously being (re)shaped in the course of the interaction, which invites them to take on multiple identities, overlapping with one another. This was especially illustrated in Example 2.2 where Paul (B1) skillfully alternated between different roles in the course of his storytelling activity, from the role of entertaining storyteller to television host, in order to build a humorous narrative. His interlocutor, Paula (B2) was shown to attentively attend to his talk without interrupting him, and by displaying tokens of appreciation and understanding. In another example, however, (Excerpt 2.3) the hearer, Alex (D1), played a bigger role in the storytelling activity performed by Jenny (D2), the speaker, by initiating another topic of conversation involving their common experience. The latter resulted in a misunderstanding, which momentarily disrupted the progressivity of the storytelling sequence, but which also provided an opportunity for participants to share common ground and display mutual understanding.

---

80. However, it should be noted that the audience probably displays tokens of participation as well, without necessarily speaking, through head nods, mutual gaze, etc. Unfortunately, this type of evidence cannot be verified, since they could not be videorecorded as part of the study.
81. Based on my experience, this is true for most French presentations at an undergraduate level in French universities, but this claim is not verified by actual evidence.

4.2.2 *Class presentations and the presenters' orientation to their talk*

In institutional settings, the main discourse objectives and orientations of the speakers differ radically from casual conversations where not much is at stake, excerpt for the need to maintain continuity and alignment between co-participants. In comparison, during class presentations, the main goal of the presenter is to deliver a successful assignment for which they will later receive a grade, and this success is mostly conditioned by their ability to provide well-constructed analyses in a given topic. While most of this work is carefully prepared at home, the challenge remains for students to give a real time performance in front of the whole classroom, and this compels them to constantly work on their own production as the presentation unfolds. As we have seen, a majority of students were fully oriented to their own talk, as indicated by the high rate of fluencemes used to manage their own communication (OCM) and the number of gestures oriented towards their own discourse. We may wonder whether fluencemes were used so frequently in this context as a result from their overburdened utterances as well as their inability to manage their online planning and engage with their audience at the same time, following the *Cognitive Burden* view of (dis)fluency (cf Chapter 1, Section II.2.2.1). However, as maintained multiple times throughout this book, I do not believe that (dis)fluency should be restricted to episodes of difficulty or trouble, as they can also function as relevant communicative signals. Note for instance the fluency behavior of a particular speaker in the following excerpt, taken from the presentation delivered by F2, pseudonymized as Matt:

Excerpt 1.4a
```
1     (0.670) par cette réforme Cléon est accusé de démagogie
      (0.670) with this reform Cléon is accused of demogagy
      (0.400) par ces detracteurs.
      (0.400) by these distractors
2     hhh. puisqu'il instaure un système de corruption en prétendant
      hhh. since he establishes a system of corruption by pretending
      soutenir le peuple.
   to support the people.
3     hhh. et en espérant surtout le soutien de celui-ci.
   hhh. and by hoping especially to gain support from the latter.
4     (0.876) il faut dire que Cléon étant le successeur de Periclès
      (0.876) one must say that Cléon being the successor of Periclès
5     (0.463) très populaire et très considéré.
      (0.463) very popular and acknowledged
6     (0.404) Périclès pas Cléon.
      (0.404) Périclès not Cléon
7     il est notamment celui qui voulut le Parthénon.
      he is also the one who wanted the Parthenon
```

As pointed out earlier, Matt is the only speaker in the data who actually produced more fluencemes in conversation than in class, as he only produced 16.5 fluencemes per hundred words during his presentation, which is significantly lower than the average of his group (28.5 phw). This is clearly illustrated in this brief excerpt of 24 seconds, during which he only produced simple fluencemes (inbreaths and unfilled pauses) mostly in utterance-initial position. His speech is loud and clear, very articulated, and he skillfully makes use of pauses to mark discourse boundaries, reflecting a stylistic function. In sum, Matt represents the ideal *fluent* speaker, who seems very good at public speaking, and whose voice is very pleasant to hear. However, over the course of these 24 seconds, Matt does not produce a single gesture, and his eyes remain fixed on the sheets of paper he is holding with both hands, giving little room for any kind of gestural activity, as illustrated in Figure 36 below.[82]

Figure 36. Matt's (F2) visible bodily behavior during his presentation (Excerpt 1.5.a)

Even though Matt sounds perfectly fluent *to the ear*, his visible bodily behavior conveys a total lack of communicativeness, as he looks like he is rehearsing his speech alone, or recording himself on the microphone, without paying any attention to his surroundings. Compare now with this second brief excerpt, also taken from Matt's presentation, a minute or so later:

---

82. In fact, he only produced 11 gestures during his presentation.

Excerpt 1.4b
Matt is analyzing a quote from a play he is presenting, which includes a list of several terms conveying the notion of cupidity, but he is having doubts about the use of the term "Harpagon". This excerpt starts from there.

```
1 (0.380) avec un doute sur Harpagon parce-que:e (0.554)
  (0.380) with doubts on Harpagon because:e (0.554)
  ((smiles, gazes towards audience, A.))
  Victor-Henri Debidour connait le personnage de Molière.
  Victor-Henri Debidour knows Molière's character
2 mai:ais j'ai pas de connaissances d'un personnage euh Harpago:on
  bu:ut I don't know about a character euh Harpago:on
            ((quickly extends his right open hand sideways, B.))
3 euh du cinquième siècle avant notre ère.
  euh from the fifth century before our era
4 Aristophane a:a aussi procédé à une création d'une telle ampleur
  Aristophane ha:ad also proceeded to the making of such a creation
  ma:ais là j'ai pas de version grecque pour m'en rendre compte.
   bu:ut then I don't have a Greek version to get a grasp of it
     ((raised eyebrows + shoulder shrug C.))
```

Here Matt deploys a high number of fluencemes to spontaneously elaborate on his interpretation of the use of the term *Harpagon* in the text. He is not reading from his notes anymore, or acting as the skilled oral performer, but rather speaks with *his own voice*, giving his own personal opinion, as he displays a series of communicative and expressive behaviors (smile, shoulder shrug, gaze towards the audience, manual gesture etc.,) as illustrated in Figure 37.

A. B. C.

Figure 37. Matt's display of visible expressive behaviors (Excerpt 1.5.b)

This time, Matt is actively oriented towards his audience and only relies occasionally on his notes. His style is now much more dialogic, as it looks like he is expecting some kind of validation from his audience through his gaze and gestures.

In sum, these brief excerpts have shown that the degree of (dis)fluency should not be restricted to examples of perfectly well-formed fluent utterances as opposed to cases of highly disfluent ones, but should include the full scope of semiotic behaviors participants have at their disposal, which further reveals how they may use them to (dis)engage with their interlocutor(s). While a particular delivery produced in the speech signal may *sound* "disfluent", it may in fact *look* rather "fluent" in the visual-gestural channel.

Conclusion to the chapter

In conclusion, the general aim of this chapter was to describe potential differences in fluency and visual-gestural behavior across two distinct styles and settings, i.e. institutional class presentations versus casual face-to-face interactions. In this chapter, I presented the notions of style and setting as *multidimensional*, encompassing a wide array of inter-related factors such as audience design, multimodal setting, turn-taking mechanisms, or register, thus going beyond differences in type of delivery (i.e. read between spontaneous) or mode (i.e. monologue versus dialogue). While a lot of research has been conducted on the different effects affecting (dis)fluency (topic, genre, task type, anxiety, register etc.,) many of these studies were designed very differently from one another, relying on different experimental procedures, sampling from different types of speakers, eliciting different types of production, hence resulting in contrasting results. Gestures, on the other hand, have received very little attention with respect to language style in corpus-based studies. The aim of this study on the DisReg corpus was to provide an overview of fluency and gesture within their situated ecology, based on semi-naturalistic data and on the same pairs of speakers across the two situations, which allows for efficient quantitative treatments, as well as micro analyses of the data.

As the findings revealed, a number of significant differences were found across the two situations, mainly a higher rate of fluencemes, longer unfilled pauses, and longer utterances in class presentations than the conversations, as well as more instances of utterance-initial fluencemes in class as opposed to more utterance-final ones in conversation. More gestures were also found during the class presentations, but a majority of them served discursive functions, as opposed to conversations which contained more interactive and representational gestures. In addition, a significant proportion of gazing towards paper was found during presentations, which reveals a lack of engagement towards the audience, despite dense gestural activity. The lack of visible engagement during the presentations (marked by the absence of mutual gaze) was further illustrated in the multimodal qualitative analyses, where students were shown to be mostly focused on their own performance and the material objects around them (their notes, their book, their pen, etc.) reflecting more intrapersonal processes and pertaining to *own communication management* (OCM). In conversations, on the other hand, several interactional practices involving embodied displays of intersubjectivity were exemplified, thus further reflecting the interactional dimension of fluencemes (*interactive communication management, ICM*).

A number of limitations in this study should also be noted. First, as explained earlier (Chapter 3) I worked on a selected sample of DisReg to approximately match the size of SITAF, but the sample is still relatively small and only representative of a selection of the students' productions, so the findings need to be taken with caution. Lastly, as pointed out before in my conclusion to Chapter 4, I am aware that the statistical methods used in the quantitative analyses are rather simple and resulting in binary outcomes, so more complex data analysis techniques, such as multiple correspondence analysis, or mixed linear regression models, containing fixed and random effects, should be used in the future to explore possible systematic relationships between fluency and other variables. However, I still believe that the quantitative analyses yielded a number of significant results, which can be of interest to researchers in (dis)fluency and gesture studies.

In addition, while the present study does not primarily intend to be pedagogical-oriented, it may still open perspectives onto future work in class pedagogy, offering tools for students to better perform their assignments in class, by making simultaneous use of their voice, body, and eye contact to increase "eloquence" (e.g., Papanas et al., 2011). The issue with a majority of oral presentations found in French universities is that they tend to be too content-oriented, which may explain why students spend most of their time dealing with the written content on their notes, instead of engaging with their audience. However, this type of hypothesis would require more data from a larger sample of speakers in different universities in order to be supported. In addition, fluencemes should not be systematically stigmatized as performance errors or "hallmarks of youth" (Fox Tree, 2007), representing poor communication skills, as I have shown them to be dynamically ambivalent systems, relying on a multiplicity of resources.

CHAPTER 6

On the relationship between inter-(dis)fluency and gesture

The goal of the present chapter is to further explore the multimodal dimension of inter-(dis)fluency by documenting the different forms and functions of gestures co-occuring with fluencemes, or occurring within their vicinity, in their situated, embodied, and multimodal environment, thus taking a step further from the initial functional classification of gestures used for the quantitative analyses. The present chapter will thus only present detailed qualitative analyses of the data across the two corpora, and pay specific attention to the temporal relationship between (dis)fluency and gesture and their synchronicity in terms of gesture phases, as well as the deployment of different articulators (i.e. hand, face, eyes, shoulders, and trunk) and the shape, configuration, orientation, movement, and position of gestural sequences in the gesture space, following a more *form-based approach* to gesture (Bressem & Müller, 2014; Ladewig & Bressem, 2013; Müller et al., 2013). Several references will also be made to the gestures analyzed in previous chapters, as to establish a typology of gestural variants in relation to inter-(dis)fluency. The present chapter is structured as follows: I first illustrate the temporal relationship between (dis)fluency and gesture phrasing through several examples on the synchronization of speech and gesture production, then document several visual-gestural practices embodying inter-(dis)fluency.

I. Synchronization of speech and gesture

In Chapter 1, I reviewed a number of studies conducted on (dis)fluency and gestures which targeted aspects of gestural and speech suspension (cf Chapter 1, Section III.3.3.4). While some showed that gestures tended to be suspended prior to the production of (dis)fluencies (e.g., Seyfeddinipur, 2006; Seyfeddinipur & Kita, 2001) others have stated that they were more likely to begin during them (e.g., Beattie & Butterworth, 1979). As Graziano & Gullberg (2018) pointed out, most of the studies that investigated the timing of gestures relative to (dis)fluency have presented contradictory findings, mostly due to methodological and theoretical differences. Following the notion that speech and gesture form a tightly integrated, orchestrated, and unified system (e.g. Kendon, 2004; McNeill, 1992) Graziano & Gullberg (2018), along with other researchers (e.g. Chui, 2004;

Esposito & Marinaro, 2007; Yasinnik et al., 2005) provided evidence that gesture suspension tended to synchronize with speech suspension, hence suggesting that gesture production is an integral component of utterance construction (Kendon, 2004). Similarly, the studies conducted on the SITAF and DisReg corpus have shown a similar tendency, with a proportion of about 25% to 35% of fluencemes[83] which occurred during phases of gestural actions, such as *preparation, hold,* or *retraction*, regardless of language or setting[84] (cf Chapters 4 and 5), further giving support to the temporal patterning of speech and gesture. The following analyses, taken from the two corpora under study, will focus specifically on this relationship by showing the deployment of gestures within different gesture phases and their relationship to (dis)fluency. The excerpts chosen are purposefully very brief as to zoom in on particular instances of gesture phases (i.e., gesture hold, retraction, and preparation) and forward gesturing.

1.1 Hold and retraction: Suspension and interruption in the two modalities

In this section, I focus on two specific gesture phases deployed after the stroke, mainly the (post-stroke) hold, and the retraction of the gesture. As explained earlier, (cf Chapter 1, Section III.3.3.4), gesture *hold* refers to hand gestures that are temporarily frozen in a static position, and *retraction* refers to a moment of relaxation, when hands return to the initial rest position, following a gesture stroke, or a previously held one. The two following examples illustrate the way speakers momentarily suspend or interrupt the course of their multimodal utterance by either holding their hands in the same position in the gesture space, or by returning them to their initial rest position. Gesture holds have already been illustrated in previous qualitative analyses (e.g. Excerpts 1.A, 2.A, and 2B in Chapter 4), but here I will focus more precisely on their timely coordination with vocal suspensions in the acoustic channel. The first example is taken from Pair 3 in French in the SITAF corpus. All examples use the gestural notation system created by Kendon (2004) (cf Appendix 1, Transcription conventions) and the fluenceme sequences that accompany these gesture phases are marked in brackets and in bold in the transcription.

---

83. However, one methodological limitation should be noted. Gesture phases were only coded during fluencemes, while gesture strokes were coded in the whole data (i.e. both within and outside fluencemes, cf Chapter 2, Section II.2.2.3), but it would have been interesting to compare the proportion of gesture holds within fluencemes with those outside fluencemes to get a more precise idea of their temporal relationship.

84. There was still a tendency, however, for the American and French groups to hold their gestures more frequently during fluencemes in their L2 than in their L1 in SITAF. No significant differences were found across the two situations in DisReg.

Chapter 6. On the relationship between inter-(dis)fluency and gesture

Ex. hold

In this excerpt, the two tandem partners are talking about differences between travelers and tourists (cf Excerpt 2A in Chapter 4), and the American non-native speaker (Julia, A03) argues that the traveler, unlike the tourist, settles down more permanently in a foreign country.

```
1 JUL: mai:is (0.460) peut-être euh il s'installe (1.080) mm mieux
   bu:ut (0.460) maybe euh he settle down (1.080) mm in a better way
                                      [FLUENCEME SEQ.]
                          1.*********************
   ((both lax open hands, palm facing up, spread bent fingers + hold))
```

           1.

```
2 MAR:                    +< d'accord.
                          +< ok.
2 JUL: ou il s'installe euh (1.280) [!] plus
   or he settles down euh (1.280) [!] more
                          [FLUENCEME SEQ.]
                       2.*******************
   ((both hands coming down, same configuration as 1. + hold))
```

2.

```
        forteme:ent (0.680) dans [/] dans le pays.
        permanently:y (0.68) in [/] in the country
                 [FLUENCEME SEQ.]
              3.*********** ~~~~~*****
        ((hold + Palm Down Open Hand))
```

     3.

In this example, Julia is producing a series of formally similar manual gestures, where both her lax flat hands are first slightly raised with spread bent fingers to the center of her trunk, then coming down to the lower part of her body, with both palms facing up (illustrations 1 and 2); the initial stroke of the gesture first coincides with the verb "installer" (*settle down*), and is then repeated with several beat movements, as she repeats the verb in line 2. Every time she held her hands in the same position (as shown in the transcription with the underlined asteriks), she also momentarily suspended the course of her vocal utterance. In line 1, she first delays the course of her vocal flow by pausing for a significant amount of time (about one second), and producing a nasal vocalization ("mm"); then in line 3, she produces another series of vocal and non-lexical fluencemes (a filled pause, an unfilled pause and a tongue click), and this time she holds her gesture during them. She also lengthens the final syllable of the adverb "fortement" (*permanently*) and produces another 680 ms pause near the end of her utterance, during which she also holds her hands in the same position. Each time, the same type of gesture is held, i.e., both lax flat open hands facing up with spread bent fingers, and each of them is also accompanied by specific facial expressions; she is either looking away (1), closing her eyes (2) or slightly frowning (3). In sum, Julia suspended various parts of her multimodal utterances as she went along with her discourse, and she did so with the help of vocal and gestural markers of suspension, which illustrates how both modalities were momentarily suspended in the multimodal communication channel, in order to build meaning.

As Kendon (2004) noted, when a speaker employs a post-stroke hold (Kita, 1993), the expression conveyed by the gesture stroke seems to be prolonged, as to extend its meaning, and it would appear to be the case in this example as well. The non-native speaker first deployed her hands in the gesture space to introduce the concept of settling down in a foreign country, and she did so by moving her hands down, with palm-up open hands and bent fingers. Her hands were also held in this very same position, as if she was *holding on* to the idea she was conveying to her partner.

Ex. retraction

In this excerpt from the DisReg corpus, Linda (F1) and Matt (F2) are talking about TV shows and the fact that whenever a new one comes out and the first season is over, they have to wait for another year before they can watch the second season, which makes it difficult to remember the plot and characters (not in the transcription). Here Linda draws a parallel with new episodes that come out every week on TV.

```
1 LINDA:  euh comme regarder euh (0.425) les [//] épisode après episode
          euh like watching  euh (0.425) the [//] one episode after the other
                      [FLUENCEME SEQ.]
          ***********-.-.-.-.-.-.-.-.-.-~~~************************
```

Chapter 6. On the relationship between inter-(dis)fluency and gesture 195

((moves her right hand forward away from her, vertical palm facing her body with extended thumb, looks up + retraction))

```
2 LINDA: (en)fin chaque semaine tu dois te remettre dans le truc euh
         I mean each week you need to get back into it euh
         ~~~~~*********************************
    ((moves her right hand with a rotating motion; gazes towards MATT))
3 MATT: bah ouais.
        well yeah
```

Here Linda first initiates a gesture that seems to convey a continuous process through time by moving her right hand further away from her body in the central space with several beat motions, her vertical palm facing her trunk and her thumb extended. This gesture is synchronized with the verb "regarder" (watch), and is then followed by a fluenceme sequence comprised of a filled pause, a silence and a syntactic repair, during which her hand moves back to rest position. Linda suddenly interrupts her speaking activity as she is trying to reformulate parts of her utterance to describe the process of watching one episode after the other every week, and this interruption is embodied in the two modalities. She then repeats the same gesture initiated at the beginning of her turn, and this time it coincides with the noun phrase "episode après episode" (one episode after the other), which offers additional verbal lexical content to the gesture's intended meaning. She is also gazing towards Matt at this moment, and the latter demonstrates his alignment through verbal backchanneling ("well yeah"). In addition, her multimodal interruption marked a transition from a self-oriented activity (i.e. reformulating a verbal expression while looking up) to an other-oriented one (i.e. sharing this piece information with her partner while looking towards him).

To conclude, the two examples analyzed above have illustrated instances of suspension or interruption in the verbal/vocal and visual-gestural modality, reflecting a unified and co-orchestrated process in the two modalities. These suspending/interrupting activities may further embody relevant interactional actions in the course of the multimodal exchange, marking a transition from a self-oriented practice to the next communicative move. This leads us to the analysis of the preparation phase, which further sheds light on the timely coordination between speech and gesture.

1.2 Preparation: Preparing speech and gesture in tandem

When a manual action enfolds, it is usually marked by a preparatory movement phase where the hand(s) move from a resting position to prepare the execution of the gesture stroke; this is known as the *preparation phase* (Kendon, 1972; Kita et al., 1997; McNeill, 1992). Unlike the post-stroke hold and the preparation phase, this one occurs before the stroke, and therefore does not mark a suspension or an interruption, but rather an initiation, or a projection. In the following example, I show how this phase also coincides with the emergence of vocal and verbal fluencemes.

Ex. preparation
This excerpt is taken from Pair 18 in the SITAF corpus. The two tandem partners, Rosie (A18) and Sophie (F18) are comparing teenage years with adulthood, and the American native speaker (Rosie) is presenting a number of arguments in favor of adulthood, stating that, as an adult, she believes that she gets more opportunities to experience life more, as opposed to when she was a teenager and things always seemed to be the same.

```
1 ROS: (0.549) um (0.330) [!] I think that (1.296)
       [/] I just think (0.451) that (1.175) the life +//.
                   [FLUENCEME SEQ.]
                        ~~~~~~~**********
((left hand moves forward in preparation in a slow motion + beat movement with her
vertical open palm))
```

```
2 ROS: (0.338) like when I was a teenager my life was very um (1.429)
       [FLUENCEME SEQ.]
       ~~~~~****************************_.-.-.-.-.-.-.-.-.-.-.-.-
```

```
((left hand moves in preparation to her left then produces a beat movement and brings
her palm down + return to rest position))
3 ROS: it was all the same.
           ~~~~~~~~~*****
```

Chapter 6. On the relationship between inter-(dis)fluency and gesture

```
                   ((performs a cyclic rotation with her left hand with her vertical open palm))
           4 SOP:  (chuckles)
           5 ROS:  it was (0.374) the same day after day.
                        ~~~~********************
                   ((performs a similar cyclic gesture with her left vertical palm open hand))
```

Rosie begins her first utterance with a very long and complex fluenceme sequence, comprised of multiple fluencemes (five unfilled pauses, one filled pause, one tongue click, and a repetition of the segment "I just think that"). During most of this fluenceme sequence, Rosie keeps her hands in rest position, but then she initiates a gesture with her left hand, as it slowly moves forward in preparation during her fifth pause of 1.175 milliseconds. Then, as she introduces a noun phrase ("the life") she produces a beat movement with her vertical left open hand. This multimodal phase of preparation, characterized by a preparation of a gestural and a linguistic unit, also marks the beginning of her discourse unit as she launches a new topic ("the life") that is later re-introduced in her next utterance, following her self-interruption. In her second utterance, she produces another unfilled pause of much shorter duration (338 ms) in utterance-initial position, during which her left hand moves once again in preparation, but this time to the left periphery of her gesture space, her palm facing down, with slightly bent fingers. The left side of her gesture space thus seems to metaphorically embody a specific region of time (her teenage years), and she performs a series of cyclic gestures in the same location, as to represent a habitual and routinely process that captures her life as a teenager ("it was all the same", "the same day after day").

As Gullberg (2006) showed, speakers consistently make use of space to introduce different discourse entities, which is known as "spatial anaphoricity" (Debreslioska et al., 2013, p. 435) i.e., when referents are introduced into multimodal discourse with gestures, as to signal their accessibility. Similarly, in this example, Rosie placed a specific referent in time (her life as a teenager, placed in the left periphery of her gesture space) perhaps to disambiguate between her adulthood and her teenage years, and she later made use of this specific location in space to express the monotonous regularity of this time period. More specifically, this deictic-anaphoric gesture was initiated during fluenceme sequences, and the gesture preparation was timely coordinated with speech preparation, showing once more a harmonious cooperation between the two modalities. This further shows that (dis)fluency processes are not only associated with discourse suspension or interruption, but may also index new sequences of multimodal talk and (re)introduce discourse topics.

II.   On the visual-gestural practices embodying inter-(dis)fluency

In this section, I explore more specifically the notions of (dis)fluency and hesitation in visible bodily behavior, and document recurrent visual affiliates of (dis)fluency, mainly thinking postures and word searching manual actions and embodied displays of intersubjectivity. Analyses are also based on the SITAF and DisReg corpus, with a number of excerpts that have already been introduced in the previous chapters, but with a slightly different take.

2.1   Doing thinking as an interactional practice

In Chapter 1, I mentioned the display of a specific facial expression in social interaction, known as the "thinking face", a term coined by Goodwin & Goodwin (1986) in their paper on joint word searches (cf Chapter 1, Section III.3.2.3). Despite what the term "thinking" entails, the authors do not view this practice as a reflection of inner cognitive processes, but rather as an interactive display of the speakers' continued engagement in a joint activity. Such facial displays may also reveal a state of uncertainty, and do not necessarily indicate a cognitive process, but rather invoke particular types of social organization, such as inviting the interlocutor to take part in a word search (Goodwin, 1987).

More recently, Heller (2021) conducted a study on joint decision making, following the work of Goodwin & Goodwin (1986). Based on a corpus of monolingual and multilingual children recorded within a school setting in which they were asked to perform a series of argumentative tasks, Heller (2021) showed how speakers and recipients combined various semiotic resources to create complex multimodal gestalts (Mondada, 2014) which embodied practices of "doing thinking". Such practices include a combination of body postures, particular gaze practices, and linguistic resources. In her analysis of thinking displays, she documented a series of multimodal gestalts including "imaginative gaze", wandering of the eyes, and thinking postures. The latter is characterized by an "inflexible" body posture where the face and hands are fixed, as a signal that neither gesture nor hand movement are expected during the display. In addition, thinking postures were shown to index an embodied change of mind, a transition into the display of doing thinking. This is also marked by gaze withdrawals, where the speaker embodies a change of orientation, and displays to his or her partner that he or she is no longer oriented towards their external surroundings, but rather directs attention "inwards, toward a world of thought, in which she first needs to make up her mind before she can share her ideas with her co-participants (Heller, 2021, p. 8). Following Goodwin & Goodwin (1986) and Heller (2021) the present section aims to document different uses of the thinking face along with other bodily manifestations, mainly body orientation and manual gestures, specifically in relation to inter-(dis)fluency and the notion of hesitation.

2.1.1 *Multimodal gestalts of doing thinking: Embodied markers of hesitation?*

In Chapter 1, I described the different uses of the term *hesitation* in the literature, and argued that this term was not truly representative of the phenomena under study. Indeed, not every fluenceme reflects an act of choice or indecision, and the term "hesitation" remains too restrictive to instances of trouble or uncertainty (cf Chapter 1, Section II.2.2.2), which does not cover the whole range of functions and uses of fluencemes. However, it may be argued that in some specific contexts the core notion of hesitation could be found within embodied displays of thinking, which may reveal the emergence of *embodied hesitation*, and therefore instances of *doing hesitation*. The following instances, taken from previous examples in Chapters 3 and 4, and summarized in Table 31, further explore this idea.

These multimodal gestalts of doing thinking, or doing hesitation, largely echo the work of Heller (2021), showing similar facial and body displays documented in her work, mainly self-touch, "imaginative" gaze, "inflexible" posture, wandering of the eyes, and gaze withdrawals. Similar facial features were also found in Bavelas & Chovil (2018) who described them as "somewhat stylized gestures in which the speaker pauses, turns his or her head or looks away, often with a blank, puzzled, or thoughtful face" (Bavelas & Chovil, 2018, p. 111). Similarly, in the examples reported (Table 33), these displays were deployed at relevant transition points during which speakers resorted to temporary solitary practices. These practices were further made visibly available to the recipients, who did not interrupt the speakers while they were delaying the course of their multimodal talk. As Bavelas & Chovil (2018, p. 111) further stated: "it is a temporary hesitation that requires nothing of the addressee but to wait". Once more, the notion of delaying or suspending speech is further embodied in recurrent, recognizable, and salient facial displays which evoke epistemic stance, and to a larger extent the notion of *hesitation*.

This act of hesitating, marked by vocal and gestural markers of suspension in the multimodal flow, may also mark a *fluent* and *smooth* transition towards a change of participation and of pace. In the case of the non-native speaker during the tandem interaction (*Excerpt 1.b*, Chapter 4), she interrupted and delayed the course of her utterance multiple times to look for the right words in her target language, while signaling her continued engagement towards the activity-in-progress.

Similar practices are reported in the following examples. In particular, I will focus on instances of *self-touch*. As Heller (2021) claimed, touching a part of one's body implies that "the individual gets entangled in the haptic-kinetic perception

Table 31. Summary of embodied displays of thinking in previous examples (Chapter 4)

Illustration	Example	Description	Context	Participant's status
	Excerpt 1.b (Chapter 4)	Squinting of the eyes, eyebrow frown, gazes away, hands in rest position	Speaker is looking for her words, marked by a series of vocal fluencemes in the acoustic channel	Non-native French speaker in tandem interaction
	Excerpt 1.b (Chapter 4)	Smiles, looks up and brings her head up, hands in rest position	Speaker explicitely signals her word-searching problems with an explicit editing phrase ("I ain't got the word here")	Non-native French speaker in tandem interaction
	Excerpt 1.b (Chapter 4)	Squinting of the eyes, winces, gazes away, hands held in the same position	Produces a series of unintelligible words before reformulating	Non-native French speaker in tandem interaction

of her own body and shields herself from other stimuli" (p. 8). Thinking postures which involve self-touch may be also regarded as *stylized*, as Heller (2021) and Bavelas & Chovil (2018) noted, and echo similar famous representations found in Art, such as "The Thinker" by Rodin, or even "The Scream" by Edvard Munch. The following examples further illustrate this point.

Ex. thinking posture 1

The first excerpt is taken from Pair 3 in English in the SITAF corpus, where the participants are discussing whether prisoners should have the right to vote. Marina, the non-native speaker, spoke first and gave her opinion, mainly that prisoners should still keep their rights as citizens even though they are in jail, since they are going to go back to society eventually (omitted from the transcription). It is now Julia's turn to speak, and she feels somewhat conflicted about this topic.

```
              *JUL: but I don't actually like um (0.878) [!]
→                                             [FLUENCEME SEQ.]
((scratches her cheek with index finger))  ((thinking posture))
```

```
    I don't [/] I do:on't (0.909) [/] I don't feel like that's valid
    (0.400) feeling like that.
```

Julia's thinking posture, characterized by several recurrent features identified earlier, mainly imaginative gaze, self-touch, and inflexible posture, closely echoes a widely recognized and conventionalized embodiment of thinking or skeptical stance, also found in digital communication in the form of an *emoji* (a small image encoded in text messages and other forms of digital communication) known as the *Thinking Face Emoji* (🤔 see Gawne & McCulloch, 2019) with the hand rested on the chin. By performing this thinking posture, Julia manages to simultaneously mark epistemic stance towards her utterance, as well as her personal involvement towards the argumentative task at hand, with her use of the emotion verb "feel". This *doing thinking* practice is also recognized as such by her conversational partner, who displays her understanding through head nods and shared gaze (not in the transcription). In addition, the display of this thinking posture is perfectly synchronized with a complex fluenceme sequence comprised of a filled pause, an unfilled pause, and a tongue click. In this context, the tongue click may function as a stance marker, illustrating another slightly different function and turn position from the ones described in Chapter 5 (see Chapter 5, Section III.3.1).

Ex. thinking posture 2
This excerpt is taken from Pair 09 in the SITAF corpus introduced in Chapter 4 (see Excerpt 3A, Chapter 4, Section III) in the exchange in French where they are also discussing whether prisoners should have the right to vote. The native speaker (Emilie, A09) speaks first and seems a bit at loss for words as she has never thought about this type of issue before, but then provides a series of arguments in favor of voting.

```
→ 1 *EMI: mais euh (0.840) euh wow (laughs) je sais pas quoi dire eum (2.120)
           but euh (0.840) euh wow (laughs) I don't know what to say eum (2.120)
```

```
((EMI gazes away, touches her ear, her body oriented to the side))
((ART gazes towards paper, hand resting on chin, body crouched))
```

```
2  bah c'est pas parce-qu'ils sont prisonniers que:e (0.410)
   well it's not because they're prisoners tha:at (0.410)
   i:ils pourraient pas voter
   the:ey couldn't vote
   ((Emilie slightly moves her body towards ART, gazes towards him))
          ((ART remains in the same inflexible thinking posture))
```

```
3  *EMI: ils font quand même parti d'une nation.
         they're still part of a nation
```

Two instances of thinking postures are deployed together almost simultaneously by the two different speakers at the beginning of the excerpt, when Emilie takes the turn with utterance-initial fluencemes (*FP+UP+FP*) as she rotates her body to the side, gazes away, and touches her right ear. She remains in this position until the end of her second fluenceme sequence comprised of an explicit editing phrase "je sais pas quoi dire" (I don't know what to say), a nasalized filled pause ("eum") and an unfilled pause of significantly long duration (2220 ms), indexing her next piece of talk. Similarly, her partner Arthur also displays a very characteristic thinking posture, which closely resembles the posture depicted by Rodin in *The Thinker*, a famous sculpture representing a male individual in deep thought; his body is crouched, his hand resting on his chin, and he displays a salient thinking face. Even though these two thinking postures were initiated at the same time by the two speakers at the beginning of the sequence, as they were engaged in collaborative joint thinking, the exchange takes a whole different turn when Emilie shifts from her solitary thinking activity and turns her body towards Arthur in line 2, as she begins to provide a number of arguments in favor of the topic. However, Arthur remains in the same inflexible posture, and completely withdraws himself from the interaction, as he shows utter disengagement from the ongoing activity, marked by his lack of vocal and visual participation, i.e., he does not respond to any of what Emilie is saying with either vocal or visual backchanneling (e.g. head nods) at *backchannel relevant spaces* (Heldner et al., 2013) i.e., intervals where it is relevant for other speakers to provide backchannel. Note that this type of asymmetrical positioning was also found during their exchange in English where the roles were reversed (see *Excerpt 3a*, Section III, Chapter 4) and when the French non-native speaker constantly gazed towards the piece of paper and showed little participation in the ongoing exchange.

thinking posture 3
The final excerpt is taken from the conversational exchange between Dan (D1) and Laura (D2) from the DisReg corpus. They are talking about assignments they are preparing for their class presentations, and more specifically about the relationship between servants and masters in Molière's play *Le Malade Imaginaire*.

```
 1 *LAU: hhh. elle est plutôt du côté bon de son autre maîtresse la fille
        hhh. she is rather on well her other mistress' side the girl
→2 *LAU: mais en l'occurrence (0.571) mmm +/.
        but in this case (0.571) mm +/.
                       [FLUENCEME SEQ.]
   ((thinking posture + leans her head to her left and right))
```

```
 3 *DAN: bah moi j'ai plus l'impression que (0.572) es [//] euh fin
        well I have more the impression that (0.572) es [///] euh well
        que Argan c'est vraiment son maître.
        that Argan really is her master
```

Laura displays another type of thinking posture in line 2 in turn-final position which presents slightly different characteristics. We find instances of frowning, looking up, and wincing, which are, so far, recurrent features of doing thinking, but the speaker also brings both her palms to her cheeks, her fingers almost touching her ears. She also leans her head to her left and right in alternated motions, further embodying the action of decision-making, which may be another recurrent feature of doing thinking and doing hesitation. Once more, this posture is perfectly synchronized with the emergence of a fluenceme sequence (following the VOC+NL pattern), which also becomes a transition relevant place for Dan, who takes his turn and gives his opinion on the current matter.

This specific posture may also echo another famous art work *The Scream*, a painting by Expressionist artist Edvard Munch, depicting a man standing by a bridge, screaming, with a horrified look on his face, his palms placed on his cheeks, covering his ears. Even though the facial expressions are radically different, the two speakers displayed a similar posture, hinting once more to the fact that embodied displays of thinking in social interaction bear stylized or iconic properties, and are in permanent interaction with popular culture and art (Boutet, 2018). As Müller (2014, p. 453) rightly put it: "Gesturing hands are so intricately bound to the act of speaking that they function as an icon for speaking in the visual arts". This was shown across the different excerpts, where several references to works of art or digital illustrations were mentioned, as summarized in Figure 38.

Figure 38. Thinking displays as stylized and iconic postures imbricated into art and popular culture

To conclude, the different analyses of embodied displays of thinking or hesitation documented in this section have illustrated several recurrent features of this social practice, emerging within complex multimodal gestalts (Heller, 2021, Mondada, 2014) or compound enactments (Debras, 2017, Streeck, 2009b). Following the work of Heller (2021), I introduced several embodied practices of doing thinking, which were shown to function as relevant displays in specific interactional sequences (repair, disaffiliation, or turn projection) involving multiple modalities (vocal fluencemes and a series of facial and body displays). This further acknowledges the embodied nature of hesitation, and to a larger extent of inter-(dis)fluency, characterized by a number of multimodal markers of suspension (speech, hand gesture, and body suspension) to manage the fluency of multimodal discourse. Table 32 summarizes the different visual and vocal resources identified in this section.

Table 32. Summary of features embodying practices of doing thinking

FACIAL AND BODY DISPLAYS
- Imaginative gaze
- Squinting and wandering of the eyes
- Eyebrow frown
- Raising one's head up and looking up
- Self-touch (hand resting on chin, or touching one's ear or face)
- Body crouched, or oriented to the side in an inflexible posture
- Head leaning back and forth to the left and right

VERBAL AND VOCAL DISPLAYS
- Nasalized vocalizations and filled pauses *(mm, eum, um)*
- Tongue clicks *(tsk, ttut)*
- Silent pauses
- Explicit editing phrases *(je sais pas quoi dire, I ain't got the word)*

2.1.2 *Gestural practices of doing thinking*

While Heller (2021) or Bavelas & Chovil (2018) focused more specifically on stylized inflexible postures, we may also find other instances of *doing thinking* that involve a richer gesturing activity. In Chapter 3, I mentioned Gullberg's use of the term *thinking gestures*, which are metapragmatic gestures that do not relate to referential content but rather comment on "the breakdown itself" (Graziano & Gullberg, 2018), and the latter are also known as *Butterworth* or "conduit" gestures (in McNeill, 1985 and Tellier & Stam, 2012), and refer to gestures used for word searches specifically (cf Chapter 3, Section II.2.2.3). As Graziano & Gullberg (2018) pointed out, many of these word-searching gestures involve a rotation of the wrist, and they have in fact been extensively documented in Ladewig's work on recurrent gestures (Ladewig, 2011, 2014; Ladewig & Bressem, 2013) under the label "cyclic gesture". As explained earlier in the methodology (cf Chapter 3, Section II.2.2.3) the category "thinking gesture" was used in the functional classification to refer to a large class of metapragmatic gestures used to enact word searching and thinking activities, in line with Gullberg (2011) and Graziano & Gullberg (2018), but without annotating their formal features, to remain consistent with functional criteria.

We shall now turn to a more formal analysis of these gestural practices of doing thinking from the two corpora. The first one is the finger snap. This involves a forceful and rapid movement of the thumb towards the index finger, usually performed with a single hand, creating a snapping or clicking sound. A quick reference to this gesture is found in Poggi's (2001) paper on her typology of gestures. In one section, she focuses on the semantic content of gestural actions, whether they communicate about abstract or concrete objects, or convey speakers' mental states (i.e., beliefs, goals, and emotions). In particular, she mentions the types of gestures that display metacognitive information towards a speaker's utterance, which is very similar to the types of metacommunicative functions described earlier. She claims (Poggi, 2011, p. 3):

> we provide metacognitive information as we inform about the source of what we are saying: we may be trying to retrieve information from our long-term memory, as we imply when we "snap thumb and middle finger" (=I am trying to remember); or we may try to concentrate, that is, to draw particular attention to our own thinking, as we imply by "leaning chin on fist"   (Rodin's Thinker posture)

Interestingly, Poggi also makes a reference to the thinking posture described earlier in Section 2.1, but she does not provide any example or illustration of these gestures in context. In addition, while she focuses on the externalization of "mental states" through gesture (in line with the *cognitive-psychological* approach to gesture, cf Chapter 1, Section III. 3.3.2), I maintain that such manifestations should be regarded as relevant social and interactional displays, which emerge from specific participation frameworks in particular multimodal settings, following Heller (2001) and Goodwin & Goodwin (1986). In addition, as Streeck (2020) further emphasized, manual gestures should not be viewed as *mere reflections* of the inner workings of the mind, but rather as dynamic actions abstracted from haptic acts, i.e., touch, physical actions, or manipulation of objects. It is still relevant to note, however, that finger snaps perform meta-communicative functions, as they embody the process of thinking, searching, or "remembering", according to Poggi. In Chapter 4, I briefly mentioned the emergence of a finger-snap gesture in Excerpt 1a, illustrated in Figure 39.

In *Excerpt 1a*, the finger-snap gesture emerged in a word-searching context in L2 during a complex fluenceme sequence within Sally's discourse, as she explicitly signaled her word-finding difficulties ("I don't know how the word") thus directing her attention (and her interlocutor's) towards the current search-in-progress, presenting it as a relevant activity to pursue the ongoing exchange. Here the snapping motion was performed twice with the left hand, which was previously held, as Sally expressed her expressive difficulties. A very similar pattern is also found in the following example.

Chapter 6. On the relationship between inter-(dis)fluency and gesture 207

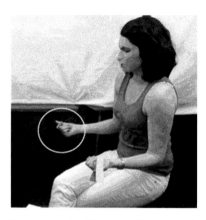

Figure 39. Occurrence of finger snap in Chapter 4 (Excerpt 1.a)

Ex. thinking gest – finger snap
This excerpt is taken from Pair C in the conversation-session (DisReg) where Laura (C2) and Dan (C1) are still talking about the role of Toinette in Molière's *Le Malade Imaginaire (cf* Excerpt *Thinking Posture (D)*. Dan suggests that Toinette (the servant) is kind of acting like a second wife towards her master (omitted from the transcription), and he further elaborates on this idea.

```
  1 DAN: ba:ah elle est très maternelle avec lui +/.
         we:ell she's very maternal with him +/.
  2 LAU:       +< ouais c'est vrai qu'elle le gronde plus au début
              +< yeah it's true that she scolds him more at first
  3 DAN: genre euh +//.
     like euh +//.
  4 DAN: ouais
     yeah
→ 5 DAN: pıs mëme à un moment elle hhh. fin mmm comment dire euh
     and then at some point she hhh. well mmm how do I say this euh
                              [FLUENCEME SEQ.]
                                 ******
          ((head oriented to the right; snaps his fingers twice))
```

```
     un moment elle lui demande de prendre son traitement
     at some point she asks him to take his medecine
     **************************************
```

```
((right hand held + gazes towards LAU))
fi:in je trouve ça presque ironique
li:ike I find that almost ironic
```

Similarly, the finger-snap gesture performed by Dan also emerges in a searching context. Here Dan is trying to find an appropriate and relevant illustration of Toinette's role as a mother figure in the play. He does so by first qualifying her as "maternal", which Laura agrees with, and then begins to search for a specific moment from the play ("à un moment"/ at some point l. 5). This is conveyed by his complex fluenceme sequence, comprised of a nasal vocalization, an explicit editing phrase ("how do I say this") and a filled pause during which he initiates the finger-snap gesture. Just like the non-native speaker from Excerpt 1a, the snapping motion is performed twice with the left hand in the upper lower gesture space. However, unlike Sally the L2 speaker, Dan is not experiencing language-related difficulties, but is rather concerned with the relevance of what he is about to say. The snapping motion may further conceptualize the dynamic and embodied act of thinking, derived from the motor activity and clicking sound of the gesture, which further creates a kinesthetic and tactile experience for the speaker (Streeck, 2021) to seek or grasp his next piece of discourse to present to his interlocutor. This is also visible in his gaze, as he is gazing away while performing the snapping motion, further reflecting a temporary disengagement from the interactive task at hand, which echoes the previous analyses of thinking postures characterized by gaze withdrawal. In addition, this example shows that the practice of *doing thinking* is not only characterized by temporarily "frozen" thinking postures, but may involve dynamic gestural actions as well, such as cyclic or finger-snap gestures.

This leads us to a second type of thinking gesture variant found in the data, characterized by a tapping of the fingers. This is illustrated in the two examples below, taken from DisReg.

Ex. thinking gest – finger tapping (A)
This is taken from the same exchange between Laura and Dan, and Laura is talking about whether servants are truly loyal to their masters.

```
  1 LAU: hhh. mais c'est peut-être ça qui serait intéressant parce-que
         hhh. but that's what may be interesting because
         euh (0.400) du coup (0.557) est-ce que les serviteurs aussi
         euh (0.400) so (0.557) do servants also
     ils assurent la loyauté
         ensure loyalty
                ******
            ((taps fingers from her left hand on the table twice))
→ 2 LAU: mais eum (1.042) [!] d'un autre côté (1.265)
         but eum (1.042) [!] on the other hand (1.265)
                      *********
```

Chapter 6. On the relationship between inter-(dis)fluency and gesture   209

((taps her fingers four times + looks up))

et j'ai oublié que j'allais dire
and I forgot what I was about to say
3 DAN: (laughs)

Ex. thinking gest – finger tapping (B)
This is taken from Pair E of the DisReg corpus where Tina (E1) and Lea (E2) are talking about the books they had to read for the semester.

1 LEA: et toi du coup euh à part euh la littérature euh comparée et
and you so euh except for euh comparative euh literature and
Agrippat t'as quoi d'autre comme euh bouquin?
Agrippat what other euh books do you have?
2 TINA: euh olala (sighs) c'est une grande question ça hhh. ba:ah en
euh olala (sighs) that's a big question hhh. we:ell act(ually)
(f)ait euh attends à part Agripa:at bah j'ai pas d'autre livre
euh wait except Agripa:at well I don't have any other book
3 LEA: ah ouais
oh yeah
4 LEA: ah t'as de la chance (laughs)
ah you're lucky (laughs)
→ 5 TINA: ah si j'en ai t(u) sais c'est [/] c'est un cours là **eum hhh**.
*ah I do have one you know it's [/] it's a class on **eum hhh**.*
                                                               ****

((eyes closed + taps her fingers four times on the table))

c'est une UE libre!
it's on an optional course!
****
((gazes towards LEA, extends her left arm towards LEA with a PUOH))

In the two examples above, the speakers performed a similar gesture with their left hand that involves several beat motions of their fingers against the table next to them. In both cases this finger-tap gesture was produced during fluencemes (although for Laura the gesture was also initiated prior to the fluenceme sequence); and they also emerged in contexts of deep thinking, or deep search, while they were withdrawing their gaze. In Excerpt A, Laura is wondering whether servants are truly loyal to their masters, and is looking for something to add that may be insightful, which requires additional time for thinking, so she gazes up and inserts a silent pause of rather long duration (1.265 milliseconds) while tapping her fingers against the table, signaling a change of participation towards a self-oriented search. Similarly, in Excerpt B, Tina is thinking about the other books she may have read during the semester and remembers one that she had in a specific class, called an "UE libre" in French, a sort of optional class that is not part of the student's major. She does not remember the name of this class right away, so she delays her utterance for some time with a nasalized filled pause and an inbreath, and also retreats into a solitary word search, during which she closes her eyes and taps her fingers against the table. In both cases, the two speakers withdrew their gaze while performing the tapping motion, just like the previous excerpts introduced above with the finger snaps. And just like the finger-snap gesture, this gesture is performed with several motions of the fingers which create a soft noise. It is further relevant to note that the finger-tap gestures could have easily been produced on the participants' bodies (i.e. on their lap) and not necessarily on the desk, which further gives support to the close relationship between language, the body and the material environment.

To conclude, the aim of this section was to demonstrate the ways our vocal, gestural, and physical actions all interact to jointly perform specific social practices in discourse. More specifically, I focused on the practice of "doing thinking", a term coined by Heller (2021) who followed the work of Goodwin & Goodwin (1986) on specific facial displays known as "thinking" faces, and who identified multimodal gestalts of doing thinking, characterized by imaginative gaze, frowning, and inflexible posture. Similarly, I presented a number of qualitative analyses from the data which showed similar instances of doing thinking, and examined them more specifically through the lens of inter-(dis)fluency and hesitation. In addition, I included the deployment of other relevant gestural actions into the practice of doing thinking, mainly finger snaps and finger-tapping gestures. The latter were all characterized by a series of repetitive dynamic motions (either a snapping or a beat motion performed with the fingers) and were also sometimes accompanied by specific facial displays (e.g., frown, gaze withdrawal). This has further shown that the act of doing thinking can also invoke more dynamic gestural actions which make use of the material space around them. While this section has only focused on rather solitary self-oriented practices, we shall now turn to the analysis of intersubjective displays.

2.2 Embodied displays of stance and intersubjectivity

As explained in Chapters 4 and 5, fluencemes are multifunctional, and may relate to planning, monitoring, in other words, production-oriented processes (*Own Communication Management*), or may as well embody interactional and communicative actions (*Interactive Communication Management*). This section presents a selection of visible and bodily displays which deal with interpersonal mechanisms (i.e., turn-taking management, displays of understanding,), and perform or enact communicative actions in the interaction. The latter are typically known as *interactive* (Bavelas et al., 1992, 1995) or *performative* gestures (e.g., Cienki, 2004; Kendon, 2004, Müller, 2015), and very often take the form of palm-up open hands oriented towards the interlocutor as to offer, present, give, request, or handle over a piece of discourse, an argument, or a turn (Bavelas et al., 1992; Kendon, 1995, 2004; Müller, 2017; Müller et al., 2013; Streeck & Hartge, 1992). They may also involve instances of pointing towards the interlocutor, as to include them in the interactional task, or cite their previous contribution (Bavelas et al., 1992). However, performative/interactive gestures do not only deal with turn-taking matters, but may also further convey speakers' attitudes towards what they are saying (e.g., indifference, indignation, obviousness etc.,), and this is often conveyed by shoulder shrugs, or head shifts (Debras & Cienki, 2012; Kendon, 2004; Streeck, 2009b). While all these types of gestural actions have been thoroughly documented and carefully analyzed in different papers within the field of gesture studies over the past 30 years, little is known about their coordination with fluencemes. Such instances have already been illustrated in previous chapters, and are summarized in Table 33.

In Excerpt 2b (Chapter 4), the non-native speaker extended his left palm-up open hand towards his interlocutor at the end of this turn to invite her to take the floor, as he was talking about the types of sensitive topics that friends may share, further including her in the current topic of conversation. This gesture also coincided with a fluenceme sequence at a transition relevant place, when his partner took the turn.

Similarly, in Excerpt 2.2 (Chapter 5) the speaker raised his index finger from his right hand and slightly oriented it towards his interlocutor as to acknowledge her presence (and the presence of an imaginary audience as he was telling a humorous anecdote), and hand other relevant discourse material. This gesture was also produced during a pause following the production of a funny catch phrase "le saviez-vous" (*did you know*), further contributing to the humorous dimension of his story. While the gestures documented in the table served comparatively different functions (i.e., turn-taking, stance-taking, attention-seeking, etc.,) and occurred at different turn-positions (turn-medial and turn-final) they

Table 33. Summary of communicative displays deployed during fluencemes in previous chapters

Illustration	Example	Context	Visual-gestural description
	Excerpt 2 B (Chapter 4)	American NNS is inviting his interlocutor to take the turn	Left Palm-Up Open Hand extended towards the interlocutor
	Excerpt 2.2 (Chapter 5)	French native speaker is adressing his interlocutor and an imaginary audience	Stretched index finger from left hand is raised and slightly oriented towards the interlocutor
	Excerpt 2.2 (Chapter 5)	French native speaker is paying a tribute to the protagonist from his story	Stretched index finger raised in the air

all performed communicative illocutionary acts and embodied an interactional move. In fact, Kendon (1995) referred to this class of gestures as "illocutionary marker gestures". In addition, all these gestures occurred without speech, in other words, during fluencemes. This further reveals that fluencemes produced in the speech channel may provide relevant opportunities for interactants to perform multimodal communicative actions within the interaction; even though the flow of speech is momentarily suspended or interrupted, it *opens up* to another semiotic field in a different modality to build *deliberate expressiveness* (Kendon, 2004, p. 13–14). This is further illustrated in the following example.

Ex. interactive gest
This excerpt is taken from Pair 16 of the SITAF corpus during the tandem exchange in English. Here the two partners are talking about whether prisoners should get the right to vote, and after agreeing that prisoners are still citizens and must definitely keep this right (omitted from the transcription) the French non-native speaker (Elisa, F16) is wondering about the types of serious crimes that actually prevent prisoners from voting.

```
     1 *ELI: and even if you I don't know killed someone?
                             *******   ********
((right hand: points to the right)) ((left hand: performs a waving motion towards her shoulder))
→    2 *BET:                      +< ex(cept) [//] unless hhhh. [/] unless
                                  ~~~~~~~~~~~********************
((looks up, extends her index finger towards ELI from her right hand and performs
two beat motions + hold))
```

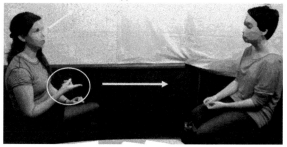

```
     you've committed um (0.620) a certain level of felony.
     *****************+.+.+.+.+.+.     **********
((bends her fingers from her right hand and sways back and forth))
```

Here the two participants are talking about the United States more specifically, so Beth, the American speaker, does not only position herself as a native speaker of American English, but also as someone who has a certain knowledge of her country's body of law and its rules and regulations. Beth first claims that prisoners do have the right to vote in the United States, which comes as a surprise to Elisa, which further prompts Beth to re-shape her previous assessment, perhaps to align with Elisa's expectations (not in the transcription). A complex fluenceme sequence emerges at the beginning of Beth's subsequent turn in line 2, during which she reconsiders the matter at hand. She first initiates a preposition ("except") but in truncated form, replaces it with another one ("unless" in its complete form), followed by an audible inbreath, and a repetition of the initial word. Beth also extends her index finger towards Elisa in her lower gesture space during the fluenceme sequence, and holds it the same position until her production of a second fluenceme sequence in mid-utterance (FP+UP) when her gesture is retracted. The gesture initiated during the first sequence shares close formal and functional properties with the one performed by Paul in Excerpt 2.2 except for the hand configuration and position in the gesture space. In Paul's case, the index finger was raised in the center space with the palm vertical, while here it is only extended in the lower gesture space with the palm up. In both cases, nonetheless, the two gestures are oriented towards the partner and can thus be considered *interactive* and be recognized more specifically as *delivery* gestures (cf Bavelas et al., (1995) i.e. gestures used to hand over information relevant to the speakers. Even though Beth is pointing towards Elisa, it is not to indicate an object, person, or location in this case (as pointing gestures often do e.g. Kendon & Versante, 2003), but rather to acknowledge her partner's presence and present an upcoming piece of discourse as potentially relevant material to the activity-in-progress. In addition, Beth is also seen gazing up, then down, and she only shifts her gaze back towards her partner when she finishes her utterance and introduces the noun phrase "a certain level of felony". This shift in gaze behavior may be interpreted as a sign that Beth is dealing with multiple orientations at the same time: on the one hand she is re-elaborating her previous assessment, which prompts her to modify parts of her talk and think about what to say next (self-oriented); and on the other she may also be wishing to capture her partner's attention and react to what they have been discussing in the prior turn (other-oriented). Once more, this example reveals the multidimensionality and multifunctionality of inter-(dis)fluency phenomena, which can further be determined by paying close attention to their co-occurring visual-gestural behavior and gaze within the turns-at-talk.

To conclude, this example further demonstrated that we cannot strictly separate the speech channel from the gestural channel, nor claim that one modality replaces the other, as the different articulators used in discourse to build meaningful language (i.e. the lips, the tongue, the mouth, as well as the limbs) do not operate independently from one another, but are rather co-deployed harmoniously in ways that are relevant to the *fluent* achievement of the interactional task at hand. In addition, these examples have further put forward the interactional dimension of *inter-fluency*, which should not only be regarded as a cognitive internal and mental process underlying planning or thinking processes, but as a dynamic interactive practice which is very sensitive to the affordances of the situation.

Conclusion to the chapter

The aim of this chapter was to further explore the multimodal dimension of inter-(dis)fluency by drawing on a number of qualitative analyses extracted from the data illustrating the different visible practices occurring during fluencemes and in their close vicinity. In this chapter I focused on a more *form-based* approach to gesture, documenting formally similar gestural patterns, thus taking a step further from the initial gesture functional typology used in the quantitative annotations. I first illustrated the tight relationship between speech and gesture production through several examples of gestural holds, retraction, and preparation coordinated with fluencemes, reflecting a unified process performed in the two modalities. I then documented a series of recurrent visible practices found during fluencemes, with several facial and body displays of doing thinking, as well as manual actions (finger snaps and finger-tapping gestures) and intersubjective displays (with palm-up open hand gestures and raised index fingers). These analyses led us to a closer understanding of the notion of *language* which captures multimodal language use grounded in situated and embodied discourse. In this view, fluency should not solely be regarded as a vocal or temporal phenomenon, restricted to mental states or proficiency levels, but as a fully multimodal process, relying on a multiplicity of resources in situated discourse. Hence the practice of *doing hesitation*, or *doing fluency*, can further be recognized as an embodied social act, rather than as a mere by-product of verbal processes.

However, this chapter also raises a few questions regarding methodology in gesture research. For the sake of clarity and consistency, I chose to work on a functional classification of gestures with a finite set of categories in the quantitative analysis, in order to get a clear idea of the gestural distribution and tendencies found in the two datasets. However, it could be argued that some gesture functions may overlap in certain situations (e.g. pragmatic and referential functions), which makes the coding process quite difficult, and ultimately requires inter-coder reliability. While I did use inter-coder reliability (cf Chapter 3), this was only performed on 15% of the data, which remains limited. In addition, I did not annotate the different forms, handshapes, or configurations of the gestures in the data at a quantitative level, which would have been highly time consuming, but which would also have resulted in a high number of different categories, making statistical analysis difficult. The solution was thus to combine quantitative annotations with qualitative analyses of the data in order to reflect different aspects of the gestures at different levels (form, function, shape, context of use etc.). However, the ideal solution would be to integrate a multi-level annotation system based on *both* the forms and functions of gestures, see for example *The MultiModal MultiDimensional* (M3D) labelling scheme for the annotation of audiovisual corpora (Rohrer et al., 2020). But such models do not incorporate the analysis of inter-(dis)fluency, which is fundamental to the present study, and which, as maintained throughout this chapter, needs to find a place within the field of gesture studies.

General conclusion

I. Beyond disfluency: Towards a multidimensional framework

The present study has stressed the need to situate inter-(dis)fluency in a larger integrated framework in order to bridge the gap between "traditional" production-based psycholinguistic studies conducted in disfluency research, and interactional, multimodal approaches to social interaction. In this framework, the core notion of *fluency*, understood here as flow, continuity, progressivity, or communicativeness, is a flexible and dynamic process which is constantly reshaping its focus, and which can potentially be interrupted, suspended, or disrupted, at different levels of analysis, as illustrated in Figure 40.

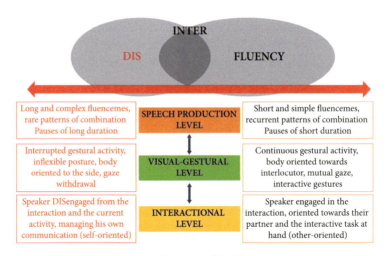

Figure 40. Multidimensional approach to inter-(dis)fluency

In the verbal and vocal level, a short and simple vocal fluenceme is not often deemed disruptive and "disfluent", since it is barely perceptive in the vocal channel, but a very long sequence containing a dozen of different markers can mark a significant delay in the speech signal, hence disrupting its initial delivery. This is the traditional view of disfluency, as cued by several temporal variables, as well as others, such as syntactic position, or co-occurrence with other markers. The visual-gestural and interactional dimensions offer entirely different views on these phenomena, since a priori "disfluent" forms in the speech signal can still perform "fluent" communicative actions in the interactional flow. For instance, in Chapter 4, I showed a series of examples from the SITAF corpus in which non-native speakers produced a number of fluencemes in the verbal channel, hence temporarily interrupting the flow of speech, but who also made use of their hands and gaze to co- construct meaning with their interlocutor, hence contributing to the interactional fluency of the exchange (Excerpts 1B, 2A and 2B). Conversely, in Chapter 5, I showed how one particular student, who was ideally "fluent" from a speech production perspective, as he produced very few fluencemes compared to the rest of the group, was in fact quite "disfluent" from a visual-gestural and interactional perspective, since he seemed very *DIS*engaged from his audience, only focusing on his own production (cf Excerpt 1.5.a). In Chapter 6, I put forward the role of gaze direction to index changes of participation, from self-oriented cognitive practices to other-oriented interactive ones (Excerpt "Interactive Gest", Section 2.2, Chapter 6). In some cases, these dimensions were shown to converge (i.e. gaze withdrawal associated with a self-oriented practice marked by a very long fluenceme sequence), and in others they were divergent (e.g. a short fluenceme disrupting the progressivity of the exchange).

This novel approach also challenges the implications of the various definitions of disfluency provided in Second Language Acquisition research, as it does not restrict it to negative notions such as lack of proficiency, or "resource deficit" (Dörnyei & Kormos, 1998). In the present work, L2 fluency has largely been associated with the notion of interactional competence (cf Galaczi, 2014, Chapter 2) and focuses on learners' ability to co-construct interaction rather than to deal with difficulties alone, in line with the interactional level of the inter-(dis)fluency model.

II. Summary of the main findings

Analyses were carried out on two video corpora, the SITAF corpus and the Dis-Reg corpus, which both include productions of undergraduate students in different languages (French and English) and settings (formal class presentations and informal conversations). The compilation of this dataset aimed to establish a comprehensive perspective by triangulating evidence from different parameters, such as language proficiency, context, task type, genre, and setting, in order to shed light on the multifunctionality and multimodality of inter-(dis)fluency within a range of contextual usages.

2.1 Study on the SITAF corpus: Native versus non-native productions

One of the main research questions this study sought to answer was whether L2 fluency differed significantly from L1 fluency, and I showed how such differences could be measured by looking at temporal variables and fluency rates, as well as sequential, positional, and visual-gestural features, leading to more subtle differences. Results showed a higher rate of fluencemes in L2 than L1 (for both groups), with a number of differences in distribution: for the American Group, more repetitions and filled pauses were found in L2, but more self-interruptions and unfilled pauses in L1. For the French group, however, more self-interruptions and prolongations were found in L1, but more non-lexical sounds in L2, exhibiting a different pattern of distribution. In addition, the American group produced more complex fluenceme sequences in their L2 than in their L1, comprising a higher number of markers combined on average. However, no significant differences were found for the French group. Differences were also found in the sequence configurations: American speakers showed a tendency to produce sequences which mainly consisted in the *VOC+MS* configuration in their L2, and the *VOC+VOC* configuration in their L1, suggesting preferences for stalling strategies in the L1, as opposed to a mixture of stalling and repair mechanisms in the L2. For the French group, however, the *VOC+MS* pattern was used more frequently in their L1 than in their L2, showing once again an opposite tendency. Overall, these results seemed to suggest that some specific patterns were more prominent than others, especially *VOC+MS* and *VOC+VOC*, but their use was not systematically determined by levels of proficiency, but rather by language preferences. Slight differences were also found in the positions of the fluenceme sequences in the two language groups: American speakers produced a slightly higher proportion of sequences in medial position in L2 than in L1, while the French group produced slightly more utterance-final fluencemes in their L1 than in the L2.

Most importantly, one of the major contributions of this study was to analyze inter-(dis)fluency with regards to gaze and gestural behavior, in order to go beyond a traditional view of L2 fluency which has too often been restricted to temporal variables in SLA research. Following previous work (e.g. Gullberg, 1998; Kita, 1993; Stam, 2006), a higher rate of gestures in L2 than in L1 was expected, and the findings confirmed this prediction, as the two speaker groups produced significantly more gestures in their L2 than in their L1, both in sequences with and without fluencemes (even though gestures did not frequently occur during fluencemes), which demonstrated a higher gestural activity in the L2 overall. In addition, I argued against cognitive-psychological approaches to gesture with theories such as the *Lexical Retrieval Hypothesis* (LRH; Krauss et al., 2000), or *Information Packaging Hypothesis* (Kita, 2000) following the work of Graziano &

Gullberg (2018). As argued, I did not believe that speakers produced more gestures in their L2 because of lexical problems (Beattie & Butterworth, 1979; Krauss & Hadar, 1999), or that they produced referential gestures during fluencemes to overcome a "lack of skill" in their L2, which would be too restrictive, suggesting that speech and gesture worked independently from one another. Indeed, as the quantitative results showed, the two speaker groups produced a higher rate of referential gestures in their L1 than in their L2 overall, which challenged the idea that speakers produced more referential gestures in their L2 to deal with lexical difficulties (Stam, 2001). In addition, the two speaker groups were found to produce a higher proportion of referential gestures in sequences *outside* fluencemes than during them, while a large majority of the gestures produced during fluencemes were pragmatic ones, contrary to what the LRH suggested. I also noted a higher rate of thinking gestures in the L2 than in the L1 overall (for both groups, and almost exclusively during fluencemes) which may reflect one prominent feature of L2 fluency as a display of *doing thinking* (Heller, 2021). Such gestures, along with thinking faces, were also examined in the qualitative analyses, and I showed how they were used as an interactional practice to display the progressivity of a word search. When it comes to gazing behavior, the two groups showed a tendency to withdraw their gaze more often during sequences of fluencemes than without them, and this was the case both in L1 and in L2, which demonstrates a notable feature of (dis)fluency in general, regardless of language proficiency.

However, it should be noted that a high degree of variability and dispersion was found in the data, with a number of crosslinguistic and individual differences, as well as inter-group variation, leading to more nuanced findings, and further suggesting that L2 fluency is highly speaker- and language- specific (De Jong, 2018). In addition, the qualitative analyses further shed light on the individual multimodal communication strategies yielded by the L2 speakers, who made use of a variety of semiotic features (voice, face, gaze, manual gestures, the body, and material objects around them) to deal with language difficulties in the course of interaction.

2.2 Study on the DisReg corpus: Individual class presentations versus dyadic conversations

One of the main questions this second study sought to answer was whether style and setting had an effect on (dis)fluency and gesture production, and whether significant differences would be found across the two situations. I further presented the notions of style and setting as multidimensional, encompassing a wide array of inter-related factors, such as audience design, multimodal environment, turn-taking mechanisms, or register, in order to identify the different types of variables characterizing the two situations (style, audience, spatial configuration etc.). All these features were shown to have an effect on the use of (dis)fluency and visual-gestural behavior: a higher rate of fluencemes was found in class presentations, with significantly longer unfilled pauses, and a higher proportion of non-lexical sounds as well as filled pauses. The latter were also more often realized with the nasal variant ("eum") in class presentations than conversations, suggesting a longer delay (Clark & Fox Tree, 2002). In addition, a slightly higher proportion of complex fluencemes was found in class, but without differences in length. A tendency for fluenceme sequences to occur in utterance-initial position was also found in presentations, which potentially reflected a rhythmic and stylistic style, in line with Duez (1982). As to the sequence configurations, the *VOC+NL* pattern was more prevalent in class presentations than conversations, which further reflected the recurrence of non-lexical sounds in this specific institutional context. Overall, the distributional differences found across the two situations (i.e., longer pauses, slightly more complex sequences, and more instances in utterance-initial position) suggested that class presentations required more time for planning and monitoring processes than conversations. This was further confirmed by the mean length of utterances which was much longer in class than in conversation, and the positive correlation found between unfilled pause duration and utterance length, with longer pauses associated with longer utterances, as well as the overwhelming proportion of fluenceme sequences which pertained to *Own Communication Management* (almost a majority of instances) in presentations.

When it comes to gesturing and gazing behavior, a number of differences were also found across the two situations. A higher rate of gestures was found in class presentations, with a higher proportion of discursive gestures. Conversations, on the other hand, comprised a higher proportion of interactional and representational gestures, in line with Bavelas et al.'s (2008). No significant differences were found for the proportion of thinking gestures however, but the latter almost occurred only exclusively during fluencemes in the two situations, which is consistent with findings from the SITAF corpus. As the qualitative analyses further showed, speakers often made use of interactional gestures in the conversations to perform a series of communicative actions, such as establishing common ground, displaying a stance, or addressing their interlocutor in the course of their interactive practices (cf Excerpts 2.2 and 2.3). During their oral presentations, however, students almost never addressed their audience but mostly made use of gestures to segment discourse and mark information structure. In addition, a considerable proportion of gazing towards the piece of paper was found in the presentation-sessions, with a relatively very small proportion of gazing towards the interlocutor, which was a significant difference with the conversations. This finding seemed somewhat at odds with the high gesturing activity found in the presentations; I thus concluded that even though the students produced more gestures in class than in conversation, they did not use them to truly engage with their audience (as they would more often do in conversations), since they were too engrossed in their notes. In addition, findings further showed that speakers were more likely *not* to establish eye contact when they produced fluencemes in both situations, which was consistent with SITAF where the two language groups were found to withdraw their gaze more frequently during fluencemes than outside them, both in their L1 and L2. This further emphasized the fact that gazing away is a very common practice of (dis)fluency, regardless of language or setting, as it enables speakers to momentarily retreat from the current activity to attend to other relevant ones, such as retrieving an item from memory, looking for a specific word, checking for a sentence in a book, etc. However, I also showed several instances of mutual gaze coordinated with fluencemes in the conversations (see excerpts 2.2 and 2.3 during which speakers were engaged in interactive practices), which further revealed the potential for fluencemes to embody interactive processes, and not only intrapersonal ones. This ambivalence was further explored in Chapter 5, where I documented a series of practices involving gaze withdrawal (i.e. with thinking gestures) and mutual gaze (i.e. with interactive gestures).

It should also be noted that just like SITAF, a great number of individual differences were found in the data, displaying different tendencies and patterns of distribution across speakers, which further confirmed that fluency is in part dependent on personal speaking style, regardless of setting or proficiency. The analyses further revealed the interplay between fluencemes, gestures, actions, and manipulation of objects, which can all be deployed together to build the fluency of multimodal discourse. I concluded that fluencemes and gestures were highly sensitive to a number of multimodal situational features, other than language proficiency, which further gives support to the claim that they should not be considered in decontextualized utterances but in situated language use.

2.3 Synthesis

Inter-(dis)fluency can be characterized by a number of recurrent features, or traits, such as form, duration, type, pattern of co-occurrence, etc., and some of them were found to be more prominent in certain situations. For example, *combination type* was shown to be affected by language proficiency specifically in the American group from the SITAF corpus, with a higher proportion of complex sequences containing more fluencemes in the L2 than in the L1, suggesting a more complex pattern of co-occurrence in L2 fluency. However, these differences did not reach statistical significance within the French group, which may further reveal language characteristics, or individual differences.

In addition, some aspects of inter-(dis)fluency and gesture were found to differ significantly in SITAF, but not DisReg, or the other way around. For instance, no significant differences were found in the proportion of fluencemes performing *Own Communication Management* (OCM) versus *Interactive Communication Management* (ICM) in SITAF, as a majority of them served intrapersonal functions, regardless of language proficiency or language group. In DisReg, however, significant differences were found between the two situations, with a quasi-absent proportion of fluencemes serving interpersonal functions in class presentations, contrary to the conversations. This is not surprising, given the number of differences characterizing the two situations (level of interactivity, type of audience, task type etc.) which inevitably had an effect on the function of fluencemes. In addition, the speakers from the SITAF corpus were shown to produce a higher proportion of held gestures during fluencemes in their L2 than in their L1 (both groups), while no significant differences were found in DisReg between the two situations. This may reveal another feature of L2 fluency marked by a higher degree of suspension in the two modalities. Similarly, no differences were found in gaze behavior between L1 and L2 in SITAF both within and outside fluencemes, while it exhibited radically different patterns across the two situations in DisReg, with an overwhelming proportion of gazing towards the piece(s) of paper in class presentations (both within and outside fluencemes) compared to the conversations which relied more on mutual gaze. This is one distinct feature of class presentations, noted in Chapter 5, which is marked by a quasi-total absence of mutual gaze and engagement with the audience. Lastly, both language groups from the SITAF corpus showed a tendency to produce more thinking gestures in their L2 than in their L1, while no differences were found in DisReg, hinting once more to the fact that the association between the activity of doing thinking and the emergence of fluencemes may be more prominent in L2 than in L1 at a quantitative level. In Chapter 6, however, I also showed how such displays could also be manifested in the L1, at a qualitative level.

III.   Perspectives for future work

As noted in Chapters 4, 5, and 6, the present study presents a number of limitations, which calls for further research in the field. First, the data sample remains quite small and limited, especially for DisReg which is based on a selective sample used to match the size of SITAF. While I justified my choice to work on a small corpus for the present study (cf Chapter 3), I intend to extend the analysis to the whole dataset for further research, in order to see if the results presented here could be generalized to a larger sample. I also mentioned the limits of the statistical analyses, which were chosen to remain quite simple, as statistical, purely quantitative descriptions were not the core approach of this study. Indeed, I chose to mostly use a binary categorization ("L1" versus "L2", "class" versus "presentations", or "gesture" versus "no gesture", etc.); given the multiplicity of factors potentially affecting (dis)fluency use, more complex statistical models, random and fixed effects, such as mixed-model regression models, or multiple correspondence analysis, should be used in the future, in order to uncover which aspects of discourse may be more affected by (dis)fluency across different contexts of use. More progress regarding the methodology could already be considered for further investigation. For instance, I used a duration threshold for the annotation of silent pauses, which is questionable to a certain extent, given the number of pauses that were left out from the analyses. In future research, I may wish to follow Campione & Véronis (2002) and Betz (2021) who did not use a cut-off point for their identification of pauses. In a similar vein, the phonetic, acoustic, and prosodic dimensions of inter-(dis)fluency remain quite underexplored in this study, since I mostly focused on visual-gestural features, which have received less attention in the (dis)fluency literature. In addition, several questions regarding methodology in gesture research were raised in Chapter 6. While I focused on a functional typology in the quantitative model to work on a finite set of categories that would be better suited to statistical treatments, other aspects of gestures, such as form, handshape, orientation, configuration, quality of movement, flow, segments involved, and the like, were completely left out from the quantitative annotations, and were only observed in the qualitative analyses. It was thus suggested to use a multi-level gestural annotation system for future work, following previous ones such as *The MultiModal MultiDimensional* (M3D) labelling scheme for the annotation of audiovisual corpora (Rohrer et al., 2020).

So far, the present study has made two central theoretical and methodological contributions to the current field of (dis)fluency research, which are, in my opinion, also relevant to the field of linguistics and the study of *language* in general. First, this study has provided several tools for the analysis of fluency on a multidimensional scale, combining several methods from different theoretical frameworks, such as Conversation Analysis, gesture studies, psycholinguistics, and Second Language Acquisition. What the quantitative findings have suggested so far is that the complexity of inter-(dis)fluency phenomena cannot easily be broken down into a finite number of categories, and that despite general tendencies in the data, it was deemed necessary to integrate all aspects of human communication to capture the intricacies of these processes. The complexity and multifunctionality of these processes were in fact highlighted in the qualitative analyses, as they shed light on the importance of individual variation and contextual features. Second, this study has introduced a fresh and innovative approach to fluency as a multifaceted, multimodal, and dynamic phenomenon, without restricting it to temporal variables, language proficiency, repair processes, or speech error, which, I hope, may further help us unravel some of the most fascinating issues surrounding these phenomena.

References

Abrahamson, D., & Bakker, A. (2016). Making sense of movement in embodied design for mathematics learning. *Cognitive Research: Principles and Implications*, *1*(1), 1–13.

Adams, T. W. (1998). Gestures in foreigner talk. [Unplublished PhD thesis]. University of Pennsylvania.

Akhavan, N., Göksun, T., & Nozari, N. (2016). Disfluency production in speech and gesture. *CogSci*. Cognitive Science Society.

Alibali, M. W., Kita, S., & Young, A. J. (2000). Gesture and the process of speech production: We think, therefore we gesture. *Language and Cognitive Processes*, *15*(6), 593–613.

Alibali, M. W., & Nathan, M. J. (2007). Teachers' gestures as a means of scaffolding students' understanding: Evidence from an early algebra lesson. *Video Research in the Learning Sciences*, 349–365.

Allwood, J. (2017). Fluency or disfluency? *Proceedings of DiSS 2017, the 8th Workshop on Disfluency in Spontaneous Speech*, 1.

Allwood, J., Ahlsén, E., Lund, J., & Sundqvist, J. (2005). Multimodality in own communication management. *Proceedings from the Second Nordic Conference on Multimodal Communication*.

Allwood, J., Nivre, J., & Ahlsén, E. (1990). Speech Management – On the Non-written Life of Speech. *Nordic Journal of Linguistics*, *13*(1), 3–48.

Azaoui, B. (2015). Fonctions pédagogiques et implications énonciatives de ressources professorales multimodales. Le cas de la bimanualité et de l'ubiquité coénonciative. *Recherches En Didactique Des Langues et Des Cultures. Les Cahiers de l'Acedle*, *12*(12–2).

Azi, Y. A. (2018). Fillers, Repairs and Repetitions in the Conversations of Saudi English Speakers: Conversational Device or Disfluency Markers. *International Journal of Linguistics*, *10*(6), 193–205.

Barlow, M. (2013). Individual differences and usage-based grammar. *International Journal of Corpus Linguistics*, *18*(4), 443–478.

Bavelas, J. B., Chovil, N., Lawrie, D. A., & Wade, A. (1992). Interactive gestures. *Discourse Processes*, *15*(4), 469–489.

Bavelas, J. B., Chovil, N., Coates, L., & Roe, L. (1995). Gestures specialized for dialogue. *Personality and social psychology bulletin*, *21*(4), 394–405.

Bavelas, J., & Chovil, N. (2018). Some pragmatic functions of conversational facial gestures. *Gesture*, *17*(1), 98–127.

Bavelas, J., Gerwing, J., & Healing, S. (2014). Effect of dialogue on demonstrations: Direct quotations, facial portrayals, hand gestures, and figurative references. *Discourse Processes*, *51*(8), 619–655.

Bavelas, J., Gerwing, J., Sutton, C., & Prevost, D. (2008). Gesturing on the telephone: Independent effects of dialogue and visibility. *Journal of Memory and Language*, *58*(2), 495–520.

Beattie, G. W., & Shovelton, H. (1999). Do iconic hand gestures really contribute anything to the semantic information conveyed by speech? An experimental investigation. *Semiotica*, *123*(1/2), 001–030.

Beattie, G. W. (1979). *Planning units in spontaneous speech: Some evidence from hesitation in speech and speaker gaze direction in conversation*.

Beattie, G. W., & Butterworth, B. L. (1979). Contextual probability and word frequency as determinants of pauses and errors in spontaneous speech. *Language and Speech*, *22*(3), 201–211.

Belhiah, H. (2013). Gesture as a resource for intersubjectivity in second-language learning situations. *Classroom Discourse*, *4*(2), 111–129.

Bell, A. (2006). Speech Accommodation Theory and Audience Design. In J. L. Mey & R. E. Asher (Eds.), *Concise encyclopaedia of pragmatics (second edition)* (pp. 992–994). Elsevier Oxford.

Benus, S., Enos, F., Hirschberg, J. B., & Shriberg, E. (2006). *Pauses in Deceptive Speech. Proceedings of ISCA, 3rd International Conference on Speech Prosody*.

Betz, S. (2020). Hesitations in Spoken Dialogue Systems [Unpublished PhD Thesis]. Bielefeld University.

Betz, S., Carlmeyer, B., Wagner, P., & Wrede, B. (2018). Interactive Hesitation Synthesis: Modelling and Evaluation. *Multimodal Technologies and Interaction*, *2*(1), 9.

Betz, S., & Gambino, S. L. (2016). Are we all disfluent in our own special way and should dialogue systems also be? *Elektronische Sprachsignalverarbeitung (ESSV) 2016*, 81.

Betz, S., & Kosmala, L. (2019). Fill the silence! Basics for modeling hesitation. *The 9th Workshop on Disfluency in Spontaneous Speech*, 11.

Betz, S., & Wagner, P. (2016). Disfluent Lengthening in Spontaneous Speech. *Elektronische Sprachsignalverarbeitung (ESSV) 2016*.

Boersma, P. (2001). Praat, a system for doing phonetics by computer. *Glot. Int.*, *5*(9), 341–345.

Bortfeld, H., Leon, S. D., Bloom, J. E., Schober, M. F., & Brennan, S. E. (2001). Disfluency Rates in Conversation: Effects of Age, Relationship, Topic, Role, and Gender. *Language and Speech*, *44*(2), 123–147.

Boulis, C., Kahn, J. G., & Ostendorf, M. (2005). The role of disfluencies in topic classification of human-human conversations. *AAAI Workshop on Spoken Language Understanding*.

Boutet, D. (2008). Une morphologie de la gestualité: Structuration articulaire. *Cahiers de Linguistique Analogique*, 5.

Boutet, D. (2010). Structuration physiologique de la gestuelle: Modèle et tests. *Lidil. Revue de Linguistique et de Didactique Des Langues*, *42*, 77–96.

Boutet, D. (2018). *Pour une approche kinésiologique de la gestualité [Habilitation à diriger des recherches]*. Université de Rouen-Normandie.

Boutet, D., Morgenstern, A., & Cienki, A. (2016). Grammatical Aspect and Gesture in French : a kinesiological approach. *Vestnik RUDN*, *20*(3), 131–150.

Brand, C., & Götz, S. (2013). Fluency versus accuracy in advanced spoken learner language. *Errors and Disfluencies in Spoken Corpora*, *52*, 117–137.

Brennan, S. E., & Schober, M. F. (2001). How listeners compensate for disfluencies in spontaneous speech. *Journal of Memory and Language*, *44*(2), 274–296.

Bressem, J., & Müller, C. (2014). A repertoire of German recurrent gestures with pragmatic functions. In *Handbücher zur Sprach-und Kommunikationswissenschaft/Handbooks of Linguistics and Communication Science (HSK) 38/2* (Vol. 2, pp. 1575–1591). De Gruyter Mouton.

Broen, P. A., & Siegel, G. M. (1972). Variations in normal speech disfluencies. *Language and Speech*, 15(3), 219–231.

Brouwer, C. E. (2004). Doing pronunciation: A specific type of repair sequence. *Second Language Conversations*, 93–113.

Butterworth, B., & Beattie, G. (1978). Gesture and silence as indicators of planning in speech. In R. N. Campbell & P. T. Smith (Eds.), *Recent advances in the psychology of language* (pp. 347–360). Springer.

Bybee, J. (2008). *Usage-based grammar and second language acquisition*. Routledge.

Bybee, J. (2010). *Language, Usage and Cognition*. Cambridge University Press.

Campione, E., & Véronis, J. (2002). A large-scale multilingual study of silent pause duration. *Speech Prosody 2002, International Conference*.

Candea, M. (2000). Contribution à l'étude des pauses silencieuses et des phénomènes dits « d'hésitation » en français oral spontané. Étude sur un corpus de récit en classe de français. [Unpublished PhD Thesis]. Université Sorbonne Nouvelle – Paris III.

Candea, M. (2017). *Pratiques de prononciation et enjeux sociaux. Approches post-variationnistes en sociophonétique du français de France* [Habilitation à diriger des recherches]. Université Grenoble Alpes.

Candea, M., Vasilescu, I., & Adda-Decker, M. (2005). Inter-and intra-language acoustic analysis of autonomous fillers. *DISS 05, Disfluency in Spontaneous Speech Workshop*, 47–52.

Cenoz, J. (1998). *Pauses and Communication Strategies in Second Language Speech*. (ERIC Document ED 426630).

Chomsky, N. (1965). *Aspects of the Theory of Syntax*. MIT press.

Christenfeld, N., & Creager, B. (1996). Anxiety, alcohol, aphasia, and ums. *Journal of personality and social psychology*, 70(3), 451.

Christenfeld, N., Schachter, S., & Bilous, F. (1991). Filled pauses and gestures: It's not coincidence. *Journal of Psycholinguistic Research*, 20(1), 1–10.

Christodoulides, G., Avanzi, M., & Goldman, J.-P. (2018). DisMo: A morphosyntactic, disfluency and multi-word unit annotator. An evaluation on a corpus of French spontaneous and read speech. *ArXiv Preprint*

Chui, K. (2005). Temporal patterning of speech and iconic gestures in conversational discourse. *Journal of Pragmatics*, 37(6), 871–887.

Cienki, A. (2004). Bush's and Gore's language and gestures in the 2000 US presidential debates: A test case for two models of metaphors. *Journal of Language and Politics*, 3(3), 409–440.

Cienki, A. (2005). Image schemas and gesture. *From Perception to Meaning: Image Schemas in Cognitive Linguistics*, 29, 421–442.

Cienki, A. (2012). Usage events of spoken language and the symbolic units we (may) abstract from them. *Cognitive Processes in Language*, 149–158.

Cienki, A. (2015a). The dynamic scope of relevant behaviors in talk: A perspective from cognitive linguistics. *Proceedings of the 2nd European and the 5th Nordic Symposium on Multimodal Communication, August 6-8, 2014, Tartu, Estonia*, 110, 5–7.

Cienki, A. (2015b). Spoken language usage events. *Language and Cognition*, 7, 499–514.

Cienki, A. (2016). Cognitive Linguistics, gesture studies, and multimodal communication. *Cognitive Linguistics*, 27(4), 603–618.

Cienki, A. (2017). Utterance Construction Grammar (UCxG) and the variable multimodality of constructions. *Linguistics Vanguard*, 3(s1).

Cienki, A. & Irishkhanova, O. K. (2018). *Aspectuality across Languages*. John Benjamins.

Clark, H., & Fox Tree, J. E. (2002). Using uh and um in spontaneous speaking. *Cognition*, 84(1), 73–111.

Clark, H. H. (1996). *Using language*. Cambridge University Press.

Clark, H. H. (2002). Speaking in time. *Speech Communication*, 36(1), 5–13.

Clark, H. H. (2006). Pauses and hesitations: Psycholinguistic approach. In K. Brown (Ed.), *Encyclopedia of Language and Linguistics* (pp. 244–248). Oxford: Elsevier.

Clark, H. H., & Wasow, T. (1998). Repeating words in spontaneous speech. *Cognitive Psychology*, 37(3), 201–242.

Corley, M., & Stewart, O. W. (2008). Hesitation disfluencies in spontaneous speech: The meaning of um. *Language and Linguistics Compass*, 2(4), 589–602.

Couper-Kuhlen, E., & Selting, M. (2001). Introducing interactional linguistics. *Studies in Interactional Linguistics*, 122.

Crible, L. (2017). Discourse markers and (dis)fluency across registers: A contrastive usage-based study in English and French [PhD Thesis]. UCL – Université Catholique de Louvain.

Crible, L. (2018). *Discourse Markers and (Dis)fluency: Forms and functions across languages and registers*. John Benjamins Publishing.

Crible, L., Degand, L., & Gilquin, G. (2017). The clustering of discourse markers and filled pauses. *Languages in Contrast*, 17(1), 69–95.

Crible, L., Dumont, A., Grosman, I., & Notarrigo, I. (2019). (Dis)fluency across spoken and signed languages: Application of an interoperable annotation scheme. In L. Degand, G. Gilquin, & A. C. Simon (Eds.), *Fluency and Disfluency across Languages and Language Varieties* (Corpora and Language in Use-Proceedings 4). Presses universitaires de Louvain.

Croft, W. (2000). *Explaining language change: An evolutionary approach*. Pearson Education.

Cucchiarini, C., Strik, H., & Boves, L. (2000). Quantitative assessment of second language learners' fluency by means of automatic speech recognition technology. *The Journal of the Acoustical Society of America*, 107(2), 989–999.

Cutting, J. (2001). The speech acts of the in-group. *Journal of Pragmatics*, 33(8), 1207–1233.

Cutting, J. (2002). The in-group code lexis. *HERMES-Journal of Language and Communication in Business*, 28, 59–80.

Danino, C. (2018). Les petits corpus – Introduction du numéro thématique. *Corpus*, 18.

De Jaegher, H., & Di Paolo, E. (2007). Participatory sense-making. *Phenomenology and the Cognitive Sciences*, 6(4), 485–507.

De Jong, N. H. (2016a). Fluency in second language assessment. In D. Tsagari & J. Banerjee (Eds.), *Handbook of Second Language Assessment*. Mouton de Gruyter.

De Jong, N. H. (2016b). Predicting pauses in L1 and L2 speech: The effects of utterance boundaries and word frequency. *International Review of Applied Linguistics in Language Teaching*, *54*(2), 113–132.

De Jong, N. H. (2018). Fluency in second language testing: Insights from different disciplines. *Language Assessment Quarterly*, *15*(3), 237–254.

De Jong, N. H., & Bosker, H. R. (2013). Choosing a threshold for silent pauses to measure second language fluency. *The 6th Workshop on Disfluency in Spontaneous Speech (DiSS)*, 17–20.

De Leeuw, E. (2007). Hesitation markers in English, German, and Dutch. *Journal of Germanic Linguistics*, *19*(2), 85–114.

De Ruiter, J. P. (2007). Postcards from the mind: The relationship between speech, imagistic gesture, and thought. *Gesture*, *7*(1), 21–38.

Debras, C. (2013). L'expression multimodale du positionnement interactionnel (multimodal stance-taking): Étude d'un corpus oral vidéo de discussions sur l'environnement en anglais britannique [Unpublished PhD Thesis]. Université Sorbonne Nouvelle -Paris III.

Debras, C. (2017). The shrug: Forms and meanings of a compound enactment. *Gesture*, *16*(1), 1–34.

Debras, C. (2018). Petits et grands corpus en analyse linguistique des gestes. *Corpus*, *18*.

Debras, C., & Beaupoil-Hourdel, P. (2019). Gestualité et construction des chaînes de référence dans un corpus d'interactions tandem. *Cahiers de Praxématique*, *72*.

Debras, C., Beaupoil-Hourdel, P., Morgenstern, A., Horgues, C., & Scheuer, S. (2020). Corrective Feedback Sequences in Tandem Interactions: Multimodal Cues and Speakers' Positionings In S. Raineri, M. Sekali & A. Leroux (Eds.), *La correction en langue(s) – Linguistic Correction/Correctness*, 91–115.

Debras, C., & Cienki, A. (2012). Some uses of head tilts and shoulder shrugs during human interaction, and their relation to stancetaking. *International Conference on Privacy, Security, Risk and Trust and 2012 International Confernece on Social Computing*, 932–937.

Debras, C., Horgues, C., & Scheuer, S. (2015). The multimodality of corrective feedback in tandem interactions. *Procedia-Social and Behavioral Sciences*, *212*, 16–22.

Debreslioska, S., Özyürek, A., Gullberg, M., & Perniss, P. (2013). Gestural viewpoint signals referent accessibility. *Discourse Processes*, *50*(7), 431–456.

Derwing, T. M., Munro, M. J., Thomson, R. I., & Rossiter, M. J. (2009). The relationship between L1 fluency and L2 fluency development. *Studies in Second Language Acquisition*, 533–557.

Deschamps, A. (1980). The syntactical distribution of pauses in English spoken as a second language by French students. In H. W. Dechert & M. Raupach (Eds.), *Temporal variables in speech: Studies in honour of Frieda Goldman-Eisler* (pp. 255–262). Mouton.

Dingemanse, M. (2020). Between sound and speech: Liminal signs in interaction. *Research on Language and Social Interaction*, *53*(1), 188–196.

Dollaghan, C. A., & Campbell, T. F. (1992). A procedure for classifying disruptions in spontaneous language samples. *Topics in Language Disorders*.

Dörnyei, Z., & Kormos, J. (1998). Problem-solving mechanisms in L2 communication: A Psycholinguistic Perspective. *Studies in Second Language Acquisition*, *20*(3), 349–385.

Duez, D. (1982). Silent and non-silent pauses in three speech styles. *Language and Speech*, *25*(1), 11–28.

Duez, D. (1991). *La pause dans la parole de l'homme politique*. Editions du Centre national de la recherche scientifique.

Duez, D. (1997). Acoustic markers of political power. *Journal of Psycholinguistic Research*, *26*(6), 641–654.

Duez, D. (2001a). Caractéristiques acoustiques et phonétiques des pauses remplies dans la conversation en français. *Travaux Interdisciplinaires Du Laboratoire Parole et Langage d'Aix-En-Provence (TIPA)*, *20*, 31–48.

Duez, D. (2001b). Signification des hésitations dans la parole spontanée. *Revue Parole*, 17–18.

Dumont, A. (2018). Fluency and disfluency: A corpus study of non-native and native speaker (dis) fluency profiles [PhD Thesis]. UCL-Université Catholique de Louvain.

Dwijayanti, I., Budayasa, I. K., & Siswono, T. Y. E. (2019). Students' gestures in understanding algebraic concepts. *Beta: Jurnal Tadris Matematika*, *12*(2), 133–143.

Edlund, J., Hirschberg, J. B., & Heldner, M. (2009). *Pause and gap length in face-to-face interaction*.

Eguchi, M. (2016). Investigating the Relationships Between Vocabulary and Clause-internal Pauses and its Development in L2 Speech. *Proceedings of the Pacific Second Language Research Forum (PacSLRF2016). Hiroshima: Japan Second Language Association*.

Eisenbeiss, S. (2010). Production methods in language acquisition research. *Experimental Methods in Language Acquisition Research*, 11–34.

Eklund, R. (2001). Prolongations: A dark horse in the disfluency stable. *ISCA Tutorial and Research Workshop (ITRW) on Disfluency in Spontaneous Speech*.

Eklund, R. (2004). Disfluency in Swedish human–human and human–machine travel booking dialogues [PhD Thesis]. Linköping University Electronic Press.

Eklund, R., & Shriberg, E. (1998). Crosslinguistic disfluency modelling: A comparative analysis of Swedish and American English human–human and human–machine dialogues. *5th International Conference on Spoken Language Processing, 30th November-4th December, 1998, Sydney, Australia*, *6*, 2627–2630.

Ekman, P., & Friesen, W. V. (1969). The repertoire of nonverbal behavior: Categories, origins, usage, and coding. *Semiotica*, *1*.

Enfield, N. J. (2005). The body as a cognitive artifact in kinship representations: Hand gesture diagrams by speakers of Lao. *Current Anthropology*, *46*(1), 51–81.

Esposito, A., & Marinaro, M. (2007). What pauses can tell us about speech and gesture partnership. *Nato security through science series human and societal dynamics*, *18*, 45.

Esposito, A., McCullough, K. E., & Quek, F. (2001). Disfluencies in gesture: Gestural correlates to filled and unfilled speech pauses. *Proceedings of IEEE Workshop on Cues in Communication*, 1–6.

Fehringer, C., & Fry, C. (2007). Hesitation phenomena in the language production of bilingual speakers: The role of working memory. *Folia Linguistica: Acta Societatis Linguisticae Europaeae*, *41*(1–2), 37–72.

Ferreira, F., & Bailey, K. G. D. (2004). Disfluencies and human language comprehension. *Trends in Cognitive Sciences*, *8*(5), 231–237.

Fillmore, C. J. (1976). Frame semantics and the nature of language. *Origins and Evolution of Language and Speech*, *280*, 20–32.

Finlayson, I. R., & Corley, M. (2012). Disfluency in dialogue: An intentional signal from the speaker? *Psychonomic Bulletin & Review*, *19*(5), 921–928.

Fischer, K. (2000). *From Cognitive Semantics to Lexical Pragmatics: The Functional Polysemy of Discourse Markers*. Mouton de Gruyter.

Foster, P., Tonkyn, A., & Wigglesworth, G. (2000). Measuring spoken language: A unit for all reasons. *Applied Linguistics*, *21*(3), 354–375.

Fox, B. A., Thompson, S. A., Ford, C. E., & Couper-Kuhlen, E. (2013). Conversation Analysis and Linguistics. In J. Sidnell & T. Stivers (Eds.), *The handbook of conversation analysis* (p. 726). Blackwell Publishing.

Fox Tree, J. E. (1995). The effects of false starts and repetitions on the processing of subsequent words in spontaneous speech. *Journal of Memory and Language*, *34*(6), 709–738.

Fox Tree, J. (2007). Folk notions of um and uh, you know, and like. *Text & Talk*, *27*, 297–314.

Fox Tree, J. E. & Clark, H. H. (1997). Pronouncing "the" as "thee" to signal problems in speaking. *Cognition*, *62*(2), 151–167.

Fraundorf, S. H., & Watson, D. G. (2011). The disfluent discourse: Effects of filled pauses on recall. *Journal of Memory and Language*, *65*(2), 161–175.

Fraundorf, S. H., & Watson, D. G. (2014). Alice's adventures in um-derland: Psycholinguistic sources of variation in disfluency production. *Language, Cognition and Neuroscience*, *29*(9), 1083–1096.

Galaczi, E. (2014). Interactional competence across proficiency levels: How do learners manage interaction in paired speaking tests? *Applied Linguistics*, *35*(5), 553–574.

Galaczi, E., & Taylor, L. (2018). Interactional competence: Conceptualisations, operationalisations, and outstanding questions. *Language Assessment Quarterly*, *15*(3), 219–236.

Gawne, L., & McCulloch, G. (2019). Emoji as digital gestures. *Language@ Internet*, *17*(2).

Gilquin, G. (2008). Hesitation markers among EFL learners: Pragmatic deficiency or difference. In J. Romero-Trillo (Ed.), *Pragmatics and Corpus Linguistics: A Mutualistic Entente* (pp. 119–149). De Gruyter Mouton.

Ginzburg, J., Fernández, R., & Schlangen, D. (2014). Disfluencies as intra-utterance dialogue moves. *Semantics and Pragmatics*, *7*, 9–1.

Ginzburg, J., & Poesio, M. (2016). Grammar is a system that characterizes talk in interaction. *Frontiers in Psychology*, *7*, 1938.

Goffman, E. (1981). *Forms of talk*. University of Pennsylvania Press.

Goldberg, A. E. (2006). *Constructions at work: The nature of generalization in language*. Oxford University Press.

Goldin-Meadow, S. (1999). The role of gesture in communication and thinking. *Trends in Cognitive Sciences*, *3*(11), 419–429.

Goldin-Meadow, S., Alibali, M. W., & Church, R. B. (1993). Transitions in concept acquisition: Using the hand to read the mind. *Psychological Review*, *100*(2), 279.

Goldman, J.-P., Avanzi, M., & Auchlin, A. (2010). Hesitations in read vs. Spontaneous French in a multi-genre corpus. *DiSS-LPSS Joint Workshop 2010*.

Goldman-Eisler, F. (1958). The predictability of words in context and the length of pauses in speech. *Language and Speech*, 1(3), 226–231.

Goldman-Eisler, F. (1968). *Psycholinguistics: Experiments in spontaneous speech*. Academic Press.

Goodwin, C. (1981). *Conversational Organization: Interaction Between Speakers and Hearers*. Academic Press.

Goodwin, C. (1987). Forgetfulness as an interactive resource. *Social Psychology Quarterly*, 115–130.

Goodwin, C. (2000). Action and embodiment within situated human interaction. *Journal of Pragmatics*, 32(10), 1489–1522.

Goodwin, C. (2003). The body in action. In *Discourse, the body, and identity* (pp. 19–42). Springer.

Goodwin, C. (2007). Participation, stance and affect in the organization of activities. *Discourse & Society*, 18(1), 53–73.

Goodwin, C. (2010). Multimodality in human interaction. *Calidoscopio*, 8(2).

Goodwin, C. (2017). *Co-operative action*. Cambridge University Press.

Goodwin, C., & Goodwin, M. H. (1996). Seeing as a situated activity: Formulating planes. In D. Middleton & Y. Engestrom (Eds.), *Cognition and Communication at Work*. Cambridge University Press.

Goodwin, C., & Goodwin, M. H. (2004). Participation. *A Companion to Linguistic Anthropology*, 222–224.

Goodwin, C., & Heritage, J. (1990). Conversation analysis. *Annual Review of Anthropology*, 19(1), 283–307.

Goodwin, M. H., & Goodwin, C. (1986). Gesture and coparticipation in the activity of searching for a word. *Semiotica*, 62(1–2), 51–76.

Götz, S. (2013). *Fluency in native and nonnative English speech* (John Benjamins Publishing, Vol. 53). John Benjamins Publishing.

Graziano, M., & Gullberg, M. (2013). Gesture production and speech fluency in competent speakers and language learners. *Presentado En TIGER, Tilburg University, Holanda*.

Graziano, M., & Gullberg, M. (2018). When speech stops, gesture stops: Evidence from developmental and crosslinguistic comparisons. *Frontiers in Psychology*, 9, 879.

Grosjean, F., & Deschamps, A. (1972). Analyse des variables temporelles du français spontané. *Phonetica*, 26(3), 129–156.

Grosjean, F., & Deschamps, A. (1975). Analyse contrastive des variables temporelles de l'anglais et du français: Vitesse de parole et variables composantes, phénomènes d'hésitation. *Phonetica*, 31(3–4), 144–184.

Grosman, I. (2018). Évaluation contextuelle de la (dis) fluence en production et perception: Pratiques communicatives et formes prosodico-syntaxiques en français [Unpublished PhD Thesis]. UCL-Université Catholique de Louvain.

Grosman, I., Simon, A. C., & Degand, L. (2019). Empathetic hearers perceive repetitions as less disfluent, especially in non-broadcast situations. *Proceedings of DiSS, 2019, the 9th Workshop on Disfluency in Spontaneous Speech*.

Guaïtella, I. (1993). Functional, acoustical and perceptual analysis of vocal hesitations in spontaneous speech. *ESCA Workshop on Prosody*.

Gullberg, M. (1995). Giving language a hand: gesture as a cue based communicative strategy. *Working Papers, Lund University, Dept. of Linguistics*, 44, 41–60.

Gullberg, M. (1998). *Gesture as a communication strategy in second language discourse: A study of learners of French and Swedish* (Vol. 35). Lund University.

Gullberg, M. 2006. Some reasons for studying gesture and second language acquisition. *International Review of Applied Linguistics in Language Teaching (IRAL)* 44.103–24.

Gullberg, M. (2011). Multilingual multimodality: Communicative difficulties and their solutions in second-language use. *Embodied Interaction: Language and Body in the Material World*, 137–151.

Gullberg, M. (2014). Gestures and second language acquisition. In C. Müller, A. Cienki, S. H. Ladewig, D. McNeill, & S. Tessendorf (Eds.), *Body- Language- Communication: An International Handbook on Multimodsality in Human Interaction*. Mouton de Gruyter.

Gullberg, M., & McCafferty, S. G. (2008). Introduction to gesture and SLA: Toward an integrated approach. *Studies in Second Language Acquisition*, 30(2), 133–146.

Gürbüz, N. (2017). Understanding fluency and disfluency in non-native speakers' conversational English. *Kuram ve Uygulamada Egitim Bilimleri*, 17(6), 1853–1874.

Hai, T. (2017). Hesitation phenomena expressed in native Russian and Chinese and accented Russian* spontaneous speech. *Phonetics Without Borders*, 86–92.

Harrison, S. (2009). *Grammar, gesture, and cognition: The case of negation in English*. Unpublished Doctoral Dissertation, University of Bordeaux.

Hartsuiker, R. J., & Notebaert, L. (2009). Lexical access problems lead to disfluencies in speech. *Experimental Psychology*.

Hashemi, M. R., & Babaii, E. (2013). Mixed methods research: Toward new research designs in applied linguistics. *The Modern Language Journal*, 97(4), 828–852.

Hayashi, M. (2003). Language and the body as resources for collaborative action: A study of word searches in Japanese conversation. *Research on Language and Social Interaction*, 36(2), 109–141.

Heath, C., & Luff, P. (2011). Gesture and institutional interaction. *Embodied Interaction: Language and Body in the Material World*, 276–288.

Heldner, M., Hjalmarsson, A., & Edlund, J. (2013). Backchannel relevance spaces. *Nordic Prosody XI, Tartu, Estonia, 15–17 August*, 2012, 137–146.

Heller, V. (2021). Embodied Displays of "Doing Thinking." Epistemic and Interactive Functions of Thinking Displays in Children's Argumentative Activities. *Frontiers in Psychology*, 12, 369.

Hieke, A. E. (1981). A Content-Processing View of Hesitation Phenomena. *Language and Speech*, 24(2), 147–160.

Hilton, H. (2009). Annotation and analyses of temporal aspects of spoken fluency. *Calico Journal*, 26(3), 644–661.

Hoetjes, M., & Van Maastricht, L. (2020). Using Gesture to Facilitate L2 Phoneme Acquisition: The Importance of Gesture and Phoneme Complexity. *Frontiers in Psychology*, 11.

Hoey, E. M. (2015). Lapses: How people arrive at, and deal with, discontinuities in talk. *Research on Language and Social Interaction*, 48(4), 430–453.

Hoey, E. M. (2020). Waiting to inhale: On sniffing in conversation. *Research on Language and Social Interaction*, 53(1), 118–139.

Holmes, V. M. (1988). Hesitations and sentence planning. *Language and Cognitive Processes*, 3(4), 323–361.

Holt, B., Tellier, M., & Guichon, N. (2015, September). The use of teaching gestures in an online multimodal environment: The case of incomprehension sequences. *Gesture and Speech in Interaction 4th Edition*. https://hal.archives-ouvertes.fr/hal-01215770

Horgues, C., & Scheuer, S. (2015). Why some things are better done in tandem. In *Investigating English Pronunciation* (pp. 47–82). Springer.

Horgues, C., & Scheuer, S. (2017). Misunderstanding as a two-way street: Communication breakdowns in native/non-native English/French tandem interactions. *International Symposium on Monolingual and Bilingual Speech 2017*, 148.

Hough, J., Tian, Y., De Ruiter, L., Betz, S., Kousidis, S., Schlangen, D., & Ginzburg, J. (2016). Duel: A multi-lingual multimodal dialogue corpus for disfluency, exclamations and laughter. *10th Edition of the Language Resources and Evaluation Conference.*

Hwang, J., Brennan, S. E., & Huffman, M. K. (2015). Phonetic adaptation in non-native spoken dialogue: Effects of priming and audience design. *Journal of Memory and Language*, 81, 72–90.

Ibbotson, P. (2013). The scope of usage-based theory. *Frontiers in Psychology*, 4, 255.

Iverson, J. M., & Thelen, E. (1999). Hand, mouth and brain. The dynamic emergence of speech and gesture. *Journal of Consciousness Studies*, 6(11–12), 19–40.

Jefferson, G. (1974). Error correction as an interactional resource. *Language in Society*, 181–199.

Johnson, R. B., Onwuegbuzie, A. J., & Turner, L. A. (2007). Toward a definition of mixed methods research. *Journal of Mixed Methods Research*, 1(2), 112–133.

Johnson, W. (1961). Measurements of oral reading and speaking rate and disfluency of adult male and female stutterers and nonstutterers. *Journal of Speech & Hearing Disorders. Monograph Supplement*.

Kahng, J. (2014). Exploring utterance and cognitive fluency of L1 and L2 English speakers: Temporal measures and stimulated recall. *Language Learning*, 64(4), 809–854.

Kärkkäinen, E. (2006). Stance taking in conversation: From subjectivity to intersubjectivity. *Text & Talk-An Interdisciplinary Journal of Language, Discourse Communication Studies*, 26(6), 699–731.

Kasper, G., & Færch, C. (1983). *Strategies in interlanguage communication*. Longman Publishing Group.

Keevallik, L., & Ogden, R. (2020). Sounds on the Margins of Language at the Heart of Interaction. *Research on Language and Social Interaction*, 53(1), 1–18.

Kelly, S. D., McDevitt, T., & Esch, M. (2009). Brief training with co-speech gesture lends a hand to word learning in a foreign language. *Language and Cognitive Processes*, 24(2), 313–334.

Kendon, A. (1967). Some functions of gaze-direction in social interaction. *Acta Psychologica*, 26, 22–63.

Kendon, A. (1972). Some relationships between body motion and speech. In A. W. Siegman & B. Pope (Eds.), *Studies in dyadic communication* (pp. 177–210). Pergamon Press.

Kendon, A. (1980). A description of a deaf-mute sign language from the Enga Province of Papua New Guinea with some comparative discussion. *Semiotica*, *32*(1/2), 81–117.

Kendon, A. (1995). Gestures as illocutionary and discourse structure markers in Southern Italian conversation. *Journal of Pragmatics*, *23*(3), 247–279.

Kendon, A. (2004). *Gesture: Visible action as utterance* (Cambridge University Press). Cambridge University Press.

Kendon, A. (2014). Semiotic diversity in utterance production and the concept of 'language.' *Philosophical Transactions of the Royal Society B: Biological Sciences*, *369*(1651), 2–13.

Kendon, A. (2017). Languages as semiotically heterogenous systems. *Behavioral and Brain Sciences*, *40*.

Kendon, A., & Versante, L. (2003). Pointing by hand in Neapolitan. *Pointing: Where Language, Culture, and Cognition Meet*, 109–137.

Kita, S. (1993). *Language and thought interface: A study of spontaneous gestures and Japanese mimetics*. University of Chicago.

Kita, S. (2000). How representational gestures help speaking. *Language and Gesture*, *1*, 162–185.

Kita, S. (Ed.). (2003). *Pointing: Where language, culture, and cognition meet*. Lawrence Erlbaum.

Kita, S., & Özyürek, A. (2003). What does cross-linguistic variation in semantic coordination of speech and gesture reveal?: Evidence for an interface representation of spatial thinking and speaking. *Journal of Memory and Language*, *48*(1), 16–32.

Kita, S., Van Gijn, I., & Van der Hulst, H. (1997). Movement phases in signs and co-speech gestures, and their transcription by human coders. *International Gesture Workshop*, 23–35.

Kjellmer, G. (2003). Hesitation. In defence of er and erm. *English Studies*, *84*(2), 170-198.

Koester, A. (2010). Building small specialised corpora. *The Routledge Handbook of Corpus Linguistics*, *1*, 66–79.

Kormos, J., & Dénes, M. (2004). Exploring measures and perceptions of fluency in the speech of second language learners. *System*, *32*(2), 145–164.

Kosmala, L. (2020a). (Dis)fluencies and their contribution to the co-construction of meaning in native and non-native tandem interactions of French and English. *TIPA. Travaux Interdisciplinaires Sur La Parole et Le Langage*, *36*, Article 36.

Kosmala, L. (2020b). On the distribution of clicks and inbreaths in class presentations and spontaneous conversations: blending vocal and kinetic activities. *Proceedings of Laughter and Other Non-Verbal Vocalisations Workshop*.

Kosmala, L. (2021). On the Specificities of L1 and L2 (Dis)fluencies and the Interactional Multimodal Strategies of L2 Speakers in Tandem Interactions. *Journal of Monolingual and Bilingual Speech*.

Kosmala, L., & Morgenstern, A. (2017). A preliminary study of hesitation phenomena in L1 and L2 productions: A multimodal approach. *Proceedings of DiSS 2017, the 8th Workshop on Disfluency in Spontaneous Speech*, 37.

Kowal, S., Wiese, R., & O'Connell, D.C. (1983). The use of time in storytelling. *Language and Speech*, *26*(4), 377–392.

Krauss, R. M., Chen, Y., & Gottesman, R. F. (2000). Lexical gestures and lexical access: A process. *Language and Gesture*, 2, 261.

Krauss, R. M., Dushay, R. A., Chen, Y., & Rauscher, F. (1995). The communicative value of conversational hand gesture. *Journal of Experimental Social Psychology*, 31(6), 533–552.

Krauss, R. M., & Hadar, U. (1999). The role of speech-related arm/hand gestures in word retrieval. In R. Campbell & L. Messing (Eds.), *Gesture, speech, and sign* (pp. 93–116). Oxford University Press.

Labov, W. (1966). *The social stratification of English in New York City*. Center for Applied Linguistics.

Ladewig, S. H. (2011). Putting the cyclic gesture on a cognitive basis. *CogniTextes. Revue de l'Association Française de Linguistique Cognitive, Volume 6*.

Ladewig, S. H. (2014). Recurrent gestures. In C. Müller, A. Cienki, S. H. Ladewig, D. McNeill, & S. Tessendorf (Eds.), *Body- Language- Communication: An International Handbook on Multimodsality in Human Interaction*. Mouton de Gruyter.

Ladewig, S. H., & Bressem, J. (2013). New insights into the medium hand: Discovering recurrent structures in gestures. *Semiotica*, 2013(197), 203–231.

Landis, J. R., & Koch, G. G. (1977a). An application of hierarchical kappa-type statistics in the assessment of majority agreement among multiple observers. *Biometrics*, 363–374.

Landis, J. R., & Koch, G. G. (1977b). The measurement of observer agreement for categorical data. *Biometrics*, 159–174.

Langacker, R. W. (1987). *Foundations of Cognitive grammar, vol. 1 theoretical prerequisites*. Stanford University press.

Langacker, R. W. (1995). Cognitive grammar. In *Concise History of the Language Sciences* (pp. 364–368). Elsevier.

Langacker, R. W. (1999). *Grammar and conceptualization*. Mouton de Gruyter.

LeBaron, C. D., Mandelbaum, J., & Glenn, P. J. (2003). An overview of language and social interaction research. *Studies in Language and Social Interaction*, 12–42.

Lennon, P. (1990). Investigating fluency in EFL: A quantitative approach. *Language Learning*, 40(3), 387–417.

Lerner, G. H. (1992). Assisted storytelling: Deploying shared knowledge as a practical matter. *Qualitative Sociology*, 15(3), 247–271.

Levelt, W. J. (1983). Monitoring and self-repair in speech. *Cognition*, 14, 41–104.

Levelt, W. J. (1989). *Speaking. From intention to articulation*. MIT Press.

Levelt, W. J. (1999). Producing spoken language. *The Neurocognition of Language*, 83–122.

Levelt, W. J., & Schriefers, H. (1987). Stages of lexical access. In *Natural language generation* (pp. 395-404). Springer.

Levy, E. T., & McNeill, D. (1992). Speech, gesture, and discourse. *Discourse Processes*, 15(3), 277–301.

Lickley, R. J. (2001). Dialogue moves and disfluency rates. *ISCA Tutorial and Research Workshop (ITRW) on Disfluency in Spontaneous Speech*.

Lickley, R. J. (2015). Fluency and Disfluency. In M. A. Redford (Ed.), *The Handbook of Speech Production* (pp. 445–474). John Wiley.

Lopez-Ozieblo, R. (2019). Cut-offs and co-occurring gestures: Similarities between speakers' first and second languages. *International Review of Applied Linguistics in Language Teaching, 1*(ahead-of-print).

Lopez-Ozieblo, R. (2020). Proposing a revised functional classification of pragmatic gestures. *Lingua, 247*, 1–47.

Ma, W., & Winke, P. (2019). Self-assessment: How reliable is it in assessing oral proficiency over time? *Foreign Language Annals, 52*(1), 66–86.

Maclay, H., & Osgood, C. E. (1959). Hesitation phenomena in spontaneous English speech. *Word, 15*(1), 19–44.

MacWhinney, B. (2000). *The CHILDES Project: Tools for analyzing talk. transcription format and programs* (Vol. 1). Psychology Press.

Matzinger, T., Ritt, N., & Fitch, W. T. (2020). Non-native speaker pause patterns closely correspond to those of native speakers at different speech rates. *PloS One, 15*(4), e0230710.

Mazeland, H. (2006). Conversation analysis. *Encyclopedia of language and linguistics, 3*, 153–162.

McCafferty, S. G. (1998). Nonverbal expression and L2 private speech. *Applied Linguistics, 19*(1), 73–96.

McCafferty, S. G. (2004). Space for cognition: Gesture and second language learning. *International Journal of Applied Linguistics, 14*(1), 148–165.

McCarthy, M. (2009). Rethinking spoken fluency. *ELIA, 9*, 11–29.

McLaughlin, S. F., & Cullinan, W. L. (1989). Disfluencies, utterance length, and linguistic complexity in nonstuttering children. *Journal of Fluency Disorders, 14*(1), 17–36.

McNeill, D. (1985). So you think gestures are nonverbal? *Psychological Review, 92*(3), 350.

McNeill, D. (1992). *Hand and mind: What gestures reveal about thought.* University of Chicago press.

Menn, L., & Dronkers, N. F. (2016). *Psycholinguistics: Introduction and applications.* Plural Publishing.

Merlo, S., & Barbosa, P. A. (2010). Hesitation phenomena: A dynamical perspective. *Cognitive Processing, 11*(3), 251–261.

Merlo, S., & Mansur, L. L. (2004). Descriptive discourse: Topic familiarity and disfluencies. *Journal of Communication Disorders, 37*(6), 489–503.

Meteer, M. W., Taylor, A. A., MacIntyre, R., & Iyer, R. (1995). *Dysfluency annotation stylebook for the switchboard corpus.* University of Pennsylvania Philadelphia, PA.

Michel, M. C. (2011). Effects of task complexity and interaction on L2 performance. *Second Language Task Complexity: Researching the Cognition Hypothesis of Language Learning and Performance, 2*, 141–173.

Michel, M. C., Kuiken, F., & Vedder, I. (2007). Effects of task complexity and task condition on Dutch L2. *International Review of Applied Linguistics, 45*(3), 241–259.

Mondada, L. (2001). Pour une linguistique interactionnelle. *Marges Linguistiques, 1*, 142–162.

Mondada, L. (2007). Multimodal resources for turn-taking: Pointing and the emergence of possible next speakers. *Discourse Studies, 9*(2), 194–225.

Mondada, L. (2013). Interactional space and the study of embodied talk-in-interaction. *Space in Language and Linguistics: Geographical, Interactional and Cognitive Perspectives*, 247–275.

Mondada, L. (2014). Bodies in action: Multimodal analysis of walking and talking. *Language and dialogue*, 4(3), 357–403.

Mondada, L. (2016). Challenges of multimodality: Language and the body in social interaction. *Journal of Sociolinguistics*, 20(3), 336–366.

Mondada, L. (2018). Multiple temporalities of language and body in interaction: Challenges for transcribing multimodality. *Research on Language and Social Interaction*, 51(1), 85–106.

Mondada, L., & Pekarek-Doehler, S. (2004). Second language acquisition as situated practice: Task accomplishment in the French second language classroom. *Canadian Modern Language Review*, 61(4), 461–490.

Mondada, L., & Traverso, V. (2005). (Dés) alignements en clôture. Une étude interactionnelle de corpus de français parlé en interaction. *Lidil. Revue de Linguistique et de Didactique Des Langues*, 31, 35–59.

Moniz, H. (2019). Processing disfluencies in distinct speaking styles: Idiosyncrasies and transversality. *The 9th Workshop on Disfluency in Spontaneous Speech*, 1–2.

Moniz, H., Batista, F., Mata, A. I., & Trancoso, I. (2014). Speaking style effects in the production of disfluencies. *Speech Communication*, 65, 20–35.

Moniz, H. (2013). Processing disfluencies in European Portuguese [Unpublished PhD Thesis] Universidade de Lisboa.

Moniz, H., Trancoso, I., & Mata, A. I. (2009). Classification of disfluent phenomena as fluent communicative devices in specific prosodic contexts. *Tenth Annual Conference of the International Speech Communication Association*.

Morel, M. A., & Danon-Boileau, L. (1998). *Grammaire de l'intonation l'exemple du français*. Editions OPHRYS.

Morgenstern, A. (2014). Children's multimodal language development. *Manual of Language Acquisition*, 123–142.

Morgenstern, A. (2020). The Other's Voice in the Co-Construction of Self-Reference in the Dialogic Child. *Bakhtiniana: Revista de Estudos Do Discurso*, 16, 63–87.

Morgenstern, A., Caët, S., Debras, C., Beaupoil-Hourdel, P., & Le Mené, M. (2021). Children's socialization to multi-party interactive practices: Who talks to whom about what in family dinners. In Letizia Caronia (ed.) *Language and Social Interaction at Home and in School*. Amsterdam: John Benjamins, 46–85.

Mori, J., & Hayashi, M. (2006). The achievement of intersubjectivity through embodied completions: A study of interactions between first and second language speakers. *Applied Linguistics*, 27(2), 195–219.

Moro, L., Mortimer, E. F., & Tiberghien, A. (2020). The use of social semiotic multimodality and joint action theory to describe teaching practices: Two cases studies with experienced teachers. *Classroom Discourse*, 11(3), 229–251.

Müller, C. (1998). *Redebegleitende Gesten: Kulturgeschichte, Theorie, Sprachvergleich* (Vol. 1). Spitz.

Müller, C. (2014). Gesture as 'deliberate expressive movement.' *From Gesture in Conversation to Visible Action as Utterance: Essays in Honor of Adam Kendon*, 127–151.

Müller, C. (2017). How recurrent gestures mean: Conventionalized contexts-of-use and embodied motivation. *Gesture*, 16(2), 277–304.

Müller, C., Bressem, J., & Ladewig, S. H. (2013). Towards a grammar of gestures: A form-based view. In C. Müller, A. Cienki, S. H. Ladewig, D. McNeill, & S. Tessendorf (Eds.), *Body-Language – Communication. An International Handbook on Multimodality in Human Interaction* (Vol. 1, pp. 707–733). De Gruyter Mouton.

Nicholson, H. B. M. (2007). Disfluency in dialogue: Attention, structure and function [Unpublished PhD thesis]. University of Edinburgh.

Notarrigo, I. (2017). Marqueurs de (dis) fluence en langue des signes de Belgique francophone [Unpublished PhD Thesis]. Université de Namur.

Ogden, R. (2013). Clicks and percussives in English conversation. *Journal of the International Phonetic Association*, *43*(3), 299–320.

Ogden, R. (2020). Audibly not saying something with clicks. *Research on Language and Social Interaction*, *53*(1), 66–89.

Ogden, R. (2018). The actions of peripheral linguistic objects: Clicks. *Proceedings of Laughter Workshop 2018*, 2–5.

O'Shaughnessy, D. (1992). *Analysis of False Starts in Spontaneous Speech*. The International Conference on Spoken Language Processing, Banff, Alberta, Canada.

Oviatt, S. (1995). Predicting spoken disfluencies during human-computer interaction. *Computer Speech and Language*, *9*(1), 19–36.

Pallaud, B., Bertrand, R., Prevot, L., Blache, P., & Rauzy, S. (2019). *Suspensive and Disfluent Self Interruptions in French Language Interactions*.

Pallaud, B., Rauzy, S., & Blache, P. (2013). Auto-interruptions et disfluences en français parlé dans quatre corpus du CID. *TIPA. Travaux interdisciplinaires sur la parole et le langage*, *29*.

Papanas, N., Maltezos, E., & Lazarides, M. K. (2011). Delivering a powerful oral presentation: All the world's a stage. *International Angiology: A Journal of the International Union of Angiology*, *30*(2), 185–191.

Pekarek-Doehler, S. (2006). «CA for SLA»: Analyse conversationnelle et recherche sur l'acquisition des langues. *Revue Française de Linguistique Appliquée*, *11*(2), 123–137.

Pekarek-Doehler, S. (2018). Elaborations on L2 interactional competence: The development of L2 grammar-for-interaction. *Classroom Discourse*, *9*(1), 3–24.

Pekarek-Doehler, S., & Pochon-Berger, E. (2011). Developing "methods" for interaction: A cross-sectional study of disagreement sequences in French L2. *L2 Interactional Competence and Development*, *56*, 206.

Peltonen, P. (2017). L2 fluency in spoken interaction: A case study on the use of other-repetitions and collaborative completions. *AFinLA-e: Soveltavan Kielitieteen Tutkimuksia*, *10*, 118–138.

Peltonen, P. (2019). Gestures as Fluency-enhancing Resources in L2 Interaction: A Case Study on Multimodal Fluency. *Fluency in L2 Learning and Use*, *138*, 111.

Peltonen, P. (2020). Individual and Interactional Speech Fluency in L2 English from a Problem-solving Perspective: A Mixed-methods Approach [Unpublished PhD Thesis]. University of Turku.

Peters, A. M. (2001). Filler syllables: What is their status in emerging grammar? *Journal of Child Language*, *28*(1), 229.

Pinto, D., & Vigil, D. (2019). Searches and clicks in Peninsular Spanish. *Pragmatics*, *29*(1), 83–106.

Poggi, I. (2001). From a typology of gestures to a procedure for gesture production. *International Gesture Workshop*, 158–168.

Pomerantz, A. (1984). Agreeing and disagreeing with assessments: Some features of preferred/dispreferred turn shaped. In J. M. Atkinson & J. Heritage (Eds.), *Structures of Social Action* (pp. 57–108). Cambridge University Press.

Pomerantz, A., & Fehr, B. J. (2011). Conversation analysis: An approach to the analysis of social interaction. *Discourse Studies: A Multidisciplinary Introduction*, *2*, 165–190.

Rasier, L., & Hiligsmann, P. (2007). Prosodic transfer from L1 to L2. Theoretical and methodological issues. *Nouveaux Cahiers de Linguistique Française*, *28*(2007), 41–66.

Rendle-Short, J. (2005). Managing the transitions between talk and silence in the academic monologue. *Research on Language and Social Interaction*, *38*(2), 179–218.

Riazantseva, A. (2001). Second language proficiency and pausing a study of Russian speakers of English. *Studies in Second Language Acquisition*, *23*(04), 497–526.

Riggenbach, H. (1991). Toward an understanding of fluency: A microanalysis of nonnative speaker conversations. *Discourse Processes*, *14*(4), 423–441.

Rohr, J. L. (2016). Acoustic and Perceptual Correlates of L2 Fluency: The Role of Prolongations [PhD Thesis].

Rohrer, P. L., Vilà-Giménez, I., Florit-Pons, J., Esteve-Gibert, N., Ren, A., Shattuck-Hufnagel, S., & Prieto, P. (2020). The MultiModal MultiDimensional (M3D) labelling scheme for the annotation of audiovisual corpora. *Gesture and Speech in Interaction (GESPIN)*.

Rose, R. L. (1998). The communicative value of filled pauses in spontaneous speech [M.A Diss.]. University of Birminghman.

Rossano, F. (2013). Gaze in Conversation. In J. Sidnell & T. Stivers (Eds.), *The handbook of Conversation Analysis*. Blackwell Publishing.

Rydell, M. (2019). Negotiating co-participation: Embodied word searching sequences in paired L2 speaking tests. *Journal of Pragmatics*, *149*, 60–77.

Sacks, H. (1992). *Lectures on Conversation* (Vol. 1–2). Basil Blackwell.

Sacks, H., Jefferson, G., & Schegloff, E. A. (1974). A simplest systematics for the organization of turn-taking for conversation. *Language*, *50*(4), 696–735.

Schachter, S., Christenfeld, N., & Bilous, F. (1991). Speech Disfluency and the Structure of Knowledge. *Journal of Personality and Social Psychology*, *60*(3), 362–367.

Schegloff, E. A. (1991). Conversation analysis and socially shared cognition. In L. B. Resnick, J. Levine, & S. D. Teasley (Eds.), *Socially Shared Cognition*. American Psychological Association.

Schegloff, E. A. (1996a). Confirming allusions: Toward an empirical account of action. *American Journal of Sociology*, *102*(1), 161–216.

Schegloff, E. A. (2007). *Sequence organization in interaction: A primer in conversation analysis I* (Vol. 1). Cambridge university press.

Schegloff, E. A. (2010). Some other "uh(m)" s. *Discourse Processes*, *47*(2), 130–174.

Schegloff, E. A., Sacks, H., & Jefferson, G. (1977). The preference for self-correction in the organization of repair in conversation. *Language*, *53*(2), 361–382.

Schettino, L., Di Maro, M., & Cutugno, F. (2020). Silent pauses as clarification trigger. *Laughter and Other Non-Verbal Vocalisations Workshop: Proceedings (2020)*.

Scheuer, S., & Horgues, C. (2020). Potential pitfalls of interpreting data from English-French tandem conversations. *Interpreting Languagelearning Data*, 197.

Schnadt, M. J., & Corley, M. (2006). The influence of lexical, conceptual and planning based factors on disfluency production. *Proceedings of the Annual Meeting of the Cognitive Science Society*, 28(28).

Schneider, U. (2014). *Frequency, Hesitations and Chunks. A Usage-based Study of Chunking in English*. Albert-Ludwigs-Universität.

Segalowitz, N. (2016). Second language fluency and its underlying cognitive and social determinants. *International Review of Applied Linguistics in Language Teaching*, 54(2), 79–95.

Selting, M., Barth-Weingarten, D., Reber, E., & Selting, M. (2010). Prosody in interaction. *Prosody in Interaction*, Amsterdam/Philadelphia, John Benjamins, 3–40.

Seo, M.-S., & Koshik, I. (2010). A conversation analytic study of gestures that engender repair in ESL conversational tutoring. *Journal of Pragmatics*, 42(8), 2219–2239.

Seyfeddinipur, M. (2006). Disfluency: Interrupting speech and gesture [Unpublished PhD Thesis]. Radboud University.

Seyfeddinipur, M., & Kita, S. (2001). Gesture as an indicator of early error detection in self-monitoring of speech. *ISCA Tutorial and Research Workshop (ITRW) on Disfluency in Spontaneous Speech*.

Shames, G. H., & Sherrick, C. E. (1963). A discussion of nonfluency and stuttering as operant behavior. *Journal of Speech and Hearing Disorders*, 28(1), 3–18.

Shriberg, E. (2001). To 'errrr' is human: Ecology and acoustics of speech disfluencies. *Journal of the International Phonetic Association*, 31(1), 153–169.

Shriberg, E. (1995). Acoustic properties of disfluent repetitions. *Proceedings of the International Congress of Phonetic Sciences*, 4, 384–387.

Shriberg, E. (1996). Disfluencies in switchboard. *Proceedings of International Conference on Spoken Language Processing*, 96(1), 11–14.

Shriberg, E. E. (1994). Preliminaries to a Theory of Speech Disfluencies [Unpublished PhD Thesis]. University of California.

Sidnell, J. (2016). *Conversation Analysis*. Oxford Research Encyclopedia of Linguistics.

Silverman, K., Blaauw, E., Spitz, J., & Pitrelli, J. F. (1992). A prosodic comparison of spontaneous speech and read speech. *Second International Conference on Spoken Language Processing*.

Simpson, R., Eisenchlas, S., & Haugh, M. (2013). The functions of self-initiated self-repair in the second language Chinese classroom 1. *International Journal of Applied Linguistics*, 23(2), 144–165.

Skehan, P. (2001). Tasks and language performance assessment. In M. Bygate, P. Skehan, & M. Swain (Eds.), *Researching Pedagogic Tasks: Second language learning, teaching, and testing* (pp. 167–185). Harlow: Longman.

Skehan, P. (2003). Task-based instruction. *Language Teaching*, 36(1), 1–14.

Slobin, D. I. (1987). Thinking for speaking. *Annual Meeting of the Berkeley Linguistics Society*, 13, 435–445.

Sloetjes, H., & Wittenburg, P. (2008). Annotation by category-ELAN and ISO DCR. *6th International Conference on Language Resources and Evaluation (LREC 2008)*.

Smith, V. L., & Clark, H. H. (1993). On the course of answering questions. *Journal of Memory and Language, 32*, 25–38.

Stam, G. (2001). Lexical failure and gesture in second language development. In C. Cavé, I. Guaïtella, & S. Santi (Eds.), *Oralité et gestualité: Interactions et comportements multimodaux dans la communication* (pp. 271–275). L'Harmattan.

Stam, G. (2006). Thinking for speaking about motion: L1 and L2 speech and gesture. *International Review of Applied Linguistics, 143*.

Stam, G. (2008). What gestures reveal about second language acquisition. *Gesture: Second Language Acquistion and Classroom Research, 231*.

Stam, G. (2018). Gesture and speaking a second language. *Speaking in a Second Language, 49*, 67.

Stam, G., & Tellier, M. (2017). The sound of silence. *Why Gesture?: How the Hands Function in Speaking, Thinking and Communicating, 7*, 353.

Sterponi, L., & Fasulo, A. (2010). "How to go on": Intersubjectivity and progressivity in the communication of a child with autism. *Ethos, 38*(1), 116–142.

Stivers, T. (2008). Stance, alignment, and affiliation during storytelling: When nodding is a token of affiliation. *Research on Language and Social Interaction, 41*(1), 31–57.

Stivers, T. (2015). Coding social interaction: A heretical approach in conversation analysis? *Research on Language and Social Interaction, 48*(1), 1–19.

Stivers, T., & Robinson, J. D. (2006). A preference for progressivity in interaction. *Language in Society, 35*(3), 367–392.

Stivers, T., & Sidnell, J. (2005). Introduction: Multimodal interaction. *Semiotica, 2005*, 1–20.

Streeck, J. (2008a). Depicting by gesture. *Gesture, 8*(3), 285–301.

Streeck, J. (2008b). Gesture in political communication: A case study of the democratic presidential candidates during the 2004 primary campaign. *Research on Language and Social Interaction, 41*(2), 154–186.

Streeck, J. (2008c). Metaphor and gesture. A view from the microanalysis of interaction. In C. Müller & A. Cienki (Eds.), *Metaphor and gesture* (pp. 259–264). John Benjamins Publishing.

Streeck, J. (2009a). Forward-gesturing. *Discourse Processes, 46*(2–3), 161–179.

Streeck, J. (2009b). *Gesturecraft: The manu-facture of meaning* (Vol. 2). John Benjamins Publishing.

Streeck, J. (2010). Ecologies of gesture. *New Adventures in Language and Interaction*, 223–242.

Streeck, J. (2014). Mutual gaze and recognition. In M. Seyfeddinipur & M. Gullberg (Eds.), *From Gesture in Conversation to Visible Action as Utterance. Benjamins, Amsterdam* (pp. 35–55). Benjamins.

Streeck, J. (2015). Embodiment in human communication. *Annual Review of Anthropology, 44*, 419–438.

Streeck, J. (2020). Self-Touch as Sociality. *Social Interaction. Video-Based Studies of Human Sociality, 3*(2).

Streeck, J. (2021). The emancipation of gestures. *Interactional Linguistics, 1*(1).

Streeck, J., Goodwin, C., & LeBaron, C. (2011). *Embodied interaction: Language and body in the material world.* Cambridge University Press.

Streeck, J., & Hartge, U. (1992). Gestures at the transition place. In P. Auer & A. Di Luzio (Eds.), *The contextualization of language* (pp. 135–157). John Benjamins Publishing.

Sweetser, E. (1998). Regular metaphoricity in gesture: Bodily-based models of speech interaction. In *Actes du 16e Congrès International des Linguistes.* Amsterdam: Elsevier.

Sweetser, E. (2007). Looking at space to study mental spaces. *Methods in Cognitive Linguistics, 18,* 201–224.

Sweetser, E., & Sizemore, M. (2008). Personal and interpersonal gesture spaces: Functional contrasts in language and gesture. *Language in the Context of Use: Discourse and Cognitive Approaches to Language,* 25–51.

Sweetser, E., & Stec, K. (2016). Maintaining multiple viewpoints with gaze. *Viewpoint and the Fabric of Meaning: Form and Use of Viewpoint Tools across Languages and Modalities, 237,* 257.

Swerts, M. (1998). Filled pauses as markers of discourse structure. *Journal of Pragmatics, 30*(4), 485–496.

Szymanski, M. H. (1999). Re-engaging and dis-engaging talk in activity. *Language in Society, 28*(1), 1–23.

Tarone, E. (1980). Communication strategies, foreigner talk, and repair in interlanguage 1. *Language Learning, 30*(2), 417–428.

Tashakkori, A., & Creswell, J. W. (2007). *The new era of mixed methods.* Sage Publications.

Tavakoli, P. (2011). Pausing patterns: Differences between L2 learners and native speakers. *ELT Journal, 65*(1), 71–79.

Tavakoli, P., & Skehan, P. (2005). Strategic planning, task structure and performance testing. In *Planning and task performance in a second language* (pp. 239–273). John Benjamins.

Tellier, M. (2008a). Dire avec des gestes. *Le Français Dans Le Monde. Recherches et Applications, 44,* 40–50.

Tellier, M. (2008b). The effect of gestures on second language memorisation by young children. *Gesture, 8*(2), 219 235.

Tellier, M., & Stam, G. (2012). Stratégies verbales et gestuelles dans l'explication lexicale d'un verbe d'action. In Rivière, V. *Spécificités et diversité des interactions didactiques.* Paris : Riveneuve éditions. 357 – 374.

Tellier, M., Stam, G., & Bigi, B. (2013). Gesturing while pausing in conversation: Self-oriented or partner-oriented?". *The Combined Meeting of the 10th International Gesture Workshop and the 3rd Gesture and Speech in Interaction Conference, Tillburg (The Netherlands).*

Tomasello, M. (2003). *Constructing a language: A usage-based theory of language acquisition.* Harvard university press.

Tottie, G. (2011). Uh and Um as sociolinguistic markers in British English. *International Journal of Corpus Linguistics, 16*(2), 173–197.

Tottie, G. (2014). On the use of uh and um in American English. *Functions of Language, 21*(1), 6–29. R.

Tottie, G. (2015). Uh and um in British and American English: Are they words? Evidence from co-occurrence with pauses. In N. Dion, A. Lapierre, & R. T. Cacoullos (Eds.), *Linguistic Variation: Confronting Fact and Theory* (pp. 38–55). NY: Routledge.

Tottie, G. (2016). Planning what to say: Uh and um among the pragmatic markers. In G. Kaltenböck, E. Keizer, & A. Lohmann (Eds.), *Outside the Clause. Form and function of extra-clausal constituents.* (pp. 97–122). John Benjamins.

Tottie, G. (2019). From pause to word: Uh, um and er in written American English. *English Language & Linguistics,* 23(1), 105–130.

Vasilescu, I., & Adda-Decker, M. (2007). A cross-language study of acoustic and prosodic characteristics of vocalic hesitations. *Fundamentals of Verbal and Nonverbal Communication and the Biometric Issue,* 18, 140.

Vaughan, E., & Clancy, B. (2013). Small corpora and pragmatics. In *Yearbook of Corpus Linguistics and Pragmatics 2013* (pp. 53–73). Springer.

Ward, N. (2006). Non-lexical conversational sounds in American English. *Pragmatics & Cognition,* 14(1), 129–182.

Watanabe, M., & Rose, R. (2012). Pausology and hesitation phenomena in second language acquisition. *The Routledge Encyclopedia of Second Language Acquisition,* 480–483.

Witton-Davies, G. (2014). The study of fluency and its development in monologue and dialogue [PhD Thesis]. Lancaster University.

Wood, D. (2001). In search of fluency: What is it and how can we teach it? *Canadian Modern Language Review,* 57(4), 573–589.

Wright, M. (2005). Studies of the phonetics-interaction interface: Clicks and interactional structures in English conversation [PhD Thesis]. University of York.

Wright, M. (2011). On clicks in English talk-in-interaction. *Journal of the International Phonetic Association,* 41(2), 207–229.

Wulff, S., & Ellis, N.C. (2018). Usage-based approaches to second language acquisition. *Bilingual Cognition and Language: The State of the Science across Its Subfields,* 54, 37.

Yasinnik, Y., Shattuck-Hufnagel, S., & Veilleux, N. (2005). Gesture marking of disfluencies in spontaneous speech. *Disfluency in Spontaneous Speech.*

Yule, G. (1996). *Pragmatics.* Oxford University Press.

Zhang, Y., Baills, F., & Prieto, P. (2020). Hand-clapping to the rhythm of newly learned words improves L2 pronunciation: Evidence from training Chinese adolescents with French words. *Language Teaching Research,* 24(5), 666–689.

Zuniga, M., & Simard, D. (2019). Factors influencing L2 self-repair behavior: The role of L2 proficiency, attentional control and L1 self-repair behavior. *Journal of Psycholinguistic Research,* 48(1), 43–59.

Appendices

Appendix 1

Table 34. Transcription conventions

CHAT conventions (MacWhinney, 2000, pp. 48–74)	
+/	interruption by other participant
+//	self-interruption
[/]	word repetition
[//]	self-repair
+…	trailing off
(0.250)	unfilled pause (number in milliseconds)
wo:rd	prolonged vowel or consonant
+ < <>	overlapping talk
(a)bout	shortenings
+/ +"/.	quoted utterance
xxx	unintelligible words
CA conventions (Jefferson, 2004; Ogden, 2018, 2013)	
[!]	tongue click
.hhh	inbreath
hhh	outbreath
creaky	creaks
(( ))	description of events, or analyst's comment
Gesture annotation (Kendon, 2004)	
~ ~ ~	preparation of gesture stroke
***	gesture stroke
***	hold
-.-.-	return to rest position

Appendix 2

Table 35. Rate of individual fluencemes (raw and relative frequency) for the SITAF corpus

PAR	L1 phw (raw values)		L2 phw (raw values)	
A02	24.5	(43)	61.7	(118)
A03	19.9	(97)	45	(188)
A07	8.9	(28)	32.6	(90)
A09	9.5	(39)	56.8	(110)
A10	30.6	(28)	41.7	(28)
A11	7.9	(34)	32.2	(75)
A13	19.3	(67)	52.6	(122)
A15	14.7	(38)	41.7	(73)
A16	20.5	(53)	25.5	(37)
A17	19.5	(41)	81.6	(275)
A18	22.3	(48)	48.9	(70)
Total	16.1	(516)	49.2	(1186)
F02	19.4	(38)	24.8	(30)
F03	17.3	(43)	16.5	(34)
F07	25.6	(127)	23.3	(93)
F09	34.5	(205)	58.7	(181)
F10	35.2	(43)	68.2	(84)
F11	22	(38)	31	(133)
F13	5.9	(19)	28.8	(62)
F15	24.3	(63)	39.4	(93)
F16	6.7	(8)	20.9	(41)
F17	22.5	(51)	26.9	(41)
F18	20.5	(22)	30.4	(21)
Total	23	(657)	33.1	(813)

Table 36. Rate of fluencemes per hundred words (American group, SITAF)

	L1 (raw)		L2 (raw)		LL score	P
Morpho-syntactic markers					
lexical repair	0.2	9	0.3	9	0.36	<
morphological repair	0.4	13	1.04	25	8.03	<
syntactic repair	0.4	14	1.9	48	30.61	<0
identical repetition	1.8	60	7.5	181	102.80	<0
self-interruption	0.7	24	0.7	17	0.04	<
truncated word	0.9	29	2.03	49	12.43	<0
Vocal markers					
filled pause	1.53	49	8.01	193	137.3	<0
prolongation	2.25	72	11.7	283	201.4	<0
unfilled pause	6.03	193	10.7	260	38.07	<0
Peripheral markers					
NL sound	1.50	48	4.73	114	49.68	<0

Table 37. Rate of fluencemes per hundred words (French group, SITAF)

	L1 % (raw)		L2 % (raw)		LL score	P
Morpho-syntactic markers					
lexical repair	0.3	11	0.2	5	1.49	<
morphological repair	0.3	11	1.02	25	7.92	<
syntactic repair	0.9	27	0.8	20	0.25	<
identical repetition	3.08	88	3.8	95	2.38	<
self-interruption	0.84	24	0.6	15	0.95	<
truncated word	1.02	29	1.4	36	2.19	<
Vocal markers					
filled pause	4.94	141	7.41	182	13.29	<0
prolongation	4.2	121	3.9	98	0.19	<
unfilled pause	5.25	150	9.57	235	34.02	<0
Peripheral markers					
NL sound	1.6	48	3.8	94	22.9	<0

Table 38. Average duration of filled pauses in SITAF (in ms)

PAR	L1	Stdev	L2	Stdev
A02	792.29	366.11	512.9	211.86
A03	682.57	224.53	506.81	162.63
A07	689	222.82	524.53	176.84
A09	602.5	116.67	462.76	230.55
A10	N/A	N/A	675	212.13
A11	510	N/A	641.33	389.63
A13	790	257.39	529.67	159.85
A15	330	N/A	422.57	294.37
A16	471.25	63.82	622.75	231.67
A17	552.14	148.21	522.31	206.43
A18	598.57	124.04	578.38	265.46
Total	658.6	238.8	514.6	192.3
F02	406.36	175.74	533.25	72.2
F03	372.6	251.45	496.67	192.94
F07	361.82	255.6	567	209.23
F09	373.2	176.19	450.75	169.51
F10	498	170.23	407.4	160.11
F11	491.43	191.7	537.24	248.47
F13	N/A	N/A	616.55	121.8
F15	301.92	181.16	399.07	171.86
F16	534	524.67	586.67	330.81
F17	189.27	83.9	471.7	174.8
F18	850	N/A	309.13	168.45
Total	371.78	214.9	465	190.5

Table 39. Average duration of prolongations in SITAF (in ms)

PAR	L1	Stdev	L2	Stdev
A02	435	138.14	479.23	227.04
A03	400.07	126.84	475.66	174.95
A07	588.75	170.64	401.82	137.89
A09	575.13	123.28	511.67	295.92
A10	266.67	50.33	371.29	66.93
A11	700	N/A	427.18	190.39
A13	546.43	118.22	497.8	161.64
A15	387.25	98.01	382.25	126.25
A16	312.86	58.87	380.77	113.08
A17	372	135.17	434.98	120.32
A18	396.5	192.29	465.64	154.04
Total	**433.5**	**149.4**	**461.5**	**177.6**
F02	442.83	86.14	576.14	87.43
F03	236.67	90.18	366.67	75.06
F07	450.5	172.32	717.27	280.79
F09	423.84	105.36	430.9	115.95
F10	369.5	134.56	428.09	164.4
F11	328.33	53.45	406.75	100.55
F13	347.25	84.66	623.25	168.79
F15	304.33	121.11	343.33	110.03
F16	334	48.08	337.5	84.6
F17	317.67	69.07	326.22	102.02
F18	480	145.33	366.33	63.89
Total	**383.4**	**122.1**	**459.3**	**187.1**

Table 40. Average duration of unfilled pauses in SITAF (in ms)

PAR	L1	Stdev	L2	Stdev
A02	1067.83	1007.55	820.25	344.32
A03	758.42	343.51	629.39	249.7
A07	747	429.34	633.21	238.71
A09	693.42	351.8	785.56	465.96
A10	878.55	426.62	1048.25	584.96
A11	729.6	282.44	695.59	290.67
A13	794.83	423.97	834.69	412.12
A15	717.47	291.76	643.65	288.43
A16	637.11	435.23	579.31	279.21
A17	816.67	282.54	778.2	376.44
A18	692.93	353.3	640.3	238.07
Total	754.7	444.3	683.9	300.8
F02	646.5	238.67	889.64	943.56
F03	672.92	395.98	598.23	165.4
F07	591.62	187.72	754.6	300.41
F09	582.44	320.83	820.78	558.62
F10	707.06	376.85	544.27	225.11
F11	876.67	460.9	813.08	410.89
F13	444.57	100.72	757.9	541.57
F15	613.14	279.23	674.9	308.22
F16	625.25	303.51	599	332.44
F17	697.36	237.57	615.87	268.62
F18	748.67	325.37	765.33	202.93
Total	629.4	292.3	717.3	443.1

Table 41. Count of non-lexical sounds for the American speakers (raw values, SITAF)

NL	L1	L2	Total
click	13	44	57
cough	1	0	1
creaky-voice	4	7	11
hunhun	0	1	1
inbreath	23	47	70
laughter	1	4	5
mm	3	7	10
sigh	3	4	7

Table 42. Count of non-lexical sounds for the French speakers (raw values, SITAF)

NL	L1	L2	Total
click	12	30	42
creaky-voice	5	16	21
inbreath	25	35	60
laughter	3	1	4
mm	1	7	8
sigh	2	4	6
unintelligible	0	1	1

Table 43. Z scores and p values for the distribution of NL sounds (SITAF)

	American speakers		French speakers	
click	$z=-1.401$	$p=0.1$	$z=-0.854$	$p=0.3$
inbreath	$z=0.785$	$p=0.4$	$z=-0.235$	$p=0.8$
other	$z=0.681$	$p=0.4$	$z=0.994$	$p=0.3$

Table 44. Average number of markers combined within a sequence (SITAF)

PAR	L1	Stdev	L2	Stdev
A02	1.9	0.8	2.4	1.4
A03	2.0	1.4	2.6	1.7
A07	1.4	0.6	2.2	1.7
A09	1.5	0.8	2.4	1.9
A10	1.9	1.0	1.9	1.4
A11	1.4	0.5	2.1	1.5
A13	1.6	0.9	2.2	1.6
A15	1.6	0.9	2.0	1.5
A16	1.7	1.1	1.8	1.1
A17	1.6	0.8	2.7	1.9
A18	1.6	0.9	1.9	1.2
Total	1.7	1.0	2.4	1.6
F02	2.4	1.7	2.4	1.3
F03	1.7	0.9	1.4	0.7
F07	2.0	1.4	1.9	1.2
F09	2.1	1.4	2.3	1.5
F10	2.3	1.6	2.4	1.4
F11	2.4	1.5	2.1	1.7
F13	1.6	0.8	2.2	2.6
F15	1.7	0.9	1.9	1.2
F16	1.5	0.8	1.6	0.9
F17	1.5	0.8	1.6	1.1
F18	1.7	1.2	1.6	0.9
Total	1.9	1.3	2.0	1.5

Table 45. Raw values and z scores for the proportion of pragmatic and referential gestures in (dis)fluent cycles of speech in L1 and L2

	\multicolumn{6}{c}{American group}
	\multicolumn{3}{c}{L1}	\multicolumn{3}{c}{L2}
	DIS	FLUENT	Z (p)	DIS	FLUENT	Z (p)
Pragmatic	41	200	0.74 (0.4)	87	214	0.84 (0.3)
Referential	13	82	−0.74 (0.4)	18	57	−0.84 (0.3)

	\multicolumn{6}{c}{French group}
	\multicolumn{3}{c}{L1}	\multicolumn{3}{c}{L2}
	DIS	FLUENT	Z (p)	DIS	FLUENT	Z (p)
Pragmatic	43	156	0.58 (0.5)	81	218	1.79 (0.07)
Referential	14	62	−0.58 (0.5)	13	63	−1.79 (0.07)

Table 46. Annotation of gaze direction in SITAF (raw values)

Gaze	American group		French group	
	L1	L2	L1	L2
away	385	419	262	323
in different directions	54	62	62	82
towards interlocutor	434	450	435	459
towards paper	60	129	111	138
Total	933	1060	870	1002

Table 47. Rate of gestures in L1 and L2 in SITAF (raw frequencies and per hundred words)

PAR	L1 Phw	L1 Raw frequency	L2 Phw	L2 Raw frequency
A02	6	11	12	23
A03	21	107	15	63
A07	7	21	12	33
A09	5	22	11	22
A10	12	11	37	25
A11	13	55	10	24
A13	2	6	16	37
A15	8	20	3	5
A16	12	30	12	17
A17	13	27	26	89
A18	12	26	27	38
Total	11	336	16	376
F02	9	17	9	11
F03	4	11	16	33
F07	11	53	16	65
F09	4	22	13	41
F10	25	30	33	40
F11	24	42	18	77
F13	11	36	20	44
F15	9	24	9	22
F16	13	15	15	29
F17	9	20	6	9
F18	5	5	6	4
Total	10	275	15	375

Table 48. Results on the Z test on gaze direction in SITAF (Z scores and p values)

	American group	French group
away in different directions	$z = 0.78; p = 0.4$	$z = -0.98; p = 0.3$
	$z = -0.05; p = 0.9$	$z = -0.85; p = 0.3$
towards interlocutor	$z = 1.82; p = 0.06$	$z = 1.811; p = 0.07$
towards paper	$z = -4.36; p < 0.002$	$z = -0.64; p = 0.5$

Table 49. Annotation of gaze in fluent and disfluent stretches of speech (raw values, American group, SITAF)

	L1 DIS	L1 FLUENT	L2 DIS	L2 FLUENT
away	164	221	245	174
in different directions	17	37	50	12
towards interlocutor	84	350	138	312
towards paper	14	46	59	70
Grand Total	279	654	492	568

Table 50. Annotation of gaze in fluent and disfluent stretches of speech (raw values, French group, SITAF)

	L1 DIS	L1 FLUENT	L2 DIS	L2 FLUENT
away	127	135	181	142
in different directions	27	35	44	38
towards interlocutor	117	318	105	354
towards paper	51	60	54	84
Grand Total	322	548	384	618

Appendix 3

Table 51. Rate of fluencemes in DisReg (raw frequency)

PAR	Class	Conversation
A1	117	103
A2	153	93
B1	156	58
B2	103	43
C1	155	154
C2	151	115
D1	83	141
D2	103	75
E1	134	119
E2	103	170
F1	125	198
F2	89	129
Total	1472	1398

Table 52. Rate of individual fluencemes (raw values and per hundred words)

	Class (raw)		Conversation (raw)		LL	P value
Morpho-syntactic markers						
lexical repair	0.4	19	0.2	16	1.77	<0.05
morphological repair	0.9	45	0.4	29	9.39	<0.01
syntactic repair	0.9	44	0.8	56	0.04	<0.05
identical repetition	2.3	121	2.4	161	0.01	<0.05
self-interruption	0.1	7	0.7	45	21.41	<0.0001
truncated word	1.1	56	0.9	63	0.77	<0.05
Vocal markers						
filled pause	7.5	387	4.1	281	59.42	<0.0001
prolongation	3.1	162	4.1	280	7.54	< 0.01
unfilled pause	6.7	345	4.7	319	21.15	<0.0001
Peripheral markers						
NL sound	5.4	278	2	134	99.58	<0.0001
explicit editing phrase	0.2	8	0.2	11	0.01	< 0.05

Table 53. Average duration values of filled pauses in DisReg

PAR	Class Average	Stdev	Conversation Average	Stdev
A1	429.32	182.13	221.57	114.02
A2	414.11	217.32	241.05	168.63
B1	410.54	180.77	469.12	447.61
B2	521.44	324.45	353.33	118.16
C1	464.43	256.36	390.82	137.4
C2	375.34	272.73	314.65	95.3
D1	413.23	250.43	338.87	221.65
D2	240.95	129.08	353.82	187.6
E1	388.28	191.88	348.39	267.78
E2	467.35	335.01	326.19	161.83
F1	421.69	190.95	356.07	153.91
F2	242.25	65.12	308.87	118.53
Total	412.09	240.18	340.05	199.77

Table 54. Average duration values of unfilled pauses in DisReg

	Class Average	Stdev	Conversation Average	Stdev
A1	674.45	268.46	591.81	331.72
A2	687.74	301.06	661.81	433.77
B1	478.84	117.95	410.00	17.32
B2	645.68	228.19	578.85	393.07
C1	646.48	191.42	639.74	352.79
C2	637.52	272.42	764.83	410.32
D1	755.06	731.27	578.93	352.83
D2	668.21	649.90	556.23	260.62
E1	849.79	875.02	516.00	136.34
E2	794.06	435.20	574.07	288.66
F1	827.11	666.58	527.52	222.44
F2	630.34	676.95	539.85	218.26
Total	695.78	543.37	594.20	323.55

Table 55. Average duration values of prolongations in DisReg

	Class		Conversation	
	Average	Stdev	Average	Stdev
A1	281.78	102.09	382.55	167.54
A2	397.27	106.11	313.06	103.75
B1	325.88	126.69	356.00	47.75
B2	316.14	55.63	400.17	129.99
C1	448.00	213.27	377.83	159.57
C2	259.31	62.37	325.24	105.14
D1	280.67	70.82	341.65	86.29
D2	281.11	120.40	295.75	90.54
E1	401.18	119.58	414.04	341.31
E2	393.90	188.06	346.78	119.99
F1	281.90	96.20	325.02	98.55
F2	348.30	88.62	328.24	102.17
Total	351.32	142.45	350.14	155.70

Table 56. Count of non-lexical sounds in DisReg (raw values)

NL	Prepared	Spontaneous	Total
click	63	15	78
creaky-voice	4	4	8
inbreath	206	99	304
laughter	0	4	4
mm	5	8	13
sigh	0	4	4

Table 57. Average number of markers combined in a sequence (DisReg)

	Class Average	Class Stdev	Conversation Average	Conversation Stdev
A1	2.8	1.3	3.7	1.9
A2	3.1	1.2	2.6	0.7
B1	2.9	1.1	2.6	0.9
B2	2.5	0.9	2.7	1
C1	3.3	1.6	2.6	1.2
C2	2.9	1.8	2.6	0.9
D1	2.3	0.6	2.6	0.9
D2	2.3	0.6	2.9	0.9
E1	2.8	1.2	2.9	1.3
E2	3	1.2	2.6	0.9
F1	3.3	1.8	2.7	1
F2	2.7	1.6	2.7	1.3
Total	2.9	1.3	2.7	1.1

Table 58. Count of gestures in class and conversation (raw values)

PAR	Class	Conversation	Total
A1	41	27	68
A2	38	36	74
B1	92	38	130
B2	43	35	78
C1	14	44	58
C2	92	48	140
D1	36	47	83
D2	61	35	96
E1	68	51	119
E2	9	40	49
F1	23	59	82
F2	11	31	42
Total	528	491	1019

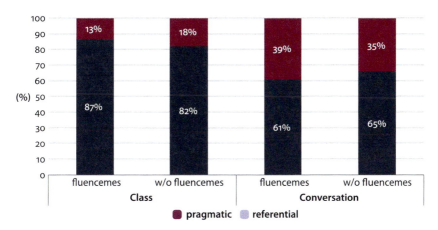

Figure 41. Proportion of the two main gesture types in class and conversation with/without fluencemes

Table 59. Annotation of gaze direction in DisReg (raw values)

	Class	Conversation
away	67	737
in different directions	53	62
towards camera	25	1
towards interlocutor	478	1199
towards paper	1211	23
Total	1834	2022

Table 60. Count and proportion of gaze direction for participant F1 (Linda)

Gaze	Class	Conversation
away	0%	31% (77)
in different directions	0%	4% (9)
towards interlocutor	9% (10)	60% (151)
towards paper	91% (110)	6% (15)

Table 61. Annotation of gaze direction in DisReg with and without fluencemes (raw values)

Gaze	With fluencemes		W/O fluencemes	
	Class	Conversation	Class	Conversation
away	33	326	34	411
in different directions	35	47	18	15
towards camera	7	0	18	1
towards interlocutor	129	359	349	840
towards paper	531	7	680	16
Total	735	739	1099	1283

Index

A
affiliation 37–38, 133, 242
alignment 37–38, 56, 61, 100, 186, 242
Allwood 3, 10, 14, 19–20, 22–23

C
Candea 3, 21, 22, 24, 25, 53, 55, 58, 82, 86–90, 101, 104, 139
Cienki 3, 27, 39–40, 43–47, 52, 54–56, 74, 94, 96, 105, 142, 211
common ground 40, 166, 173, 184, 220
complexity 2–3, 7, 21, 67, 104, 127, 143, 154, 181–182, 223, 233, 237
communicative context 39
context of production 37
context of use 8, 27, 29, 42–43, 52, 56, 98, 136, 215, 223 *see also* context of production, communicative context, interactional context
co-participation 61, 96, 133, 136, 143
Crible 3, 22–25, 28–29, 31–32, 52–55, 73, 86, 89–90, 93, 101, 104, 127, 138
cyclic gesture, cyclic gestures 45, 96, 128–129, 197, 205, 208, 236

D
discursive gestures 44, 96, 147, 162, 165, 178, 220 *see also* parsing gestures
disengagement 37, 40–41, 56, 162, 179, 202, 208
disruption, disruptions 3, 13, 17, 24, 25, 55–56, 229
doing fluency 3, 215
doing hesitation 199, 203, 215

E
engagement 37, 40, 179, 180, 189, 198–199, 222

F
flow 2–3, 6–7, 12, 14–16, 20, 23–25, 30, 37–38, 47, 53–56, 101, 127, 134, 136, 138, 143–144, 180, 194, 199, 212, 216–17, 223
fluidity 3, 7, 29, 54, 56

G
gaze aversion 19
gaze away 121, 163
gaze withdrawal, gaze withdrawals 121, 122, 124, 141, 198–199; 208, 210, 217, 221 *see also* gaze away, gaze aversion, 19
gesture space 5–6, 40, 44, 71, 180, 184, 191–192, 194, 197, 208, 213–214, 243
gesture suspension 50, 139, 192
Goodwin 3, 34–35, 38, 40–41, 51, 60, 71, 96, 127, 129, 136, 162, 173, 198, 208, 210
Götz 22, 24–25, 29, 31, 52–55, 59–60, 86, 104
Grosman 22, 29–31, 52–55, 144
Gullberg 45, 47, 49–50, 60, 64–65, 94, 97, 104–105, 118, 125–126, 129, 136, 139–140, 142, 144, 191, 197, 205, 218–219

I
individual differences 9, 60, 106–107, 137, 147, 149, 156, 160, 165, 183, 219, 221–222
interactional context 178
interactional flow 37, 55–56, 127, 217
interactional fluency 143, 173, 217
interactive gesture, interactive gestures 45–46, 70, 120, 147, 160, 162, 172, 184, 211, 221

K
Kendon 7, 42–47, 49, 55, 73, 94–96, 98, 158, 162, 192, 194, 196, 211–212, 214

M
McCarthy 3, 16, 22, 24–25, 52, 54, 62, 143–144
Morgenstern 3, 6, 55, 73, 76, 79
Müller 6, 42–47, 55, 94–95, 98, 133, 173, 191, 204
multifunctionality 8, 214, 217

P
patterns of combination 28, 104
patterns of co-occurrence 114, 137
parsing gestures 94, 96
planning 10–11, 13, 14, 16, 18, 24, 32–33, 36, 48–50, 58–59, 63, 68, 93, 96, 124, 140, 147, 158, 181–182, 184, 186, 211, 214, 220
preference structure 36, 93, 100
presentation-relevant activities 179–180
progressivity 6, 54, 93, 126–128, 136, 140, 142–143, 174–176, 185, 216–217, 219

R
read speech 1, 66, 147, 164, 181
representational gestures 45, 64–65, 162, 183, 189

S
Segalowitz 27, 29, 31–32, 52, 54–55
Shriberg 1–2, 11–12, 21, 23–24, 28, 31, 66, 68, 86–87, 89–90, 93, 101, 147, 181
spontaneous speech 12, 16–17, 20–21, 48, 66, 68, 87, 146
Streeck 3, 6, 38–40, 42, 44–45, 47, 55, 71, 94–95, 133, 136, 162, 204, 206, 208, 211

T
Tellier 65, 84, 93, 126, 188
thinking face, thinking faces 40–41, 60, 97, 128–129, 140, 198, 201, 219
thinking gesture, thinking gestures 60, 94, 96–97, 118, 120, 124, 140–141, 160–161, 165, 184, 205, 208, 219–222
Tottie 10, 17–22, 32, 52, 68–69, 73, 147, 181–182
transition relevant place 131, 169, 211
turn-taking 5, 20, 33, 36, 37, 64, 68, 100, 124, 140, 158, 189, 211